The Virago Story

WITHDRAWN

Protest, Culture and Society

General editors:
Kathrin Fahlenbrach, Institute for Media and Communication, University of Hamburg
Martin Klimke, New York University Abu Dhabi
Joachim Scharloth, Waseda University

Protest movements have been recognized as significant contributors to processes of political participation and transformations of culture and value systems, as well as to the development of both a national and transnational civil society.

This series brings together the various innovative approaches to phenomena of social change, protest and dissent which have emerged in recent years, from an interdisciplinary perspective. It contextualizes social protest and cultures of dissent in larger political processes and socio-cultural transformations by examining the influence of historical trajectories and the response of various segments of society, political and legal institutions on a national and international level. In doing so, the series offers a more comprehensive and multi-dimensional view of historical and cultural change in the twentieth and twenty-first centuries.

For a full volume listing, please see back matter

The Virago Story

Assessing the Impact of a Feminist Publishing Phenomenon

Catherine Riley

berghahn
NEW YORK • OXFORD
www.berghahnbooks.com

First published in 2018 by
Berghahn Books
www.berghahnbooks.com

Library of Congress Cataloging-in-Publication Data

A C.I.P. cataloging record is available from the Library of Congress

British Library Cataloguing in Publication Data

A catalogue record for this book is available from the British Library

ISBN 978-1-78533-808-3 hardback
ISBN 978-1-78533-855-7 paperback
ISBN 978-1-78533-809-0 ebook

Contents

Acknowledgements

This book has been many years in the making.

I began researching what is now 'The Virago Story' in the early noughties, and since then have been grateful to receive input and advice from Virago's key women, past and present. Thank you to them all, and especially to Lennie Goodings, for their time and for their generous, tenacious advocacy of women's writing and women writers.

I am grateful to the many teachers – beginning with my parents – who have given me the tools with which to write this book, and to family, friends and colleagues who have supported me materially and intellectually during the (long!) process of its composition.

Thank you to Susan Greenhill for allowing me to use her brilliant portrait of Virago's brilliant women on this book's cover, and to my editors and production team at Berghahn Books.

Finally, thank you to Natalie Koffman for teaching me – at last – the art of patience. This is for you.

Introduction

The UK publishing house Virago, founded in 1973 and running today as an imprint of Little, Brown publishers, is perhaps the most famous – and certainly the longest-running – of the women-only presses that sprung up as the second-wave feminist movement began. These publishing ventures, including but not limited to The Women's Press, Pandora, Sheba and Only-women, were critical to the early formulations and activities of second-wave feminism. Virago and its contemporaries enabled both the dissemination of feminist intellectual discourse and the discovery of women's cultural and literary history through publication of women's writing from the past. Of all these second-wave feminist publishers, Virago alone survives, making the publisher a useful prism through which to examine evolving feminisms and the changes in women's writing and in wider culture since the 1970s. Its story is unique and vital.

The importance of Virago's example lies both in its status as a female-run venture and in its provision of women's fiction and non-fiction writing. Virago, and its founder Carmen Callil in particular, regarded the act of publishing *as itself* a moment of feminist praxis – an enactment of feminist politics through the incursion into 'male' areas of economic and cultural authority. Callil has always been explicit in arguing that such practical acts are as critical to feminism as the exploration of theory and the dissemination of positive images of women that was also part of Virago's remit. Virago's feminism can therefore be defined in terms of both praxis and theory – deeds as well as words. Accordingly, this book is split into four parts roughly defined by the span of ten years, each of which is divided in two: separate chapters look in turn at the practical aspects of the work of the press, followed by an exploration of its literary output. It will, I hope, play its part in addressing the lack of writing on the phenomenon of women's publishing. In her 2004 text *Mixed Media,* Simone Murray identifies this gap in literary material which chronicles and/or quantifies feminist publishing history (Murray 2004). Crucially, she also begins the task of describing the effects of feminist publishing (see the section entitled 'Situating Feminist Publishing Analysis' later on in this chapter).

In the pages that follow, I rely on, and am grateful for, the words of Virago's key women themselves, gathered during interviews in which they expand on the commentary written of their press by others, reflect on the cultural context into which Virago was launched, and give their opinions of Virago's continued relevance for women, feminist or otherwise. Founder Carmen Callil, co-founder Marsha Rowe, founder-publisher Ursula Owen, former managing and editorial directors Harriet Spicer and Alexandra Pringle, current Chair Lennie Goodings and authors Ali Smith and Sarah Waters all provided their own analyses of the feminist publishing phenomenon and Virago's role in directing feminist politicking and polemic.

Context and Framing

Virago is a UK publisher, and so the focus of this book is the UK feminist and publishing scene from the second wave to the contemporary. However, while it prioritizes discussion of UK feminist politics and UK authors, it of course recognizes and examines the overlap and interplay between, especially, UK and US feminism and publishing, as well as literary and cultural trends from around the English-speaking world.

This analysis of Virago situates it as emerging from within the second-wave feminist movement, while recognizing that recent critiques of this wave metaphor has problematized its usefulness as a framing tool: 'we've reached the end of the wave terminology's usefulness. What was at first a handy-dandy way to refer to feminism's history, present, and future potential with a single metaphor has become shorthand that invites intellectual laziness, an escape hatch from the hard work of distinguishing between core beliefs and a cultural moment' (Jervis in Berger 2006, 14). While acknowledging such critiques (including others by Clare Hemmings (2011) and Sam McBean (2015)), which argue that the 'progress narrative' inherent in this analogy impedes our understanding of feminism's nonlinear development, this text nonetheless utilizes the terms first-, second-, third- and fourth-wave feminism. These 'wave' terms provide a useful framework or shorthand to more easily signpost both temporal and theoretical positions – further, I would argue that the wave analogy is appropriate because it is in fact suggestive of flux and circularity rather than linearity, each 'new' wave both a turning back on and a renewal of that which came before.

Situating Feminist Publishing Analysis

Prior to Murray's 2004 text *Mixed Media,* there were some examinations made of the emergence of women-run presses and their effects. Holding the power to publish was structured as vital to feminism's success, an idea set out neatly by Carmen Callil herself in discussion of her reasons for setting Virago up: 'in the past very few women had the power to publish. That is the point, of course: the power to publish is indeed a wonderful thing' (Callil 1980, 1001). Charlotte Bunch echoed this idea in an early second-wave analysis of women's publication traditions: 'controlling our words corresponds to controlling our bodies, our selves, our work, our lives' (Bunch 1982, 140).

As the 1970s progressed, the growing numbers of feminist presses in the UK had tangible effects on the wider book industry and arguably on culture itself – as I will examine in the first part that follows. Marsha Rowe recalls the electrifying effect of her first experience of creating published content with a group of other interested women: 'about 30 women came and it was just the most extraordinary evening, in my basement flat where I was living then . . . I mean there was one woman there, or one or two women, who were able to write articles, but everyone just supported: production roles, advertising. Very few women had any power in shaping what was produced or content or anything to do with women'.[1] Yet in industry comment, women's contributions were ignored or deliberately overlooked. John Sutherland's 1978 overview of book publishing makes not a single mention of feminist publishers, a full five years after Virago was launched and at a time when many other women's presses were beginning to make waves (Sutherland 1978).

It is this reality that provoked writers such as Dale Spender to address the situation of women in the industry. Her early examination of feminism's relationship to publishing concluded that men had created a protective system of 'gatekeeping' to exclude women from the business of books – as writers, as publishers and even as readers. 'Women who reveal their intellectual resources are often described as having "masculine minds", which is a clever device for acknowledging their contribution while at the same time it allows it to be dismissed, for a woman with a "masculine mind" is unrepresentative of her sex, and the realm of the intellectual is still retained by men' (Spender 1982, 19). Spender endorsed new feminist presses such as Virago that were directly challenging this hegemony.

Spender's sister Lynne similarly developed a theory of literary 'gatekeeping' to explain the ways in which women's writing had historically been overlooked for publication (Spender 1983). Arguing that the literary industry had always been controlled by a privileged male elite, she concludes: 'gatekeeping thus provides men with a mechanism to promote their own needs and interests at the expense of all others. In doing so, it effectively ensures the continuation of a male-supremacist culture' (Spender 1983, 6). Women's writing, remaining unpublished, is consigned to obscurity, and thus women are kept outside of the literary and intellectual arenas. Spender posits feminist publishers as vital to the reinvestment of women's writing as valuable:

'the role of feminist publishers is to break down traditional figurings of women's writing – and of women themselves – through the dissemination of literature that has historically been edged out (Spender 1983, 13).

This challenge to the orthodoxy of the traditional English canon led to more archaeological work, digging out women's publishing heritage (see Chapter 2) and theorizing its importance. Historicizing women's involvement in publishing led feminist investigators Cadman et al. to the records of the Stationer's Company in the 1600s. These show there were at least sixty women printers in Britain at that time (Cadman et al. 1981). Over the following centuries, women remained involved in small-scale publishing businesses, working from or near their homes as typesetters, proofreaders and publicists – suitably genteel work for women. As their educational opportunities improved in the nineteenth century, their newly acquired literacy, coupled with new printing technology that saw the industry suddenly expand as books became quicker and cheaper to produce, provided women with greater opportunities to enter the publishing world. During the early years of the twentieth century, publishing was regarded as a profession suitable for a woman of a certain social standing (Coser at al. 1982).

The feminist publishers of the second wave were perhaps also inspired by literary forebears such as Virginia Woolf, who had articulated the need for women to empower themselves through publishing in the wake of the first wave of feminism. As Bunch was later to reassert, Woolf argued that the power to publish necessarily lay in the hands of those who owned the presses, so seizing that power was critical: 'to enjoy freedom, if the platitude is pardonable, we have of course to control ourselves. We must not squander our powers' (Woolf 1932, 258). Simone Murray chronicles the attempt by first-wave suffragists to seek this control by setting up publishing houses in numbers before the outbreak of the First World War, citing evidence of at least eleven pro-suffrage presses in addition to the Woman's Press operating in London (Murray 1988, 199). These Edwardian feminist presses – which included among their number Virginia Woolf's Hogarth Press – can well be figured as forerunners of Virago and the rest of the second-wave feminist publishers that were established in the UK in the 1970s.

Ken Worpole observed in his 1984 overview of contemporary publishing that 'such has been the success of feminist publishing in recreating a popular feminist literary tradition as well as encouraging an extraordinary body of new writing that even the traditional mass distributors have had to take note' (Worpole 1984, 41). As the second-wave feminist publishing phenomenon took hold, there was a critical assessment of its impact and effect from within the feminist literary community. Gail Chester and Sigrid Neilsen published their radical feminist perspective of women's publishing,

In Other Words, exploring the principles and payoffs of smaller-scale feminist presses (Chester and Neilsen 1987). Their style of publishing was very different from Virago's, focusing on collectivism and more radical feminist treatises. Independent feminist presses such as Sheba and Onlywomen (who were never incorporated as part of a larger mainstream house as Virago, Pandora and The Women's Press were) defined themselves outside of capitalist business principles, measuring their success in terms of the absolute freedom they had to choose what to publish and the consequent symbolic meanings this had for women generally. 'It was the price we paid for having total control over the whole publishing process – something which as women we rarely have, and as writers, almost never. It was worth it' (Chester and Neilsen 1987, 106).

Following this, Dale Spender revisited her earlier assessment of feminist publishing to evaluate the impact of second-wave publishers after more than fifteen years of operations (Spender 1989). In *The Writing or the Sex?*, Spender argues that Virago, in blazing the trail followed by the other presses, helped women achieve authority in publishing in a way that hadn't been attained in any other cultural arena. It is, she said, 'one – if not the only – area where women have been able to set up an *alternative*, autonomous, and viable industry, and this has numerous implications for publishing and for the power configurations of the sexes' (Spender 1989, 47). This was made even more remarkable because 'publishing is (still) a markedly influential medium and one where it is [now] possible for women to go to women' (Spender 1989, 49).

In the same year, Nicci Gerrard's assessment of the second-wave publishing phenomenon concluded similarly that 'those women's presses which have sprung up over the last two decades have not only introduced women's writing to readers who were hungry for it, and provided space for writers from different backgrounds and cultures, they have also formed a pressure group upon the mainstream houses' (Gerrard 1989, 9). But she is sceptical of mainstream engagement with women's writing, believing it evidences a cynical move for profit and a usurpation of the bestselling authors nurtured by the feminist presses rather than a genuine shift in the way in which women writers and readers are figured in culture.

Certainly, it took the intervention of feminist publishers to prove the profitability and popularity of women's writing – only for mainstream presses to encroach upon women's newly won territory. Rukhsana Ahmad explained through the pages of *Spare Rib* magazine that 'though many progressive women writers do get picked up by the mainstream – once they have established a readership – and that success may be useful to the women's movement, this only happens for some. The likelihood for example of lesbian writers succeeding in mainstream houses seems remote' (Ahmad 1991, 12). Patricia Duncker's examination of the feminist publishing phenomenon echoes this view. She is fearful of the consequences of women's presses being edged out by mainstream houses: 'if they go out of business, feminist innovation, ambition and radical politics will surely go too. We are not in the majority; and I fear the political effects of majority taste' (Duncker 1992, 40).

More current explorations of the book industry have included examinations of the conglomeration of the industry, and of the rise of new phenomena such as book prizes and book clubs, which have had a profound effect on how the literary marketplace is run. They have also impacted hugely on feminist publishing – Virago is the sole survivor of the crop of presses that emerged in the UK during the 1970s and 1980s, and its identity now is radically different from that of its earlier years. It serves as a fascinating prism through which to view changing constructions of women's social, cultural and literary status – Virago's story, with its own cast of fascinating characters, is one that deserves to be told.

Note

1. Interview with Marsha Rowe, 15 July 2004.

Part I

1973–83

Chapter 1

Virago's Hands-on Brand of Feminism

Virago was founded in 1973 in the context of an emerging feminist community, a changing publishing industry and a patriarchal cultural paradigm. Its launch can be constituted as a moment of feminist praxis: an action intended to address the context of a new women's politics and to redress the lack of women in public and literary life. Callil describes her decision to take action as a publisher as her 'brand of feminism', grounded in the belief that books have the power to change lives and that controlling the means of literary production is vital.

From 1973, the year in which Virago was founded by Callil, Rowe and Rosie Boycott, to 1982 when Callil, Harriet Spicer and Ursula Owen presided over a now-established publishing phenomenon, Virago challenged the history, structures and practices of the industry in which it operated. It also innovated in its editorial and production techniques, effecting changes in the way in which publishing as a whole figured women – as business innovators but also as a ready and important market for books.

In its first ten years Virago was central to the dissemination of feminist ideology, publishing writing from important female critics such as Sheila Rowbotham and Denise Riley, and reprinting seminal texts from the United States such as Kate Millett's *Sexual Politics* and Eva Figes' *Patriarchal Attitudes* for consumption by a British audience (Figes 1978; Millet 1977; Riley 1983; Rowbotham 1983). It also innovated with the introduction of a 'Modern Classics' series, the brainchild of Callil and an unexpectedly huge success, and established links (which were to last) with hugely influential authors such as Margaret Atwood and Angela Carter. Even more important in this first decade, perhaps, was the example the press set as a women-only business venture, as Callil and the rest of the Virago team prioritized economic success alongside changing hearts and minds through literature.

Virago acted as an inspiration for a raft of other feminist presses that followed in its wake in the 1970s and early 1980s. As the women's liberation movement gained momentum during these years, the production and consumption of women's writing became a vital element of feminist activism: 'the support of women readers, along with the influence of an ongoing feminist movement, created in the seventies an extraordinary decade of continuous and impressive publishing for and about women' (Kinney 1982, 48). This sense of a feminist community sustained, and was in turn partly sustained by Virago in its early years.

By the beginning of the 1970s, a burgeoning feminist movement in the United Kingdom was drawing away from the sexually libertarian counterculture of the 1960s in a tentative attempt to establish *women's* independence and radicalism. Marsha Rowe, one of the women who helped Callil establish Virago in 1973, recalls these uncertain times: 'all the early seventies was a desperate search. You'd talk to women who'd been in the media a long time, or you'd talk to women who'd never written before, photographers who'd never photographed . . . you know, everything was just starting, and people were learning as they did things.'[1] She describes the changes in London as women within alternative culture began to look around themselves:

> What had been quite freeing to the underground press . . . sexual freedom was quite important at the time, and having a different sort of life to your parents and not thinking you just had to marry and have children and give up your job . . . all that had been rather rebounded and become over-determined so I was beginning to feel really uncomfortable with the images of the underground press. But we [women] still had no words to really say what we felt. I remember going to the Isle of Wight festival in 1970 and you know there were two women performers the entire weekend – Joan Baez and Joni Mitchell – and all the rest were men.[2]

Against this backdrop of women's growing alienation from and disenchantment with a radical movement that had promised much but delivered them the usual roles of support workers and soothers of male egos, the publication of seminal feminist texts further provoked women to agitate for change. In the United States, texts by Betty Friedan, Kate Millett and Shulamith Firestone had begun this process, while in the United Kingdom, a big catalyst for women's engagement with feminism was the publication of Germaine Greer's *The Female Eunuch* (1970). This was met with a huge response – one of outrage from the establishment and of inspiration for many hundreds of thousands of women readers. Virago writer Joyce Nicholson sums up a common response to the text: 'When I read *The Female Eunuch* by Germaine Greer, I could not sleep for three nights' (Nicholson 1977, 7). For the first time, *women's* sexual liberation was being talked about. Rowe describes the growing sense of frustration that galvanized the fledgling women's liberation movement as it gathered pace in the United Kingdom, and her own growing consciousness of women's inequality: 'men were just incredibly threatened and we found it very hard to say . . . I mean really we were, underneath, incredibly angry. I don't think we recognised what a motor it was and how it affected us in our relationships'.[3]

Rowe recalls that in spite of the support of many men she knew and had worked with, there was a strong sense of hostility to the establishment of her feminist magazine *Spare Rib* from other men in the industry: 'feminism was just derided in most of the media . . . I mean, even with starting *Spare Rib*, it was about four years until the magazine called itself feminist'.[4] Condescension, incomprehension and ridicule constituted the general mainstream (for which read 'male') attitude towards feminist activism – most apocryphal of all, perhaps, was the reportage around the 1968 Miss America pageant, where it was falsely reported that feminist activists were setting their underwear alight.[5] The gleeful appropriation of this myth of 'bra-burning' women, a term used to deride women to this day, serves as a fine (and lasting) example of the sexism and machismo that pervaded the culture into which Virago was launched.

This incident also marks a moment of continuity between events in the United States and the United Kingdom. The focus of this book is very much on the UK feminist and publishing scene, but there are many points of intersection with events across the Atlantic. Callil herself noted early on the debt she owed American feminists for igniting her ideas about women and publishing, spelling this out in some of Virago's early publicity material: 'many books have been re-printed here from the USA. Virago feel that it's time an English publishing house took Women's Liberation as seriously'.[6]

As this feminist community grew, *The Female Eunuch* was followed by other texts that set out to challenge women's position within patriarchal culture. Juliet Mitchell's *Woman's Estate,* Ann Oakley's *Sex, Gender and Society,* Sheila Rowbotham's *Woman's Consciousness, Man's World* and Anna Coote and Tess Gill's *Women's Rights: A Practical Guide* all constitute early examples of such feminist polemic (Mitchell 1971; Oakley 1972; Rowbotham 1973; Coote and Gill 1974). In fiction, too, feminist themes were emerging in the writing of Angela Carter, Margaret Atwood, Zoe Fairbairns and Cathy Porter – writers who would go on to publish with Virago once the press was established in 1973. Most of them were part of the Virago Advisory Group who gave advice and support to the press during its early years. Another member of this group was Rosalind Delmar, who wrote an introduction to *The Dialectic of Sex,* a text that was pivotal to the US women's movement in the 1970s. And in addition to these writers, many other prominent feminists, including journalists (Suzanne Lowry and Mary Stott), historians

(Sally Alexander and Anna Davin), academics (Christine Jackson and Elizabeth Wilson) and other authors, were part of Virago's advisory panel.

This clearly evidences the existence – and necessity – of a strong network of feminists working together to effect change as the 1970s got underway. Harriet Spicer, who joined Virago as Callil's secretary before progressing to the role of production manager, also notes that Virago's geographical location was important, placing it at the heart of a London scene of feminist activism that provided support in its earliest days: 'where we were located seems worth a mention, being part of this ludicrously eminent Arsenal women's group which had people like Juliet Mitchell and Sheila Rowbotham and god knows who else . . . Anna Davin and very close connections'.[7] This network was crucial to Virago's early successes, providing as it did material for the press to publish, ideas on which to commission work and a means of disseminating details about Virago's output – it also, of course, meant there was a ready and eager audience for Virago's books.

The sexist cultural paradigm against which the second-wave women's liberation movement set itself saw women limited to a set of stereotypes that had historically been considered 'appropriate': wife, mother, sex object. The emerging feminist consciousness that spurred Virago's women into action had only just begun to figure these stereotypes, and ways in which to challenge them, as Rowe notes: 'it [the women's movement] had made a big impact but not many changes had come about'.[8] Callil's decision to establish Virago was founded on a belief that a publishing house could act as a vital tool in this challenge, disseminating literature that addressed women's inferior status: 'Virago was founded to publish books which, focusing on the lives, history and literature of women, would provide some balance to dominant views of human experience' (Callil 1980, 1001). It was also born out of Callil's growing frustration at her – and all women's – containment within the confines of the 'feminine': 'I started Virago to break a silence, to make women's voices heard, to tell women's stories, my story and theirs. How often I remember sitting at dinner tables in the 1960s, the men talking to each other about serious matters, the women sitting quietly like decorated lumps of sugar. I remember one such occasion when I raised my fist, banged the table and shouted: "I have views on Bangladesh too!"' (Callil 2008).

Callil's solution was to publish books that would challenge women's containment within feminine stereotypes (see Chapter 2 for analysis of the books published in Virago's first decade). But she wanted more than this – she also wanted to enact this challenge herself by staking her place in the world of business: 'we had to make it [Virago] a success so that it could take its place in the world. And that had to be *business* success'.[9] In the very act of setting up their own business, Callil and the Virago team were challenging notions of 'appropriate' female behaviour. Making Virago a commercial success – an operation that turned a profit and made an impact in the literary marketplace – was an important feminist intervention.

Rowe recalls the cultural climate of the early 1970s within which she, Callil and Boycott were formulating their ideas for Virago. Women, Rowe noted, were not expected to work or innovate, even within the libertarian alternative community in which she lived: 'I mostly knew musicians and painters and they were all men. I mean, there was one woman painter but you were supposed to be the muse really. My boyfriend was a painter and they didn't want you to do work.'[10] Virago writer Margaret Atwood recalls, similarly, that she was discouraged from a career in journalism by male contacts who warned that she would be limited to supporting roles: 'I was told that women journalists usually ended up writing obituaries or wedding announcements for the women's page, in accordance with their ancient roles as goddesses of life and death, deckers of nuptial beds and washers of corpses' (Atwood 2005, 24).

In the year after Virago was founded, the publication of the findings of the National Council for Civil Liberties Women's Committee on Women and Work provided further evidence of the attitudes that Rowe and Atwood describe. It found that new anti-sexist legislation had failed to affect young women's expectations and experiences of work: 'rarely is a child exposed to female role models who function as pilot, surgeon, accountant, carpenter or construction worker' (Friedman 1977, ix). In addition, women were denied parity of pay even when they were carrying out work of equal value to their male colleagues, as Anna Coote (a member of Virago's Advisory Group) and Tess Gill pointed out: 'Women's average earnings are still little more than half those of men. Many employees have been able to avoid the impact of the Equal Pay Act by keeping women in low-paid grades of work or transferring them to "women's jobs" where they have no chance of comparing their pay and conditions with male workers' (Coote and Gill 1974, 18). It was noted that the assumption that women would also be caregivers – in ways not assumed of men, even if they too were parents – contributed to the discriminatory attitudes that structured the working day. 'Not only are there few women managers, employers and supervisors, but most women are employed in low-wage and low-status jobs, have little opportunity for training and promotion and are forced to work hours adapted to their other job as housewives and mothers' (Hadjifotiou 1983, 24).

Working women had to overcome deeply ingrained sexist prejudices – the notion of appropriate feminine behaviour so pervaded patriarchal culture that women were figured as incapable of being good at 'business'. Virago's women were thus a rare challenge. Their status as female publishing executives was anomalous: 'within major publishing houses, few women achieved anything other than minor positions . . . as late as November 1974 there were only six female executive heads of publishing' (Coser et al. 1982, 151). Callil confirms that she experienced her fair share of sexist prejudice along the way: 'if you knew what I had to put up with, if you *knew* what I had to put up with. *And* I haven't got any patience. But I did it'.[11]

One of Callil's earliest employments was at Chatto, where she is recalled by colleague Jeremy Lewis in his 1996 memoir of a life 'adrift in literary London': 'She had far more energy, enthusiasm and strength of character than the rest of the office combined, and was determined to involve herself not just in the publishing side . . . but in every aspect of office life, even to the extent of taking away the office towels every Friday night, putting them through her washing-machine and bringing them back, fragrant and neatly folded, on Monday morning' (Lewis 1996, 217). It is hard to imagine that Callil's male colleagues were similarly tasked with doing the laundry.

Another literary memoir published in 2000 gives further perspective to the sexist culture of 1970s publishing. In *Stet*, Diana Athill writes that when she entered the industry in 1952 at the invitation of Andre Deutsch:

> All publishing was run by many badly-paid women and a few much better-paid men: an imbalance that women were, of course, aware of, but which they seemed to take for granted. I have been asked by younger women how I brought myself to accept this situation so calmly, and I suppose that part of the answer must be conditioning: to a large extent I had been shaped by my background to please men, and many women of my age must remember how, as a result, you actually saw yourself – or part of you did – as men saw you, so you knew what would happen if you became assertive and behaved in a way which men thought tiresome and ridiculous. Grotesquely, you would start to look tiresome and ridiculous in your own eyes. (Athill 2000, 56)

In spite of this, Athill considers herself lucky in her choice of career: 'all my colleagues during the 1960s and 1970s admired and sympathised with other women who were actively campaigning for women's rights, but none of them joined in as campaigners: we could see injustice but we didn't feel the pinch of it, because we happened to be doing what we wanted to do' (Athill 2000, 57). This ambivalence evidences the real lack of career choices open to women. Athill's memoir is a powerful reminder that, as Virago came into being in the early 1970s, women had very limited options in the workplace.

Virago's establishment in 1973 was thus a real venture into 'male' territory and a challenge to the notion of appropriate female behaviour. Virago stood as a rare example of a woman-owned enterprise in 1970s Britain. Indeed, the phenomenon of woman-owned businesses was so uncommon that there were no official statistics on the proportion of UK small firms owned and controlled by women (Davidson 1985). Evidence of the patriarchal attitudes to women in business can be found in media coverage of Virago's launch – even by female commentators. Caroline Moorhead in *The Times* wrote the first article describing Virago's women as 'paper tigresses', a term that was subsequently used to disparage women in the industry, as current Chair of the press Lennie Goodings recalls: 'when Virago was first born people called it "paper tigresses", this sort of diminutive stuff'.[12] Moorhead's article on the fledgling Virago is revealing in its attempts to imbue women's presses with an air of respectability: 'the emphasis on professional is important: there is nothing amateur about either group. It shows in the jackets, the blurbs and the publicity' (Moorhead 1978). It is fairly certain she wouldn't have felt the need to make this point if she had been describing a publishing house set up by men.

Virago's Story Begins

This cultural antipathy towards women in work – and even more so towards feminism – framed the launch of Callil's fledgling enterprise in 1973. But she had a few important resources to draw on, not least her experience of the publishing industry, and contacts within this and also in the radical underground scene, the women's movement and in some other rather more unorthodox places. She explains:

> First of all I worked in paperback publishing which taught you about marketing. Secondly, I worked with a brilliant quartet of men, and a fifth man (because I worked for Granada publishing) who was not just good, he was a genius. He's now running Knopf in New York. And because they were my friends who I saw every day of my life, these five men, I saw what they did and I saw what I thought they did wrong, and I saw what I could do.[13]

Callil learnt a number of lessons from these men, both good and bad: 'I just thought "simply hopeless" – he's gone out to lunch again, he's come back three hours later, he's drunk as a skunk. . .'[14] These experiences were coupled with Callil's involvement with the radical underground press: 'then when I left publishing and started my own publicity company, one of the things I worked for was *Oz* and *Ink*. I didn't work actually for *Oz* but I knew who everybody was. I knew Richard Neville and I knew Germaine [Greer] . . . that whole Australian mafia that was part of my life in the 1960s'.[15] Callil took on the publicity for *Ink,* having by now set up her own PR company, Carmen Callil Ltd, employing Harriet Spicer as her secretary. It was through *Ink* and her involvement with the 'Australian mafia' in London's radical scene that she came to meet Marsha Rowe, who had just begun to put together a plan to launch a radical women's magazine called *Spare Rib.* Rowe had teamed up with Rosie Boycott to put the first issue of the magazine together, inspired by observation of similar feminist activity in the United States: 'I'd seen one of the [US radical magazines] called *Rat* which was usually fairly chauvinistic had been taken over by women and they'd changed it so it said *Liberation* on the cover', she recalls. 'I thought, of course, that's what we have to do. When I mentioned it at this third meeting Rosie was bowled over and was immediately – Rosie was very brave – she said yes, I'll do it with you. And we did actually, within six months.'[16]

Rowe says that, in starting *Spare Rib,* 'we just went round all the people we knew. People gave us. . . we got an office that had belonged to the designer at *Time Out. Oz* went bust and so we got their filing cabinet and their lightbox for the designer. Michael White gave us tables and chairs, and a friend bought me a typewriter – actually, lent me a typewriter. Things like that, you know'.[17] The *Spare Rib* venture was thus founded on the goodwill and sense of communality generated by the countercultural groups Rowe moved in at that time. 'We contacted friends: I knew an art director who worked on *Vogue* in Australia and had come back here. There was someone called Betty Britain who was another Englishwoman who used to work on *Vogue,* so I spoke to her . . . And there was a group called Women in Media, like Jill Tweedy who was the women's page editor for *The Guardian* and some other women who were columnists.'[18]

Callil was similarly involved with these women – it was these ties that led her and Spicer to take on the launch publicity for *Spare Rib* in 1972. Shortly afterwards, she hit on the idea of expanding what Rowe and Boycott were doing from magazines into books, also drawing on what she had learnt from the men at Quartet for inspiration. 'I said, "look, you're doing *Spare Rib* and we're doing the publicity (or rather Harriet has), I want to do the same for books". And that's how Virago started.'[19] Initially, her new publishing venture was even to have shared its name with Rowe and Boycott's magazine: 'October 1972: this is it. "Spare Rib Books" it was going to be called. So it must have been within a few months of *Spare Rib* starting.'[20] In the end, Boycott chose the name Virago, as Callil recalls: 'we were going through books of goddesses and stuff, and Rosie is very like me in one way, she's a true iconoclast, and she said, "yes" [to "Virago"].'[21]

Virago's initial board meeting was between Callil, Rowe and Boycott, and took place on 21 June 1973 in Callil's dining room. Spicer recalls being left to run the PR side of Callil's interests while Callil spent time holding 'wondrous boozy meetings with Rosie Boycott and Marsha Rowe to discuss setting up the feminist publishing company Virago' (Durrant 1993). Callil was confident of managing the marketing and business aspects of her new press, but at the start relied on the other two for help with forging contacts with writers and generating ideas for books, particularly drawing on the links they had already established through *Spare Rib*. 'Angela Carter had come into *Spare Rib* and written some articles for us', says Rowe, 'and I remember Carmen meeting her and saying to me, "she's a real writer" and she was right of course.'[22]

Very soon, however, Callil's working relationship with Rowe and Boycott came to an end as the demands of *Spare Rib* and other commitments kept them occupied away from the Virago project. 'Nothing else came from Rosie and Marsha', says Callil, and Spicer concurs:[23]

> My sense of sitting in the place doing other work at the time was that Carmen wanted to work with somebody else to get it going, talk to the likes of Marsha, Rosie and whoever else – I'm not even sure . . . They had an experience of Virago that meant nothing to Ursula [Owen] and Lennie [Goodings] and me because it went away and didn't go anywhere, but clearly they were involved in *a* Virago. The fact is that it wasn't the one that had legs, so to speak, but they informed it . . . some discussions and ideas and what it would be called and all that was clearly them.[24]

Rowe believes that she and Boycott gave Callil the advantage of their already-established links with the burgeoning feminist community: 'I think she thought of me as her street cred', she recalls.[25] In its infancy, Callil used *Spare Rib* as a tool to get Virago off the ground: 'Carmen would place tiny adverts in *Spare Rib* and so spoke to lots and lots of different people.'[26] The two enterprises – *Spare Rib* and Virago – drew on the same small community of women writers and activists: 'the arts didn't really start flourishing, I think, until around 1974, when many more women began writing poetry, and writing stories, and becoming feminist. So the lists aren't terribly long, we just looked out every possible connection we could'.[27]

Both Rowe and Boycott left Virago before the first book had been published, leaving Callil with the urgent task of finding an editor. Ursula Owen joined in 1974, and Spicer recalls: 'the combination of Ursula's publishing and feminist connections and clout combined with Carmen really got things going'.[28] Owen was introduced to Callil by a mutual friend – by coincidence, both women had spent time working for Frank Cass Publishers. Owen remembers with amusement their first meeting: 'I went up to her and I said – she used to do some work for Frank Cass – and I said "Hi, I used to work there", and she did such a Carmen thing, she said "Oh, you poor thing", and walked away. That was my first encounter with Carmen.'[29] As with Rowe, Callil saw the value of Owen's links to the new feminist movement of the early 1970s. 'I suppose she saw my connections with the women's movement . . . I had a lot of writer friends, I had a lot of friends in very much the lower ranks of the academic world. I've always sort of been around that world.'[30]

Owen acknowledges the patriarchal cultural climate of the times. 'I don't think there were many other feminists in publishing', she says. 'There may have been but I don't think they were saying so. I was already part of a women's group, I was a member of a women's group that survived for seven years, that had lots of writers in it actually, and we did last for seven years with almost weekly meetings, amazing. It was called the Arsenal women's group.'[31] In all this it is clear that the emerging feminist community was pivotal in helping Virago's women to find each other and to find out ways of getting their business off the ground.

Callil and Owen, who describes herself as a founding director of the press, spent the next year building their first list for publication, with the assistance of Spicer, who took on a range of supporting roles. She remembers 'the manic concentrations and the driven work patterns' of those years: 'it was all learning and doing things for the first time and thinking yippee! We were all battered into shape' (Durrant 1993). Virago's first eleven books were published in association with Quartet, who paid Virago £75 for each title in an arrangement which saw them take responsibility for distribution and marketing. 'They were a really nice lot of men and obviously, to get the funding, we had to find someone to back Virago and they agreed', recalls Rowe.[32] Callil had experience of working with these men while at Quartet with them, a link that was instrumental in securing this arrangement. 'She had this arrangement with Quartet books who were all sort of mates of hers. I knew them, she knew them. She had a very high profile in publishing, she was a very brilliant PR person so all the literary editors liked talking to her.'[33] Quartet itself was a very new company, having been launched on 1 May 1972 – and it owed Callil no small degree of its success due to her work on its PR operation. Naim Attallah, who would go on to buy his way into Quartet four years later, and then set up and bankroll The Women's Press, acknowledges her contribution: '[Carmen] was an astute publisher and publicist. There was no denying that the boys at Quartet owed her a great deal for her help in establishing the company' (Attallah 2007, 27).

Virago initially operated out of the same offices as Quartet, and Quartet's catalogues contained a section devoted to the feminist press. Callil was determined that her partnership with Quartet shouldn't dilute the feminist aims of her venture and is quick to point out the independence of one company from the other: '[Virago] wasn't owned by Quartet, that's all wrong in the stuff. I owned it. I owned it always, obviously, because I started it.'[34] Virago relied on other contacts within mainstream publishing too. During this early period, for example, it used Wildwood House (a publisher with its own sales force) to distribute its books. Later it also utilized Routledge & Kegan Paul's distribution network. 'We worked with some very nice people at Wildwood House', Spicer recalls, 'and they helped the company enormously and helped us spring off . . . they were offering us a service they knew more than us.'[35] Virago was bound to do better business if it made sure of a 'strong feminist base *and* a feminist venture into male territory' (Roberts 1981, 199). It was also shrewd business practice, since it meant Virago had a toehold in mainstream networks, which eased the difficulties typically associated with launching a new venture into a competitive marketplace.

The first Virago title was *Fenwomen* by Mary Chamberlain, published in September 1975. 'There was this wonderful moment at the first press conference', Owen recalls, 'where this young journalist put up his hand and said – and we were publishing eleven books – he put up his hand and said "how are you going to find your next list?" And that was just such a demonstration of that 'worlds apart' thing. Those of us who were just gaping at him thinking "Books? There are zillions of books!" And he thought eleven books would be enough!'[36] The publication of these first eleven books tapped into a huge – and growing – market of women desperate for material that described their lives and offered alternatives to their own realities. 'It was such an amazing enterprise', Owen recalls. 'It was the women's movement and we were doing this thing. The world was excited. The minute the books got into the shops people would come back to us and say, when are the next coming? So it was wonderful.'[37]

Virago also took on Quartet's innovative 'Midway' concept for its first publications, a new format that was put out simultaneously to initial hardback editions (essential for review purposes and libraries): Midways were hardback size, but with paperback binding and thus were cheaper to produce, meaning their price was kept low. This was figured as a practical move (keeping overheads low) as well as a political one in that it made the books more affordable. Duplicating Quartet's custom of publishing these Midway editions – and this innovation in itself can be linked back to Callil, who was involved with Quartet from the start as its PR manager – helped Virago attract as wide an audience of readers as possible by offering more affordable editions. Rowe recalls that Quartet's introduction of this idea in 1973, and Virago's uptake of it on publishing its first book in 1975, was radical: 'the idea was – you know it was really revolutionary for its time – that rather than just wait for the hardback to be out for a year and then introduce the paperback, you would publish immediately into paperback and it would be cheaper'.[38]

Yet in spite of this early success, Callil, Owen and Spicer quickly realized the need to be in charge of *all* aspects of their business. 'We decided to go independent. Carmen did this very well, she set up things with Quartet but she never liked, and neither did I – I mean they were nice guys – but she never liked going to talk to them about editorial choices. We wanted to be free.'[39] The co-publishing arrangement with Quartet was terminated after the first list had been printed. 'We had learned two things: how vital it is to have *total* financial control over your business (something hardly any women in publishing had at that time); and how any requirement to defer to others on editorial decisions, however benevolent those others might be, is a constraint' (Owen 1988, 89). Quartet were in some financial trouble by the end of 1976 and Virago's triumvirate of Callil, Owen and Spicer set about raising the necessary capital to establish themselves independently (Lowry 1977).

'The three of us raised money by borrowing, by bank overdrafts', recalls Callil.[40] Bob Gavron and Paul Hamlyn guaranteed Virago's three directors a £25,000 overdraft, while Owen's uncle, Ernest Grunfeld, lent them £10,000 and her friend, Alison Weir, lent a further £5,000. The Rowntree Trust pledged a further £10,000 and Callil put in a substantial amount of her own money to complete the financing of the deal. In 1976 Virago became self-financing: on page two of every book was printed its 'statement of intent', which set out its feminist principles, quoting from Sheila Rowbotham's *Women, Resistance and Revolution* (Rowbotham 1972):

> VIRAGO is a feminist publishing company: 'It is only when women start to organise in large numbers that we become a political force, and begin to move towards the possibility of a truly democratic society in which every human being can be brave, responsible, thinking and diligent in the struggle to live at once freely and unselfishly.'[41]

Their next task was to set up a new distribution network, now that they were operating outside the protection of Quartet's umbrella. Their first distributors were called the Writers and Readers Co-operative, and again were arrived at through the links that Virago's directors were forming with women in the radical and feminist movements taking shape at that time. Lisa Appignanesi, who went on to publish with Virago, was one of the Co-operative.

Lennie Goodings, who would shortly join Virago, also worked briefly for them: 'back then it was a real experiment . . . we published John Berger and Arnold Wester and the beginners series: *Marx for Beginners,* Freud, Einstein and so on . . . But they were tiny and didn't have a lot of money and so I worked for both [Virago and] them for a year'.[42]

Within twelve months of Virago buying back its independence, two more women joined the company who would go on to make up the famous quintet eventually depicted by Susan Greenhill in 1988 and selected by Anna Ford as one of her British 'Faces of the Century' portraits for a National Portrait Gallery exhibition in 1999 (Bown 1999). Alexandra Pringle and Lennie Goodings were vital additions to the Virago team and formed, with Callil, Owen and Spicer, the backbone of the press throughout the late 1970s and all of the 1980s.

Pringle first arrived at Virago in 1977, taking on the role of 'general office assistant – we used to call it the shitworker . . . I was doing odd jobs: I used to do export, I used to take the post, I would do photocopying, you know, everything – a dogsbody'.[43] Peter Townsend, her employer at *Art Monthly* magazine where she'd been (almost) earning her keep for some months, was Ursula Owen's neighbour and recommended her to Virago. 'So I started splitting between the two companies, then after a year of that Carmen asked me to go full time, and I felt that I should, and so that was it.'[44] Pringle spent her first two or three years as an admin worker at Virago before Callil asked her to work with her on the Modern Classics series.

The Classics were a vitally important innovation for Virago – indeed, for the publishing industry as a whole (for more on them, see Chapter 2). Virago Modern Classics were launched in 1978, conceived of as an attempt to broaden the scope of literature since 'many of the good and *enjoyable* novelists of our literary past and present have been swept under the carpet by an emphasis on the "great" novelists who so depressingly recur on student reading lists' (Callil 1980, 1001). The series emerged from an earlier initiative, the Virago Reprint Library, begun in 1977, which was in part inspired by Sheila Rowbotham's *Hidden from History,* and her problematization of the ways in which women's cultural, economic and social status had been concealed throughout history (Rowbotham 1974). Virago's Reprint Library was its first attempt to uncover this history, a task that was continued and expanded with the Modern Classics. The first Modern Classic was *Frost in May* by Antonia White, originally published in 1933 and reprinted by Virago on 15 July 1978.

The Classics have very much come to be associated with Callil, but the list was generated out of discussions within Virago's advisory group. 'That was where they started', Owen recalls. 'It came out of. . . we formed this

Advisory Group which was quite important actually. It was great across the board, it's listed in the catalogues. And the historians at the time, I knew a lot of historians, suggested these books.'[45] Spicer, too, is quick to acknowledge this shared genesis: 'yes, it was Carmen's baby, but ideas don't come from nowhere, so it came from the group that there then was'.[46]

Callil herself concurs: 'another important influence on the list has been the taste of colleagues, friends and readers' (Callil 1980, 1001). As editor of the series, she chose its books based on a desire to celebrate the range of female achievement in fiction, and this endeavour was to have a lasting effect on feminist and literary theory, and the notion of canon formation in particular (as I will more fully explore in the following chapter). Virago's reprints were to have an enduring influence on the literary landscape and would underpin much of the discussions constituting feminist literary theory in the 1970s and 1980s. Yet just as importantly (and unexpectedly), the series acted as a vital financial prop, swelling the company's coffers through its first decade as readers consumed the series in huge numbers: 'this business of re-issuing astonished the British publishing world with its success' (Lyndon 1984, 48).

Owen remembers the sudden demand for these reprinted texts, both fiction and nonfiction, but points out that in the writing of Virago's history by the media and other commentators, this emphasis on the Classics' success has cast a shadow over the impact made by Virago's contemporary writing at this time: 'They [the Classics] gathered momentum and they were terrifically successful. But you know other books were too. We did a sex education book called *Make It Happy* which caused a huge amount . . . sold a lot, caused a huge stir. People stood up in Parliament and said it should be removed from Dorset library, blah blah blah. You know there were masses of books doing that kind of thing. Dorset, you know! Lots of Tories!'[47]

As the Classics were becoming established, Lennie Goodings joined the press in 1978 having contacted Callil in the hope of getting involved: 'when I first came into publishing and certainly when Virago was first formed which was before I came to England, there were tons of women in publishing but they didn't run it. They didn't have the power to say what should be published as the men did.'[48] Goodings offered her services as a PR person, believing that a role at Virago would allow her to tackle these disadvantages: 'I really wanted to engage with all that. So I wrote to Carmen and said I think that I can help you, not knowing that she had run her own publicity company for fifteen years! But nevertheless she said yes, come in, so it did work.'[49] Over the course of the next three decades, Goodings would come to take on greater responsibility within the press, before eventually assuming the role of publisher in the 1990s – she now directs the press in the capacity of Chair.

Holding the Power to Publish

As Goodings described, the publishing scene during Virago's first decade saw most women collected in the lower ranks of the profession. Early second-wave appraisal showed that women 'are not in a position to influence the contents of composition texts. They are employed in large numbers because publishing is not only a low-profit enterprise but also a low-paying one, and women, as we know, are to be had cheap' (Hartman 1972, 90). Taking over the act of publishing was a vital feminist intervention, since holding the power to publish was figured as central to women's advancement. The consciousness-raising that defined early (white, middle-class) feminism was based on the act of reading, as women came together in groups to seek out explanations of, and alternatives to, their lives through literature. The centrality of writing – and reading – to the women's movement was crucial, summed up in the oft-quoted phrase 'this book changed my life'.

Holding the power to publish was a theme examined early on in the second wave. Virago's women were at odds with an old boys' network sourced from Oxbridge and sustained by nepotism and networking. Women in publishing outnumbered men by two to one, but only because, quite simply, there were many more low-ranked jobs: 'women are allowed to craft the books, and even to promote them, but the really public life of the book is left to the male' (Furman 1970, 68). At Virago, things were very different. Having the power to publish meant that Virago countered the dominance of male editors in the industry and presented new literary material that was the result of deliberately feminist editorial choices.

The figure of the female editor was critical: in mainstream houses the female editor was a rarity. Spicer says the figure of the woman editor was (and is) important: 'I think what you had was an empathy, you know you didn't have to argue a case . . . the care of your book and the way it was marketed was something that I think the women that wrote for us could have much more confidence in.'[50] Virago and the other feminist presses created a space in which women could figure themselves as writers – a space that was critical since, as Erica Jong stated, 'for women writers the systematic discouragement even to *attempt* to become writers has been so constant and pervasive a force that we cannot consider their literary productions without somehow assessing the effects of that barrage of discouragement' (Jong in Steinburg 1992, 86).

With literature being figured as so fundamental to feminism, it is not surprising that Virago was soon joined by others on the feminist publishing scene. Following Virago's lead as 'a feminist publishing imprint – the first of its kind in this country', many other women-only presses began to emerge.[51]

Onlywomen was the first of these, established just a year after Virago in 1974 by a collective of four women. Its aim was to publish 'literature that challenged gender and sexual stereotypes' and its stated intention was to 'prioritise lesbian authors'.[52] Onlywomen was set up as a collective, where all members were trained to have a wide range of publishing skills so that they could be equally involved in the running of any aspect of the organization, thus avoiding the formation of hierarchies. This collectivism was in contrast to the work structure in place at Virago – an issue that would be debated by feminists in the industry over the course of Virago's first decade – which had a clear chain of command. In reality, however, there was collectivism at work in all these fledgling feminist presses, as Callil simply could not afford to *not* have everyone chip in as and when required. And, as Spicer points out, 'there's commerce in a co-operative as well, it's just the style of commerce that's different'.[53]

In 1977, The Women's Press was founded by the entrepreneur and publishing magnate Naim Attallah, who installed Stephanie Dowrick to run the business as managing director. Attallah recalls: 'It was set up with a hundred £1 shares, with me holding fifty-three per cent and Stephanie the balance of forty-seven per cent . . . to begin with, Stephanie was the only full-time employee and the whole operation was started in her living-room in her house in Bow' (Attallah 2007, 37). Sibyl Grundberg doubled the staff number to two shortly after.

In an interesting twist, Attallah's purchase of Quartet, with whom Virago had co-published its first eleven books, enabled him to set up his new women's press, as he explains: 'with the departure of Virago from the Quartet fold and the emergence of feminism as a serious movement, I felt that there was space for a new feminist list that would both reflect one of the most exciting political currents in society and make commercial sense' (Attallah 2007, 36). The Women's Press' existence was predicated on Virago's success, which enabled it to launch independently of Quartet. Callil herself argued that The Women's Press and the other feminist presses that were to follow – these included Stramullion, Feminist Books, Honno, Black Woman Talk, Aurora Leigh, Urban Fox Press, Scarlet and many others – would not have been possible had Virago not 'already made the notion of feminist publishing respectable' (Moorhead 1978, 14a).

The Women's Press was launched in February 1978 with a reprint of Jane Austen's *Love and Freindship* [*sic*], echoing Virago's foray into historical women's writing in the Modern Classics series. In its first year The Women's Press published thirteen books, five of which were theoretical texts, the rest being fiction (of these, half were reprints). Its launch, like Virago's, provoked sexist critical comment in the press: 'when the advent of The Women's Press was reported as a "Diary" news item in the *Evening Standard,* for example, the headline given to the piece was "Yet more feminism"' (Attallah 2007, 38).

A year later, in 1979, 'Women in Publishing' (WiP) was founded. Its inaugural meeting, held in an upstairs room at the Globe pub opposite Baker Street tube station, was chaired by Anne McDermid and led by publisher Liz Calder of Cape (who was also the first woman on Cape's board) and Ursula Owen. Both Calder and Owen were taken aback by the numbers of women in attendance at this first meeting – testament to their growing number in the industry, but also to their emerging sense of the limited opportunities available to women in the mainstream. Further WiP meetings led to a more formal declaration of aims and to the election of a committee.[54] For her part, Calder went on to co-found Bloomsbury in 1986 (and in a nice continuity of the feminist community ethic, she appointed Virago's Alexandra Pringle to be her editor-in-chief).[55]

In the years after WiP was set up, two more important feminist presses were launched. The first of these, Sheba, was founded in 1980 specifically to address the fact that 'if more women writers are published now than in 1965, it remains true that the majority are white, heterosexual, and middle-class'.[56] Sheba's dedication to black women writers meant it was run as a not-for-profit workers' cooperative, situating itself outside of a system that it figured as historically both racist and sexist. This issue of racial specificity was to become very important to feminist debates and was to have a huge influence on The Women's Press under the direction of Ros de Lanerolle from 1981. De Lanerolle committed The Women's Press to third world and black women's writing, believing feminist publishing should 'provide a public platform for women who might have no other access to the mainstream media' (Benson and McDermid 1993, 30) (see Chapter 4).

Sheba was followed in 1981 by Pandora, established as an attempt to capture the burgeoning feminist academic market. 'Pandora emerged out of Routledge and Kegan Paul's [RKP] first tentative forays into women's studies publishing in the late 1970s with a feminist studies list overseen by former RKP publicity and editorial assistant, Philippa Brewster' (Murray 2004, 100). That Pandora was founded from within a reputable mainstream press gave it the advantages of financial stability, established distribution networks and a strong presence in the UK (and US) academic marketplace. However, its position as part of a mainstream imprint meant that its editorial integrity was pushed to the limit by a series of takeovers and sales endured as part of the RKP machinations of the 1980s (for more on this, see Chapter 3).

By the time of Pandora's establishment, Virago had operated as an independent press for five years. Between 1976 and 1981, the company grew in size and scale as its combination of excellent marketing and a product –

women's literature – that was in demand ensured success. Women's writing had become a big seller, as Eva Figes reveals in her preface to Virago's 1978 edition of *Patriarchal Attitudes*: 'the publisher who had accused me of having a chip on my shoulder and rejected the book [at first] was now "proud to be associated with a great cause", not least because feminist books sold like hot cakes' (Figes 1978, 8).

During this period, the Modern Classics came to have a huge impact on Virago's finances – within five years, the series generated more than half of the total annual turnover of the press (Lowry 1983, 37). The commercial success of the Classics series catapulted Virago into the book trade's big league, allowing 'the company to grow into a trade press able to bid for some of the most esteemed contemporary writers' (Altbach and Hoskins 1995, 133). It also meant that by the early 1980s, the company had to consider expanding its operation: in 1982 Virago's staff – which now numbered nine – were having to work very hard to manage their increasing workload. Wildwood was soon unable to manage the volume of book distribution required of it, so Virago turned to other alternatives. Chatto, Bodley Head and Cape (CBC) made Virago an offer to become a wholly owned subsidiary of their company. The alternatives were borrowing large sums, an option that was in no way guaranteed, or the sale of parts of the company that would have given outsiders control. The arrangement with CBC was ultimately arrived at via very complex negotiations. As with Virago's later buy-out decisions, the interplay of business acumen and personal loyalties were agonizing for the women involved.

On the surface, the offer from CBC was incredibly flattering for Virago. Eric de Bellaigue, an industry specialist, describes the new group as a formidable powerhouse: 'the creation in mid-1973 of Chatto, Bodley Head and Jonathan Cape marks the greatest concentration of literary excellence that the British publishing trade had witnessed up to then' (de Bellaigue 2004, 132). Owen confirms that 'we went to them because they were so prestigious and they had a huge reputation and could get us into lots of bookshops'.[57] Callil's close friendship with Liz Calder, who by this time was established on the board of Cape and was thus part of the CBC structure, was also a factor – an example of the kind of networking that men in the industry had for so long benefited from.

In reality, the approach to Callil is testament to her growing reputation as a publisher. This may well have been a cause for friction, with de Bellaigue voicing the view that 'within the Virago camp, the less than ego-building realisation that in the purchaser's eyes the primary attraction lay in securing the services of Carmen disturbed the other two main shareholders, who feared that their interests and those of Carmen might diverge' (de Bellaigue

2004, 143). Ursula Owen tells a different version of events: 'she wanted to be Chair. Harriet and I decided not to have a bloodbath about the move to Chatto, because originally Carmen wanted to take Virago *into* Chatto. Harriet and I resisted it and had enough shares to outvote her. For a year we struggled to work out this transfer. Carmen wanted to go to Chatto – she now says it was because she felt Virago wasn't doing what she wanted it to do. Whatever'.[58]

The effect of these machinations on Virago's triumvirate of directors was damaging, but the result was that Virago benefited from vastly improved warehousing, sales and distribution services, and the negotiations evidence Callil, Owen and Spicer's formidable bargaining power. Virago was sold for £244,000 – CBC had originally offered £150,000. The company name was changed to 'Chatto, Virago, Bodley Head and Jonathan Cape' (CVBC), and Callil was made non-executive chairman of Virago and managing director of Chatto. Owen and Spicer became joint MDs of Virago. One major change within Virago's structure was that 'after 1982 when Carmen left to go to Chatto, she didn't commission books'.[59] The merger with CBC certainly brought its own problems, not least in foregrounding tensions within the Virago camp, but Callil, Owen and Spicer were keen to emphasize that the sale was *not* to be read as Virago's assimilation into the mainstream. They continued to emphasize the feminist in their publishing company.

'The Feminism was My Brand of Feminism': Publishing as Praxis

Callil's engagement with mainstream partners in order to ensure the growth of her own company, or to secure its financial health, was part of her commitment to the act of publishing as praxis. She clearly enjoyed the *business* of publishing: 'the business side of starting the company was fun and not a real problem, taking as read that working twenty-four hours a day, seven days a week was a *sine qua non*' (Simons and Fullbrook 1998, 184). Callil's mode of feminism was literary, political and, importantly, commercial. As feminist bookseller Jane Cholmeley of Silver Moon bookshop puts it, 'there's absolutely no point in setting up a business and running it so politically that you go bust'.[60] Callil herself recognizes that this set her apart from other women-only publishing ventures – 'the feminism was my brand of feminism' – who wanted the process, as well as the product, to represent an alternative to the mainstream.[61]

Callil's 'brand' was therefore to provoke criticism from other feminists during Virago's first decade. Even from Virago's very beginnings, as Callil worked with Boycott and Rowe to get it off the ground, there was disagreement, with Rowe immediately uncomfortable with running Virago as a *business* rather than a not-for-profit outlet for women's writing: 'I thought maybe at this point, if there was going to be a women's publishing company it should, maybe, not be separated financially, shouldn't be an independent company but should somehow serve the women's movement. It was my politically correct year [smiles]. And so I began to have doubts about that, and Virago, because I knew that this was not in Carmen's mind at all.'[62] Rowe cites this struggle with her conscience as her main reason for leaving the company.

Rowe describes Callil's knack, evidenced in her earlier very successful career in PR, for anticipating trends and generating maximum coverage for her new venture: 'Carmen had a real eye too for what would be a good read, what would sell.'[63] She encouraged identification with Virago's product – women's writing – by designing a smart 'brand identity' and organizing high-profile book launches. This anticipated the way in which book marketing would go in the 1980s: 'nobody used the word "brand" then, but you wanted to make your mark in every possible way in the shops'.[64] Its marketing and design gave Virago a distinct identity. The striking combination of green spine, apple logo and classic artwork made it 'a brand that can be used as a shorthand to represent women's literary achievement, women's business achievement, women's abilities – be it in the covers that were created, the paintings that were painted. . .'[65] As author Jonathan Coe recalls: 'everything about those early Virago editions was well judged, and nothing more so than their cover illustrations' (Coe 2007).

Virago's clever use of marketing played a big part in its success, as the books' green spines and apple logo helped readers identify them quickly on the shelves and gave the company a visibility that, for its owners, went 'beyond our wildest dreams' (Owen 1988, 90). The slick packaging came at a price, but one that was justified by the belief that it attracted a wider audience. 'We just put the marketing into the cover and felt that the wider market that we gained by that would offset any price increase', says Harriet Spicer.[66] The Women's Press took a similar approach, using black-and-white striped spines and an iron logo on their books. This 'branding' provoked criticism from other feminists, however, who saw it as the prioritization of style over substance: 'I remember being torn off many strips – it was obviously a painful memory! – torn off several strips at a women's conference in Hebden Bridge because we printed four-colour varnished covers and we didn't put them out with just type and knock £2 off the price', Spicer remembers.[67] She defends Virago's approach, arguing: 'when you're a feminist, there's a world of difference between being a businesswoman and being a businesswoman who says "I'm doing this with the awareness that this is making a stand and has a political angle to it"'.[68] In its decision-making, she says Virago was always primarily and uncompromisingly feminist:

> What compromise do you have to make? A compromise to me makes it sound like you're accepting someone else's agenda and then trimming your sales accordingly. And the extent to which we used commerce, and success in commerce, was an absolute refusal to admit they had set the agenda . . . we didn't make compromises, we made decisions.[69]

Owen pays tribute to Carmen's skills in developing Virago's brand: 'it came from Carmen's long experience as a PR person, you know. The truth is, anyone can print a book, but selling a book is what you need to do. So that was our mantra really. Selling books was what we wanted, not just printing them. So you know Carmen was very good at publicity because she knew how to do that, and we all . . . people who came learnt how to have that in the back of our heads: who's the audience for this?'[70] Alexandra Pringle pays tribute to both Callil *and* Owen for the ways in which their combined skills made Virago such a success:

> I owe Carmen a huge amount because every single day of my life is affected by what I learnt from Carmen on how to publish a book. She was the sort of single most powerful influence on how I go about my publishing. But Ursula *massively* as well in intellectual terms, in a passionate commitment to books and ideals. So both of them equally but in different ways. With Carmen it's like, 'have I positioned this book, who do I talk to, who do I send it to, what should the package look like?' It's all of that thing which you have to be if you're going to be a good editor – you have to be a good publisher as well. She was brilliant at that. With Ursula it was more in the brain. So it's that sort of . . . different bits of me. So the two are my two sort of mothers in publishing, and they taught me just . . . everything really.[71]

The link between financial independence and editorial independence was the biggest challenge for second-wave feminist publishers as they struggled to balance a viable business that would see them produce women's writing that expressed feminist ideas for as wide an audience as possible. The tension between financial and editorial autonomy underpinned the efforts of all of the second-wave feminist presses. Virago's solution was to reclaim the 'male' territory of commerce to maximize the reach it could achieve for its product: women's writing. As Callil explains: 'my inspiration was always literary. It was books and writers and writing I loved. I always believed that books change lives, that writers change lives, and I still believe it . . . I started Virago to publish books which celebrated women and women's lives, and which would, by so doing, spread the message of women's liberation to the whole population and knock on the head for ever the idea that it was anything to do with burning bras or hating men' (Callil 2008). By the close of Virago's first decade of business, this task was well underway.

Notes

1. Interview with Marsha Rowe, 15 July 2004.
2. Ibid.
3. Ibid.
4. Ibid.
5. As Susan Faludi explains in *Backlash: The Undeclared War against Women* (1992, 99): 'the reason this event got so much ink: a few women tossed some padded brassieres in a rubbish bin. No one actually burned a bra that day – as a journalist erroneously reported'.
6. Copy taken from pre-launch publicity material written by Carmen Callil, undated, given to me by Marsha Rowe.
7. Interview with Harriet Spicer, 20 October 2004.
8. Interview with Marsha Rowe, 15 July 2004.
9. Interview with Carmen Callil, 10 November 2004.
10. Interview with Marsha Rowe, 15 July 2004.
11. Interview with Carmen Callil, 10 November 2004.
12. Interview with Lennie Goodings, 8 November 2004.
13. Interview with Carmen Callil, 10 November 2004.
14. Ibid.
15. Ibid.
16. Interview with Marsha Rowe, 15 July 2004.
17. Ibid.
18. Ibid.
19. Interview with Carmen Callil, 10 November 2004.
20. Interview with Marsha Rowe, 15 July 2004.
21. Interview with Carmen Callil, 10 November 2004.
22. Interview with Marsha Rowe, 15 July 2004.
23. Ibid.
24. Interview with Harriet Spicer, 20 October 2004.
25. Interview with Marsha Rowe, 15 July 2004.
26. Ibid.
27. Ibid.
28. Interview with Harriet Spicer, 20 October 2004.
29. Interview with Ursula Owen, 5 February 2009.
30. Ibid.

31. Ibid.
32. Interview with Marsha Rowe, 15 July 2004.
33. Interview with Ursula Owen, 5 February 2009.
34. Interview with Carmen Callil, 10 November 2004.
35. Interview with Harriet Spicer, 20 October 2004.
36. Interview with Ursula Owen, 5 February 2009.
37. Ibid.
38. Interview with Marsha Rowe, 15 July 2004.
39. Interview with Ursula Owen, 5 February 2009.
40. Interview with Carmen Callil, 10 November 2004.
41. Taken from frontispiece of Figes (1978).
42. Interview with Lennie Goodings, 8 November 2004.
43. Interview with Alexandra Pringle, 28 October 2009.
44. Ibid.
45. Interview with Ursula Owen, 5 February 2009.
46. Interview with Harriet Spicer, 20 October 2004.
47. Interview with Ursula Owen, 5 February 2009.
48. Interview with Lennie Goodings, 8 November 2004.
49. Ibid.
50. Interview with Harriet Spicer, 20 October 2004.
51. Carmen Callil, 'Untitled', Publicity Pamphlet, 1973.
52. Anon., 'Collection: Records of The Onlywomen Press' *Genesis Project*, retrieved 20 September 2017 from http://www.londonmet.ac.uk/genesis/search/$-search-results.cfm?CCODE=1145.
53. Interview with Harriet Spicer, 20 October 2004.
54. Anon, 'About Us', *Women in Publishing*, retrieved 20 September 2017 from http://www.wipub.org.uk/about.html (para. 4 of 11).
55. Jaggi, Maya, 2 July 2005.
56. Anon., 'About Sheba Feminist Press', *Maryland Institute for Technology in the Humanities*, retrieved 20 September 2017 from http://www.mith2.umd.edu/WomensStudies/ReferenceRoom/Publications/about-sheba-press.html (para. 2 of 10).
57. Interview with Ursula Owen, 5 February 2009.
58. Ibid.
59. Ibid.
60. Interview with Jane Cholmeley, 28 September 2004.
61. Interview with Carmen Callil, 10 November 2004.
62. Interview with Marsha Rowe, 15 July 2004.
63. Ibid.
64. Interview with Harriet Spicer, 20 October 2004.
65. Ibid.
66. Ibid.
67. Ibid.
68. Ibid.
69. Ibid.
70. Interview with Ursula Owen, 5 February 2009.
71. Interview with Alexandra Pringle, 28 October 2009.

Chapter 2

Changing the Literary Landscape

Publication of fiction and nonfiction whose themes fundamentally challenged the gender order put Virago at the centre of the UK women's liberation movement in the 1970s and 1980s, along with the other feminist presses that sprang up during this period. Virago's books were 'feminist' in that they contained examples of strong women, or threw light upon women's inequality, or set out another kind of challenge to the patriarchal culture into which the press was launched. As Callil said when her company was unveiled, the 'first aim is to rewrite the history of the world so that, for the first time, women are given their proper due' (Oakes 1974, 37c).

Writing has always been central to feminism throughout its various 'waves', and the second wave saw an outpouring of critical and fiction writing that explored women's place in culture: 'certainly, the 1970s women's movement was to an extraordinary extent a writers' movement', says Owen. 'Writing and politics became inextricably connected' (Owen 2009). Virago published many important texts in its first ten years that variously reflected, challenged or even instigated avenues of feminist investigation. The intention was always to speak to both women and men, conveying feminist messages to the widest possible audience: 'Virago has always said that feminism is central to us all, not just to women.'[1]

Although its lists of contemporary fiction were small during the first decade, Virago negotiated publishing rights to the works of writers such as Angela Carter, Margaret Atwood and Zoe Fairbairns, who created empowered and empowering portraits of women. Carter wanted 'to make money out of and for women's writing, and to rescue it from the slough of passive suffering: "the whole idea is tentative at the moment, obviously [she said in 1975]. I suppose I am moved towards it by the desire that no daughter of mine should ever be in a position to write: BY GRAND CENTRAL STATION I SAT DOWN AND WEPT, exquisite prose though it might contain. (BY GRAND CENTRAL STATION I TORE OFF HIS BALLS would be more like it, I should hope)"' (Sage 1994, 32). At Virago, such attitudes were the order of the day, as women's inequality in 1970s culture politicized a generation of female writers, as Atwood explains: 'I began as a profoundly apolitical writer, but then I began to do what all novelists and some poets do: I began to describe the world around me' (Atwood 1982b, 15).

Virago sought both fiction and nonfiction that communicated feminist ideas, while Callil also hunted out historical novels with these themes for reprinting. She describes, in 1974, the response that she was met with when Virago launched: 'masses of manuscripts poured in, most of them novels by women desperate to tell about their lives' (Oakes 1974, 37c). In addition, Virago's women were actively seeking feminist writing they felt was important to print. 'We did go out and look for it', remembers Callil. 'Women writing discussion books and that sort of polemic stuff.'[2] The press acted as a kind of conduit in its first decade between a new generation of feminist writers and a new audience of women (and some men) readers who wanted a change in their status within a hugely patriarchal culture. As women were beginning to formulate their own oppression, literature was a vital conduit in their coming-to-consciousness. Eva Figes notes with awe the response she received from women readers on publication of her book *Patriarchal Attitudes* in 1970: 'In the months after publication a massive postbag from all over the country told me that thousands, perhaps millions of women appeared to have the same chip: that for years women had been nursing a secret rage which society required them to repress for fear of ostracism and ridicule' (Figes 1978, 7).

Now-seminal feminist critiques such as those of Figes, Germaine Greer's *The Female Eunuch* and Kate Millett's *Sexual Politics* were inspiring women to seek out political meaning through reading. 'There were areas in which women were not expected to be heard', says Ursula Owen. 'At the time of Virago's launch, it was particularly difficult for women to make their presence felt in the intellectual world. Ideas were not seen as women's realm. In searching for early Virago authors, assisted by an advisory group of writers, teachers, journalists and academics, I found young women, many of them now distinguished professors, but then not even on the lowest rungs of the academic ladder, who were writing books of great originality' (Owen 2009). During Virago's first decade, there sprung up a new and increasingly suffuse feminist literary criticism, which in time began to take its place within the academy (a fact that Pandora was set up to exploit, targeted as it was at a specifically academic readership and marketplace). Virago had a role to play in its conception, production and dissemination.

How Virago's Books Challenged the Gender Order

In the early 1970s, the theoretical challenge to the imposition of gender roles was only just beginning to be formulated within the women's movement. As Marsha Rowe points out of the culture within which Virago was conceived, 'the language then was so unsophisticated . . . there's no separation of sex and gender. That sort of deconstruction hadn't really happened'.[3] The separation of sex – the biological categorization of male and female – from gender – a set of culturally, politically, economically and psychologically imposed behaviours – came to be a cornerstone of second-wave feminism, providing a basis from which women could examine the ways in which certain roles and behaviours were ascribed them.

This explication of the sex/gender binary took in re-readings of earlier texts, beginning with Virginia Woolf and the androgynous ideal first espoused by her as the solution to women's inequality. Woolf was sceptical of essentialist notions of male and female identity, and proposed instead that men and women were made up of masculine and feminine alike. She advised the writer to remember this as they worked: 'it is fatal for anyone who writes to think of their sex. It is fatal to be a man or woman pure and simple; one must be woman-manly or man-womanly . . . for anything written with that conscious bias is doomed to death' (Woolf in Lee 1984, 97).

Simone de Beauvoir's discussion of the construction of gender roles in her seminal text *The Second Sex,* first published in 1949, was another key influence on second-wave feminism. De Beauvoir describes the processes by which women are made 'feminine', assigned this gender at birth on the basis of their physiology and then taught to regard it as natural because of its deep entrenchment within cultural institutions: 'one is not born, but rather becomes a woman' (de Beauvoir 1997, 295). De Beauvoir explored women's construction as 'other', an oppressed group that, within patriarchal culture, could not organize as a unit because it lacked a history of its own: 'humanity is male and man defines woman not in herself but as relative to him; she is not regarded as an autonomous being' (de Beauvoir 1997, 16). Callil echoed this idea in 1978 in justifying the need for establishing her women-only press, saying that 'publishing deals with culture, and women are a separate culture' (Moorhead 1978, 14).

The later work of Robert Stoller examined this differentiation of sex and gender, with Stoller arguing in his 1968 text *Sex and Gender* that 'one can speak of the male sex or the female sex, but one can also talk about masculinity and femininity and not necessarily be implying anything about anatomy or physiology' (Stoller 1968, ix). Sex and gender, he explains, 'are not at all inevitably bound in anything like a one-to-one relationship', but are culturally determined: girls learn from birth to act in a 'feminine' way, boys in a 'masculine' way, yet we all have degrees of both masculinity and femininity within us (Stoller 1968, ix).

Eva Figes' influential second-wave text *Patriarchal Attitudes,* originally published in 1970 and reprinted by Virago in 1978, challenges the culturally dominant assumptions that men are intellectually, physically and emotionally superior to women. She argues that this 'myth' of masculinity has been manufactured and perpetuated under patriarchy to serve male interests: 'By assigning sex roles and sex-related interests we limit human possibilities' (Figes 1978, 12). The imposition of gender is a means by which women are prevented from full participation in (patriarchal) culture.

This explication of the difference between physiology and psychological and cultural constructs is made clear by Ann Oakley in her important book *Sex, Gender and Society* (1972). Gayle Rubin similarly identifies a 'sex/gender system' as the locus of women's oppression in her 1975 essay 'The Traffic in Women' (Rubin 1975). She uses the term 'sex/gender system' to highlight the fact that gender is organized, 'manmade'. 'Gender is a socially imposed division of the sexes', she states (Rubin 1975, 170). Oakley and Rubin's ideas were fundamental to early second-wave feminist arguments, greatly influencing the climate into which Virago was born. Oakley was an important part of the feminist community from which Virago drew inspiration and, indeed, three of her works of fiction would later be published by the press.

In addition to this construction of gender as an imposed dichotomy, Kate Millett's seminal text *Sexual Politics* became the first to specifically address the construction of gender in *literature,* concluding that 'whatever the real differences between the sexes may be, we are not likely to know them until the sexes are treated differently, that is alike' (Millett 1977, 9). Her critique of D.H. Lawrence, Henry Miller, Norman Mailer and Jean Genet reveals not only the ways in which gender roles are constructed and perpetuated in fiction, but also the sanctioning of this gendered literature as 'great' by cultural guardians whose interests are served by the biased attitudes it portrays. These ideas were absolutely crucial to Virago: the press would not only publish literature that challenged these gender norms, but would also play a critical role in challenging the criteria by which literature had historically been judged (see the section entitled 'Reading Back: A History of Reviewing Women's Writing' later on in this chapter).

The feminist publishing phenomenon was, then, an attempt to create new *literary* images that would effect change on women's lived realities. Strong or subversive fictional women exposed the categorization of the sexes into two unequal genders, thereby challenging the cultural lie that women must fall into one of three 'feminine' categories: housewife; mother; sex object. And as Ursula Owen explains, these categories were utterly pervasive at the time Virago was beginning to publish its books: 'until the late 60s, women's territory was still fundamentally seen to be confined to the domestic – birth, death, marriage, motherhood, children – and the emotional – love, friendship, nurturing, caring, with most of the feminine stereotypes still firmly in place – passivity, irrationality, compliancy, formlessness. Indeed it is hard to convey to young women today how marginal women felt in that world' (Owen 2009).

Margaret Atwood's early novels, reprinted by Virago in the late 1970s and early 1980s, took on the first of these stereotypes, 'housewife', to show how it strangled women's potential and suffocated their desires. *The Edible Woman* was written in 1965 and published initially in 1969 before being reprinted by Virago as a Modern Classic in 1980. In the introduction to this UK edition of her novel, Atwood paid testament to the influence of US writer Betty Friedan, who had first articulated the stifling limitations imposed on women by the construction of the housewife ideal: 'like many at the time I'd read Betty Friedan and Simone de Beauvoir behind locked doors' (Atwood 1980, 8). Friedan's investigation of the 'problem with no name' in her book *The Feminine Mystique* (1963) led her to conclude that the role of housewife led to abject misery for women constrained into it: 'In 1960 the problem that has no name burst like a boil through the image of the happy American housewife. . . the actual unhappiness of the American housewife was suddenly being reported' (Friedan 1963, 19).

Following Friedan (and Atwood), the role of housewife became central to second-wave feminist inquiry. In the United Kingdom, Hannah Gavron provided quantitative evidence of women's allocation to domestic drudgery in *The Captive Wife*, arguing that such work was always cast as inferior to that undertaken in the public domain: 'nothing has prepared young wives for the relentless boredom of scrubbing floors and ironing shirts, but on the other hand there is the feeling that being at home is not as important as being at work' (Gavron 1968, 132). Ann Oakley's *Housewife* (1974) similarly attacked the notion that women were first and foremost to fulfil the role of housebound serf. Virago's first lists featured several critiques of the housewife role (Adams and Laurikietis 1976; Nicholson 1977; Spring Rice 1981; Black 1983; D. Thompson 1983). This nonfiction was supplemented by novels like Zoe Fairbairn's *Benefits*, which examines the idea of wages for housework, and Diane Harpwood's *Tea and Tranquillisers*, which chronicles the misery of a woman prevented from enjoying a working life outside the home (Fairbairns 1979; Harpwood 1981).

In addition, there were explorations of the parallel issue of working women. Beginning with *Fenwomen*, Virago's first title, the press published critical examinations of women's status in the workplace (Chamberlain 1975). Author Mary Chamberlain notes the difficulties faced by women in conforming to cultural expectations that they won't work, as well as the limited opportunities available to women who *do* seek work outside the home. One of her interviewees recalls her desire, as a young woman, to work as a technical illustrator: 'I realised I couldn't get in anywhere. There didn't seem to be any firm round here that would take in girls. I gave the idea up then . . . I was ever so disappointed when I wrote round the firms and they said they didn't take girls' (Chamberlain 1975, 46–47). Virago followed up this text with other explorations of women in work, including Carol Adams and Rae Laurikietis' *The Gender Trap* (1976) and Joyce Nicholson's *What Society Does to Girls* (1977), in which the author argues that a female worker, in order to achieve the same rewards as her male equivalent, 'will always have to be much better than a man' (Nicholson 1977, 29).

Alongside this problematization of women's role as housewife, motherhood came to be figured as a key issue for second-wave feminist writers and readers. Greer set the terms of the debate, arguing that 'there is no reason, except the moral prejudice that women who do not have children are shirking a responsibility, why all women should consider themselves bound to breed. A woman who has a child is not then automatically committed to bringing it up' (Greer 1970, 262–63). The dual assumptions – that women ought to bear children and then ought to be mainly responsible for raising them – behind the motherhood imperative provoked a great deal of critical writing that set out to challenge this naturalizing of women's status as caregivers.

Following Greer, Firestone argued that reproduction was itself the basis of women and men's unequal status (Firestone 1970). She imagines a utopia in which conception and gestation occur artificially, free from the human body, as the end goal of feminism: 'not just the elimination of male *privilege* but of the sex *distinction* itself: genital differences between human beings would no longer matter culturally' (Firestone 1970, 11–12). Firestone's radical thesis was hugely important to the women's liberation movement as it gained momentum in the early 1970s, and was reprinted by The Women's Press in 1979. Rosalind Delmar, a member of the Virago Advisory Group, wrote the introduction to the UK edition.

Virago published several key texts in these debates about motherhood, including Adrienne Rich's *Of Woman Born,* published in 1977. In this text, Rich set out the idea that motherhood was a cultural imposition: 'the patriarchal institution of motherhood is not the "human condition" any more than rape, prostitution, and slavery are' (Rich 1977, 34). She argues that cultural, psychological and medical discourses of motherhood have come to naturalize the link between the female sex and childcare, an idea that was expanded by Nancy Chodorow in her text *The Reproduction of Mothering* (1978), which would go on to be hugely influential for feminist discussions of parenting. Chodorow similarly questions the seemingly 'natural' imperative for women to parent, an expectation based on cultural convention, and instead proposes equal parenting responsibilities for women and men – something that remains a feminist target to this day.

Virago also reprinted Margaret Llewellyn Davies' *Maternity* and Olsen's *Silences* (the first UK edition of Olsen's text) as well as publishing Catherine Itzin's *Splitting Up: Single Parent Liberation* and *War in the Nursery: Theories of the Child and Mother* by Denise Riley, all of which examined the impact and import of women's role as mother. Owen takes credit for the effect these texts had on an emerging feminist engagement with motherhood. 'With re-markable insight, Denise Riley opened up questions about the determining factors in historical change and redefined the notions of the "biological" and the "social"', she argues. 'In a post-1968 world of demonstrations, marches, sit-ins, workshops, questioning of authority, the enormously active women's liberation movement challenged the received view of women's place, and made it possible for women to test their own capacities in work and personal life – to make their stories central, not marginal' (Owen 2009).

The other feminist publishing houses that had sprung up alongside Virago were also examining the theme of motherhood. The managing director of The Women's Press, Stephanie Dowrick, co-wrote *Why Children?* with Sibyl Grundberg to problematize the ways in which women are seen pri-marily as mothers: '"Choice" is meaningless in a society which refuses to accept that responsibility for the care of children should be shared by all who benefit from their existence. So we "choose" between economic dependence within the family structure or the double load of work in the home as well as outside – or punitive welfare payments if we cannot or will not choose either' (Dowrick and Grundberg 1980, 10). The Women's Press also published Ju-dith Arcana's *Our Mothers' Daughters* and *Every Mother's Son,* as well as Eliz-abeth Baines' fictional representation of motherhood in *The Birth Machine.* Sheba reprinted *Rocking the Cradle,* in which the potential of gay parenting models to chip away at the edifice of patriarchy was explored (Hanscombe and Forster 1982).

Alongside this problematizing of motherhood, the feminist presses also took on the third female stereotype, that of 'sex object'. The issue of female sexuality was an important catalyst for the emergence of the women's liber-ation movement of the late 1960s and early 1970s. In spite of the so-called 'free love' era of the 1960s, women were still socially and psychologically constrained to one of two sexual categories – the active, desiring 'whore' or the passive, inhibited 'virgin'. Inevitably, as they began to organize po-litically, they sought new formulations of their sexual identities, beginning with Greer's demand in *The Female Eunuch* for women to embrace a more liberated, even promiscuous sexuality.

Virago published two important titles early on in this exploration of female sexual identity. Its second publication was Nancy Friday's *My Secret Garden* (1975), a collection of women's sexual fantasies and one of the first of the new genre of feminist texts to look closely at women's figuring of their own sexuality. *The Hite Report on Female Sexuality* (1976), published by Virago a year after Friday's text, continued this trend, with women writers focusing on reclaiming female pleasure in their sexual behaviour. Further books included Jane Mills' *Make it Happy* (1978), Anne Hooper's *The Body Electric* (1980), *Female Sexuality* by Janine Chasseguet-Smirgel (1981) and Jane Lazarre's *On Loving Men* (1981), while the other feminist presses also published a good number of similar 'self-help' sex texts. Sheba's author Anja Meulenbelt caused controversy in 1981 when her book *For Ourselves: From Women's Point of View: Our Bodies and Sexuality* was published:

> At the same time as elements of the American New Right were trying to get the feminist self-help manual *Our Bodies, Ourselves* banned from public libraries, their British equivalents attempted to hinder the publication by a feminist press of a book about female sexuality called *For Ourselves*. (Root 1984, 34)

These self-help books were perceived as a threat to the status quo that had long served to limit women sexually – and hence socially, psychologically and *materially*. Their publication was important for the emerging feminist critique of women's sexual figuring within patriarchal culture.

Reading Back: A History of Reviewing Women's Writing

We can also read through the publication of Virago's earliest lists the intention to change the literary landscape. For women to write was figured as an important feminist act, one that feminist publishers had the power to facilitate. As Margaret Atwood surmised in 1978, 'writers, both male and female, have to be selfish just to get the time to write, but women are not trained to be selfish [hence] it *is* more difficult for a woman writer in this society than for a male writer' (Atwood 1978, 33).

Contextualizing the literary culture of 1973 into which Virago's women launched their venture requires an examination of the traditions of reviewing as well as the commercial aspects of the industry outlined in Chapter 1. Atwood describes an experience from 1971 that encapsulates the literary establishment's attitudes towards female authors. Writing to ten women writers and ten male writers to ask if they'd ever been the subject of sexual bias in reviews, she found that most of the men said no: three-quarters of the women said yes. Atwood's own analysis of a selection of review pages showed most reviews were written by men and most of the books reviewed were also the work of male writers. In addition, 'the books written by women that were reviewed were more likely to be assigned to a female reviewer' (Atwood in Dybikowski et al. 1985, 151).

When women are judged to have written well, Atwood argues, it is because they have written in a 'masculine' way or, conversely, when a man writes in a 'feminine', it is to be applauded: 'when a man writes about things like doing the dishes, it's realism; when a woman does, it's an unfortunate feminine genetic limitation' (Atwood 1982b, 199). She also finds that women writers themselves are derogated through being sexualized, thus trivializing their work: 'the ploy diverts attention from the woman's achievement as a writer – the area where the man feels threatened – to her sexuality, where either way [through insult or compliment] he can score a verbal point' (Atwood 1982b, 202).

This exposure of the sexist culture of the review press was to become an important area for second-wave feminist investigation and complaint (see also Chapter 3). Following Atwood, Elaine Showalter (who would likewise become closely associated with Virago) took up the case: 'the very term "feminine", applied to literature, has been a pejorative', she said (Showalter 1971, 859). Germaine Greer identified in 1974 what she called a 'critical double standard' – reviewers not only distinguish what deserves to be read from what is mediocre, but also figure the ability to make this critical distinction as male (Greer 1974, 785). Dale Spender's in-depth critique of the reviewing establishment argued that male critics maintain literature as male territory by subjecting women writers to harassment: 'Women who reveal their intellectual resources are often described as having "masculine minds", which is a clever device for acknowledging their contribution while at the same time it allows it to be dismissed, for a woman with a "masculine mind" is unrepresentative of her sex, and the realm of the intellectual is still retained by men' (Spender 1982, 19).

Author Doris Lessing conducted her own experiment in the early 1980s to illustrate this reviewing bias. Deciding that 'I wanted to be reviewed on merit, as a new writer, without the benefit of a "name"; to get free of that cage of association and labels that every established writer had to learn to live inside', she pseudonymously submitted her novel *The Diaries of Jane Somers* to a number of publishers (Lessing 1983). Her usual publishers, Jonathan Cape in the United Kingdom and Granada in the United States, both declined it. It was submitted to Michael Joseph, publisher of Lessing's first book in the United Kingdom, who agreed to publish (even going as far as noting that the text was reminiscent of Doris Lessing's work). Bob Gottlieb of Knopf in the United States saw through the ruse immediately and agreed to be involved, so both he and the editors at Michael Joseph were brought in on the experiment.

The *Diaries* were submitted to a number of reviewers: none realized it was Lessing's work. It was instead treated like any other novel by an unknown woman writer: with a mixture of indifference and patronization. Lessing's experiment illustrated how mechanical the processes of reviewing can be and how little reviews can have to do with the actual text being considered. Lessing found that it was easy to predict what reviewers would say as they wrote to fulfil an editorial brief within the stylistic conventions of a literary review. She found, too, that it was mostly reviewed by women, but of those men who did review the book, none recognized the style they had found so unique and exciting in Lessing's earlier work (although when she came clean, some were able retrospectively to find merit). The critical reception afforded Lessing's work evidences the misogynist literary culture into which Virago and the other feminist presses were launched.

Review coverage of Angela Carter's writing also evidences this bias. Her work, although lauded, did not receive critical attention comparable to that of male peers because it fell foul of established literary codes. Carter herself notes:

> 'It would be whingeing, to say that men who are no better than I are very much more famous and very much richer and also regarded as the right stuff. It would ill become me. But it's amazing what the Old Boys club does for itself. They list the important British Con- temporary Writers, and they'll list Malcolm Bradbury and Kingsley Amis, and they'll leave out Doris Lessing who's the only one with a really huge international reputation. And they'll leave out Beryl Bainbridge. And. . .' she doesn't say it, but they also leave out Angela Carter. (Harron 1984)

Carter was a marginal writer in the early 1970s, in spite of having written prolifically and won many notable prizes. Her marginality meant that she made moves between several different publishers in the years before Virago was established, publishing her first four novels with Heinemann, before moving to Rupert Hart-Davis and then Quartet. As Marina Warner wrote on Carter's untimely death in 1992, finding a permanent home with Virago put Carter at the centre of a new, exciting force in publishing: 'her great friend Carmen Callil published her in Virago and her presence there helped establish a woman's voice in literature as special, as *parti pris,* as a crucial instrument in the forging of an identity for post-imperial, hypocritical, foss- ilised Britain' (Warner 1992, 25).

The traditions and biases of the review press bias inevitably had repercus- sions for feminist publishers. The literary establishment had historically long overlooked women's contributions as both writers and readers, as Marsha Rowe explains:

> I mean you must remember that newspaper editors in the seventies really did think of their newspapers as being sold to men, so most of them had a women's page and things that were supposedly interesting to women went on the women's page . . . so the idea of books for and about women that were of equal importance to anything else in the world just wasn't there. The idea just wasn't there. Let alone the market.[4]

Feminist publishers had to first circumvent this bias in order to get their books out to their readership before, second, dismantling it. In their favour, they could tap into a growing demand for women's writing from within the women's movement, as Goodings explains: 'there was a huge independent network. There was even the Radical Booksellers Association so you could sell, you could have a whole network of selling. In fact *Time Out* or *City Limits* – I can't remember, it could have been both – had an alternative bestseller list so you had *The Sunday Times'* bestseller list and then you had that one. And you know we had tons of stuff on that list, whereas we wouldn't necessarily always get on to *The Times'* list – and that reflected the culture of the time as much as the bookselling at the time'.[5] So to some extent feminist publishers were able to circumvent the bias of mainstream reviewers during Virago's first decade, but this didn't diminish the desire to see that bias broken down.

Uncovering Women's Literary Past

In beginning to tackle the problem of sexist review culture, feminist researchers first turned back to history, where they found a rich seam of material revealing the many ways in which women writers had long been ignored. These critics began to explore the absence of women from literary history, noting that canonical inclusion was almost exclusively a privilege reserved for men: 'of all the reading and study material available for stylistic imitation, inspiration, and stimulation of ideas, *over ninety per cent is prepared and written by men*' (Mullen 1972, 80, original emphasis). Works such as Ian Watt's charting of the rise of the novel reinforced the perception that's women engagement with literature was only ever as readers, not writers – his list of novelists is almost entirely male, and those women who do feature are described as imitators, not innovators (Watt 1974, 296).

Sheila Rowbotham's 1974 text *Hidden from History* challenged such received wisdoms. The conclusion she drew – that literary records of women's lives exist, but have become lost or deliberately obscured – were echoed a year later by Annette Kolodny, who demanded that the record be put straight: 'one vital goal of feminist scholarship must be the rediscovery and unearthing of texts by women which have, for one reason or another, been either lost or ignored' (Kolodny 1975, 88). Second-wave feminist literary critics took up the call to uncover this lost history, and Virago became central to the execution of this task upon the launch of its Modern Classics series in 1978.

These arguments, and specifically the influence of Rowbotham as a close friend of Virago's directors, had led to the institution of the Virago Reprint Library a year before, which was quickly developed into the Modern Classics series. The series challenged the review tradition that had consigned women authors – even those who had been a critical and commercial success in their day – to obscurity. One of its earliest published authors, Rosamond Lehmann, is a case in point: 'Lehmann's reputation remains problematic. In her day, she was certainly considered an important writer, and she was popular, too; but still, to look back on some of the reviews she received is to be reminded that notions of what constitutes a "serious" writer can be heavily weighted with assumptions; and also that the Virago Modern Classics project was (and remains) a necessary one' (Coe 2007).

Elaine Showalter's *A Literature of Their Own,* published by Virago in the same year that the Classics were launched, was a critical guide to the texts that were included in the early years of the series, as well as an influence on which texts were selected for it. The Classics put Virago right at the centre of the feminist attempt to reinsert women's writers into literary history, as author Hilary Mantel notes:

'I was living abroad when the list began', says Hilary Mantel. 'When I came back briefly in the 1980s – not a published writer then – the green spines were everywhere. I remember thinking that the world had changed while my back was turned, and changed very much for the better, as if a subtle rebalancing was occurring. Probably young women won't realise what it was like before. The star names among women – Murdoch, Spark – were treated like honorary men. Older, less-known women writers were only to be found in tatty library editions . . . Suddenly, women had become powers in the publishing industry, and they were using that fact to publicise the vitality and enduring quality of women's writing . . . I remember a man sneering at me at a dinner party circa 1975: "Women have no tradition." Actually, they had, and here was some of it in print.' (Cooke 2008)

And alongside Virago, the Women's Press' first list similarly included re-printed texts from nineteenth- and twentieth-century women writers, as feminist critics began to look back through history to find the spaces occupied by women writers. The 'rediscovery' of all these rescued texts evidenced the ways in which the parameters of 'great' literature had been drawn to exclude women. The Modern Classics were a crucial aspect of Virago's work in a political as well as commercial sense, a deliberate attempt to counter the historical pejoration and suppression of women's writing. The rapid expansion of the series during Virago's first decade was down to a combination of this political intent and financial necessity: 'the importance given to reprints is partly a reflection of their aim to establish the existence of women's culture more firmly in the public mind, and partly a financial consideration, since not only do reprints cost less than publishing a book for the first time, they also sell fairly well' (Cadman et al. 1981, 31). This explains why, of the fiction published during Virago's first decade, 136 texts were Modern Classics, while only twenty-four were new works of fiction.

In the Classics series, then, business acumen collided with feminist principle. 'The information about the series came from Carmen's literary experience and wish to replicate Penguin's success, and Ursula's experience of places like Frank Cass [Penguin and Frank Cass had also reprinted a number of obscure and out-of-print literary texts]', Spicer explains.[6] Callil and Owen had seen the success of reprinting historical fiction while working in mainstream houses, and applied the same principle to their feminist press. But however pragmatic the reasons for reprinting these texts were, the Modern Classics also fulfilled a political purpose – and they became a sales phenomenon, vital to sustaining Virago through its first decade.

The Classics were identifiable on the bookshelves because of their distinctive styling, created by designer Mick Jarvis with Callil's input – she chose the pictures to reproduce on the front covers, sourcing them from provincial galleries across the United Kingdom, as well as the Hayward and her own collection (Lowry 1983, 37). Goodings believes this branding helped bring the Classics to a wider audience. 'The Classics had that kind of way of infiltrating. They could go to places that other bits of Virago couldn't go in those days', she says. 'People just thought they were ok, they were not frightened of them.'[7] But the series was criticized by more radical feminists who saw them as pandering to middle-class sensibilities, lacking the edge of new feminist writing. Alexandra Pringle, who edited the series after Callil began working at Chatto in 1982, is clear that the Classics were as political as the new writing Virago published: 'it was a very straight reclamation of women's lives and publishing novels that deal with women's lives in all their aspects . . . it was looking at all sort of writers . . . and finding completely hidden voices like an Indian writer, Attia Hosain, or the lesbian writer Eliot Bliss, and so all the different aspects of women's lives were illuminated'.[8]

The Modern Classics had a huge impact on the reshaping of literary history and the expansion of the canon to include many more women's voices. Virago published hundreds of 'lost' British women writers and the Classics list became, perhaps, its most famous hallmark. The series proved 'there was rich value to be had from writing which stood outside the Great Tradition of English Literature' and provided concrete evidence of the flimsiness of arguments that women had not written in the past or had not written well (Lyndon 1984, 48).

The validity of traditional formulations of the canon thus came under fire during the second wave, with the Classics being at the centre of these debates. Inclusion within the boundaries of the canon denoted authority, as literary critic John Sutherland explains: 'there are, in fact, few better preservatives of a novel and its author's fame than to be set for examination, to be judged as suitable research material by the committees which approve PhD topics, or to be approached by an American university offering the curatorship of manuscript material' (Sutherland 1981, 11). Feminist literary critics thus set about tackling the absence of women in the canon, with early texts such as *Rediscovery: 300 Years of Stories by and about Women,* published by The Women's Press (Dinesen 1981). The Women's Press also went on to publish a number of important texts by Dale Spender, who made the theme of women's canonical exclusion central to her work. Her sister Lynne developed a theory of literary 'gatekeeping' to show that canonical inclusion was protected by gatekeepers whose interests were served by the texts they granted entry (Spender 1983). She posited feminist publishers as vital to the reinvestment of women's writing with value by, crucially, making that writing publicly known.

In her 1978 text *Silences,* reprinted by Virago in 1980, Tillie Olsen similarly argues that feminism's role is to unearth women's writing that can broaden our understanding of women's lives. Virago published other books such as Nicola Beauman's *A Very Great Profession,* in which the author refutes the claim that women have no literary history, and cites a range of women's historical texts for inclusion in a new, feminist canon that paid greater attention to women writers (Beauman 1983). This interrogation of the canon resulted in more women's texts being incorporated more university curricula in the late 1970s and early 1980s as new courses were structured and indeed new disciplines developed that set about redressing women's long history of exclusion from literary valuation. This is one of second-wave feminism's great successes, in which Virago and the other feminist publishers that emerged during the 1970s and early 1980s had a crucial hand. They helped change the literary landscape for good, expanding the canon so that it included a more fair representation of the writing of great female as well as male authors.

At the end of its first ten years, then, Virago had become an important cornerstone of the UK feminist and literary scenes, an achievement that perhaps exceeded even Callil's own high expectations. It had grown into a much larger operation than most of its contemporaries on the feminist publishing scene, giving it broader reach. By 1982, Virago's directors presided over a prosperous imprint situated within a mainstream publishing house that offered financial security as well as editorial freedom – the ideal arrangement, as Owen described it at the time. All this was to change in its second decade, however, as the complexities of new commercial paradigms and fragmented and fractured feminist politicking threw up a whole new set of problems, requiring new solutions.

Notes

1. Anon, 'Books and Book Women', *Sunday Times,* 25 November 1984, magazine section, p. 12.
2. Interview with Carmen Callil, 10 November 2004.
3. Interview with Marsha Rowe, 15 July 2004.
4. Ibid.
5. Interview with Lennie Goodings, 8 November 2004.
6. Interview with Harriet Spicer, 20 October 2004.
7. Interview with Lennie Goodings, 8 May 2008.
8. Interview with Alexandra Pringle, 28 October 2009.

Part II
1983–94

Chapter 3

'Alternative, Autonomous, and Viable'

Feminist Publishing and the Mainstream

By 1983, as Virago's second decade got underway, there was a new, flour-ishing network of feminist writers, publishers and bookshops. The Women's Press, Sheba, Pandora and Onlywomen were up and running, as were wom-en's bookshops Sisterwrite and Silver Moon, and support networks in the form of, most notably, Women in Publishing. Virago, the longest-established of these feminist publishers, also had the largest output. It published more than three times as many books as its nearest rival in the years 1983–92: 747 in total, compared to 229 by The Women's Press during the same period. Onlywomen published just twenty-six books. Sheba, another independent collective, published a total of thirty-seven.

Virago's business structure lay behind its larger literary output. At the start of its second decade, it was an imprint within the 'Chatto, Virago, Bodley Head and Jonathan Cape' group, enjoying the financial security and established links in the industry brought about by this merger. Later on in this ten-year period, Callil, Owen, Spicer, Pringle and Goodings forced a management buy-out, reinstating Virago as an independent in 1987. In spite of this, the company continued to publish more books than its rivals on the feminist publishing scene and punch above its weight in terms of visibility in the literary marketplace.

The 1987 buy-out is important, as Spicer argues: 'to me it is complete fact that a great deal changes once a company is not a standalone business, where the women involved in it are choosing to create their own organiza-tion and existence in the world by their own efforts drawing on the work of others'.[1] Virago had benefited hugely from its incorporation into CBC, but the sacrifice in terms of editorial freedom was clearly weighing on the direc-tors after four years of the arrangement (as had been the case with Quartet right at Virago's beginning). The cultural and political climate in which Vi-rago operated in the 1980s was also very different from that of its early years. By 1983, Margaret Thatcher was well established as the United Kingdom's first female Prime Minister, under whose tenure the welfare state was dismantled, public services privatized and a free market economy fostered, fundamentally shifting the economic setting within which Virago worked. In addition, assaults on individual rights, such as the passing into law in 1988 of the Section 28 clause outlawing the 'promotion' of homosexual lifestyles, created a sense of embattlement for LGBT+ communities, other minorities and the feminist movement more broadly.

It is of course ironic that this erosion of the rights of working-class, black and gay men and women occurred under the leadership of a female prime minister who came, somewhat perversely, to offer 'her own life and career as a proof of the folly of feminism. Since she has achieved power and success she sees no reason why other women could not do so if they wanted' (Webster 1990, 4). Thatcher constituted a hugely problematic emblem of 'woman', an anomaly that during the course of the 1980s was theorized by feminist thinkers and critiqued in books printed by the feminist presses as women's publishing houses played their part in challenging Thatcher's orthodoxy.

Virago itself expanded rapidly during its second decade, as the UK economy boomed and growing consumer spending meant there was an expanding market for publishers to exploit. Owen describes this change in the publishing environment: 'By the eighties, places like Bloomsbury were starting up with £1.5 million from the City. We started up with a £25,000 bank overdraft and a couple of loans.'[2] During its second decade, Virago's published list more than trebled in size. Between 1983 and 1992, 747 books were published compared to 208 in the previous ten years. It capitalized on the booming economy of the 1980s by focusing on what it knew best: clever marketing of excellent literature. It also ventured into new territory with the opening, for example, of a dedicated bookshop in Covent Garden. This project, described as 'tasteful but trendy' by the press and by Callil as 'a general bookshop with a radical slant', was opened in December 1984 by Rosamond Lehmann. The shop in Covent Garden (which also stocked non-Virago titles as part of the project to make women's writing available to as wide a market as possible) was short-lived, but points to the new opportunities that arose within a literary marketplace in which there was plenty more money to go round.

In this context, Virago's marketing and promotion was crucial to its ongoing success during this period. Virago's brand identity helped foster enormous loyalty among its readers who trusted the press to provide them with a good read as well as a female perspective of the world. Goodings says that the books' distinctive format and design – the green spines and apple logo – were a political statement: 'some people call the Virago green livery a ghetto. I call it the stylish and highly visible evidence of women writers and publishers who boldly continue to call themselves feminists' (Goodings 1993a, 20). But it was a contentious issue, as more radical feminist publishers and critics argued that their 'branding' of women's writing was detrimental to feminism itself. They contended that Virago's expensive marketing strategies were putting smaller-scale feminist and radical publishers out of business: publicity 'makes or breaks – and the shoestring operations cannot afford much' (Jones 1991b, 16). Gail Chester and Sigrid Neilsen wrote passionately about the need for feminism to maintain its grassroots, and for feminist publishing in particular to avoid pricing out poorer women, at the time that Thatcher's assault on the Greater London Council (GLC) meant that cheaply rented premises for such grassroots organizations were being rapidly revoked.

Thatcher's determined and ultimately successful attempt to shut down the GLC and especially its women's committee had a serious impact on feminist writers and readers. The GLC had allocated much-needed funds to important feminist projects such as the women's bookshop Silver Moon, as Jane Cholmeley, the shop's founder, recalls. She notes that without the GLC, her business would never have got off the ground: 'that is where we got incredibly lucky, because it was the time of Ken Livingston and the GLC'.[3] Sheba's closure in the early 1990s is also due to the cutting off of these monies: 'founded in the earliest months of the first Thatcher government, the Sheba collective may not have predicted how devastating an impact that government's later abolition of the GLC and its slashing of the arts budget were to have on their publishing enterprise' (Murray 2004, 157).

At the same time, books were becoming big business: 'over the past ten years, demand for books as reflected in the sales of the publishing industries of developed countries has led to sizeable sales increases by value', wrote an industry expert in 1984 (de Bellaigue 1984, 152). The contrast between the boom in book sales and the assault on liberal political positions during Thatcher's era defines Virago's challenges in the 1980s. Publishing is, after all, a *business* – feminist publishers could not afford to ignore the realities of the marketplace: 'feminism's discomfort with profit in connection with the arts, or with the lucrative business of packaging, marketing and selling creativity, has to be resolved', argued Dale Spender. 'For the uncomfortable paradox of the publishing tale is that some houses have been rescued by the new internationalism of the book world, and that some writers have never had it so good''' (Jones 1991b, 16–17). Certainly, Virago was prospering, and its success helped to popularize not only the books on its own lists but also women's writing more generally (see the section entitled 'In and around the Mainstream: Feminist Publishing Makes Inroads . . . and is Invaded' later on in this chapter). Virago's success during its second decade was predicated on two very contrasting – indeed, conflicting – circumstances. It had to strike a fine and often precarious balance between exploiting the opportunities offered by the 1980s boom in business and maintaining its feminist politics. This was not an easy path to tread.

'Alternative, Autonomous, and Viable'

Towards the end of Virago's second decade, Dale Spender claimed that publishing was 'one – if not the only – area where women have been able to set up an *alternative,* autonomous, and viable industry, and this has numerous implications for publishing and for the power configurations of the sexes' (Spender 1989, 47). This claim warrants further examination. Undoubtedly the feminist presses represented a still-rare example of women as powerful economic players. Marion Boyars, the first woman in Britain to set up her own publishing company (doing business to this day), knew why this female executive was such a rare creature: 'men feel uncomfortable with women in positions of competitive power' (Owen 1988, 121). We can see evidence of this male unease in the easy caricaturing of Virago's women as shrewish harridans – indeed, as 'viragos' – which was common in media comment on Callil and the others in the 1980s. It betrays the threat inherent in a woman's accession to a position of economic and cultural authority.

This unease was further manifested in the sustained campaign to delegitimize the figure of the female executive that emerged in the 1980s. As Virago writer Jane McLoughlin notes in her 1992 text on women in business, 'the consensus view of a woman who makes no secret of her competitiveness is that she is a bitch', while the positive aspects of business behaviour – confidence, assertiveness and acumen – continue to be figured as male (McLoughlin 1992, 122). The category of female executive was derogated since it troubled the patriarchal construction of ideal womanhood within culture. This meant, for example, that Naim Attallah could expect to be taken seriously as a male publisher of women's writing, while women publishers were made ridiculous: in the coverage given to Ros de Lanerolle's departure from The Women's Press in 1991, Attallah was described as intervening 'to sort out what he calls "arguments among the women"' (Pallister 1991).

Feminist coverage of this event in *Spare Rib* magazine highlighted the sexism of its media coverage: 'Mainstream papers which covered the story found in it a reassuring confirmation of all their suspicions: that professional women are incompetent and squabble like fishwives' (Ahmad 1991, 10). Noting that the story might have been cast as a boardroom coup if the cast had been all-male, Ahmad says that instead the event was presented as a rivalry in which powerful and committed feminist women competed for male approval. Attallah himself did not help dispel this impression, either at the time or in subsequent recollections of the event. He was quoted shortly after de Lanerolle's dismissal in terms that reveal a perception of his own role as benevolent patriarch. 'Despite the hullabaloo over his temporary donning of the MD's hat of The Women's Press, he [Attallah] claimed: "Men need to be strong and powerful to support women."'[4]

Virago's women were similarly stereotyped in sexual or gendered terms, as Harriet Spicer confirms: 'Carmen was treated entirely differently, Ursula was treated entirely differently from the way analogous people in Cape or something . . . they did not get that kind of flack. So I think really the media sexism has been in the treatment of the personalities.'[5] Gail Rebuck, another powerful female publisher, suffered her share of attempts to position her as sexual object, returning her to the age-old stereotype so effective in the limitation of women in the past. She notes that many of the men she dealt with 'feel threatened if negotiations are not undertaken in a flirtatious way because they can't place you within the comfortable stereotypes that they have grown up with' (Kinnock and Millar 1993, 169).

As these sexist parameters continued to define the workplace, Virago's example of a *successful* female-run business venture was important. And as the 1980s wore on, the women challenging this prejudice by setting up their own publishing businesses were growing in number, as Boyars notes: 'we now have a nice clutch of females such as Judith Piatkus, the Virago women, and quite a few male/female partnerships without marital ties, and their track record would indicate that entrepreneurship is not a male preserve' (Owen 1988, 121). Enterprises such as Virago showed women (and men for that matter) that success in 'male' arenas – politics, commerce, literature – was achievable. Writer Margaret Drabble saluted their example: 'the eighties have produced new images of Power Woman. Articulate, confident, and often combative, she manifests herself in Mrs Thatcher, Benazir Bhutto, Tessa Blackstone, Carmen Callil, Margaret Atwood and Glenys Kinnock, and innumerable others who are speaking up around the world'.[6] There were limits, of course, to the achievements of women publishers. While at the end of the 1980s some were arguing that 'publishing seems to have let women through to the very top – at the business end – in a way that, so far, no other industry in this country can equal', the reality was rather different, and the limited extent to which women had broken through publishing's glass ceiling was comprehensively highlighted by an important piece of research commissioned by Women in Publishing (WiP) in 1989 (Dix 1988, 10).

Published in *The Bookseller* as 'Twice as Many, Half as Powerful', this WiP research showed the publishing world to be still firmly demarcated along gender lines (Tomlinson and Colgan 1989). It detailed the industry's lack of provision for training, career development and equal opportunities for women. The report's authors made it clear that women in mainstream publishing houses were poorly paid support workers, limited to publicity and administrative work, while men took charge of editing and finance: the arenas of *real* cultural and economic authority. 'Men and women are not evenly distributed across functional areas of publishing; women are highly concentrated in the areas of secretarial, junior administrative and clerical work, desk editing, publicity and rights' (Tomlinson and Colgan 1989, 19).

The results of the Women in Publishing survey were greeted with resigned recognition by women working in the mainstream industry: 'it will come as no surprise to anyone with any experience of British publishing to hear that, though female employees outnumber men in the industry, there are fewer women directors and managers . . . There are the prominent exceptions: Carmen Callil who crossed the divide from women's publishing as co-founder and chair of Virago press to mainstream publishing to become managing director and publisher at Chatto and Windus as well' (Macaskill 1989, 256). But in spite of the exceptions of Callil and a few others (her friend Liz Calder, for example), the mainstream publishing industry on the whole excluded women from its highest echelons: 'women are under-represented in the top tiers of publishing. Men are more than twice as likely to become managers, and more than five times as likely to become a company board director. The larger the company and the more senior the board, the fewer the women directors' (Tomlinson and Colgan 1989, 8). Calder, who by the late 1980s was the publishing director of Bloomsbury, sums up the situation:

> On the whole I'd say the eighties have been a three-steps-forward-and-two-back affair for women. Certainly in publishing progress is painfully slow and tokenism reigns supreme. Several notable appointments elevated women to positions of considerable power in leading publishing houses, only to be knocked back into place by corporate manoeuvring, removing much of their effective control.[7]

There were honourable exceptions – not least the example of the feminist publishing houses – but on the whole the industry remained dominated by men.

The 1987 Buy-out: What it Meant to Be in Charge Again

The concept of publishing as praxis continued to be important for Virago during its second decade. It was during this period that Callil, Owen, Spicer,

Pringle and Goodings made the decision to buy back their independence, leaving the umbrella of Chatto, Bodley Head and Cape in 1987. While the arrangement had certainly had its positives – a wider distribution for Virago's books, greater profit and a corresponding expansion of the press' list – it also had its drawbacks. De Bellaigue explains: 'one issue that rankled with all the publishing companies revolved around the attribution of central overheads, which had the effect of giving them control over less than half the overheads they bore' (de Bellaigue 2004, 153). Virago had to shoulder its share of these communal costs, in spite of the three other companies in the umbrella group foundering in the five years after the 1982 merger. Pringle says: 'very quickly, because of the overheads, we were no longer profitable and so the decision was made to try to buy ourselves out and then get ourselves back into shape, and profitable. Because huge overheads bring you right down'.[8]

Owen recalls the chain of events that culminated in the buy-out: 'in 1986, it was Carmen actually who went to the board meeting, a Chatto, Bodley Head and Cape board meeting and represented Virago there. And she started warning us that there was a problem, there were problems with profit, they were deeply in debt. Virago was doing well, but you see they were doing everything, distribution, you know . . . But she said, you know, it's really big trouble and it was'.[9] Virago's management team decided to act: 'it proposed a management buyout. In October, this was formally presented to the board by Ursula Owen and accepted in principle. By April 1987 negotiations had advanced sufficiently for *The Bookseller* to announce the imminent completion of the management buyout' (De Bellaigue 2004, 154).

Amid these negotiations, Random House acquired CVBC through a subsidiary in May 1987. 'Towards the end of the negotiations, Random House swooped down and bought the group', Owen remembers. 'And they tried to persuade us to stay too, but by then we didn't want to, we were sort of in another place in our heads.'[10] Virago was not easily let go: 'Random House's Simon Masters, now the top executive in charge of Chatto, Bodley Head and Cape, had invited Virago to remain with the group' (Sage 1987, 742). Tough negotiations ensued, with Virago's women leveraging finance through selling their shares to both Rothschild Ventures and Bob Gavron. 'In order to raise the funds we had to get somebody to give us some money, basically', Pringle explains. 'It was the venture capital part of Rothchild's that decided, and they vetted us, and we all had to be interviewed. And I . . . it was the day of my son's first birthday and so I had to go first so I could hare across town to go to his birthday.'[11]

In July 1987, Virago completed its buy-out, with Callil retaining her posts as non-executive chairman of Virago and managing director of Chatto & Windus. Virago's management team continued much as it had: Callil remained at Chatto day-to-day, but held her role as Chair of Virago; Owen and Spicer remained MDs of Virago with Pringle and Goodings closely involved in directing the press. However, even after Virago bought back its independence, there remained a balance to strike between economic and editorial priorities. Virago still had to answer to its shareholders and this meant it was required to remain profitable. NM Rothschild was now the majority shareholder in the company, which brought with it another set of complications.

Rothschild was a corporate institution whose focus was profit, not publishing. The economy was changing and recession was setting in again, and Virago had to streamline its management and look to its future. Pringle was offered the job of editorial director at Hamish Hamilton, prompting her twelve years at the company to come to an end in 1990. This left a vacancy, which was filled by Goodings' promotion to editorial director. Very soon after, Owen decided the time was right to move on too: 'I got offered this rather yummy temporary job of being the Cultural Policy Adviser to the Labour Party, which was funded by Paul Hamlyn . . . so I decided that I would make a leap and do that. Alexandra . . . left before me, I think in the autumn of 1990, and I left at the end of 1990.'[12] These events evidence the difficulty Virago faced in balancing profits against its politics. This conflict will perhaps always lie at the heart of a political publisher's operations – as Callil says, 'no publishing house is independent, in truth, the economic and creative sides are not separable' (Sage 1987, 742).

Reviewing the Reviews: The Challenge Continues

Virago also had to operate within the parameters of *literary* traditions and structures. The exclusion of women writers from the review page had by now become a major theme of feminist literary criticism (see Chapter 2), with one of the effects of this critical appraisal of review culture being the attempt, throughout the 1980s, to establish a new *feminist* reviewing tradition. Examples such as the *Women's Review* magazine, which launched in 1985, set a different brief from that of the mainstream review press: '*Women's Review* is not launching itself into the women's magazine world. Rather, it sits firmly facing the intellectual marketplace, and is a challenge and addition to the male-dominated literary, arts and politics publications' (Ardill and O'Sullivan 1985, 12). It complemented feminist magazines such as *Spare Rib,* which had always carried book reviews, but rather than being a general feminist title, it focused *specifically* on literature.

There were other, similar magazines such as *Writing Women,* and events such as Feminist Book Fortnight also sprung up as women set about redressing the imbalance of their representation in reviews. The first of these took place in 1984, and the Fortnights gained momentum as the popularity – and profitability – of women's writing continued to grow throughout the 1980s. The events were also figured as a rebuttal to the representation of feminism put across in the mainstream review pages:

> 'It's not a man-the-barricades promotion', says Katy Nicholson, of The Women's Press. 'It's to say, look, there is this wealth of really enjoyable writing, and we want books that can easily be stocked in a wide range of places, and enjoyed by a wide range of people. We want to say that feminism isn't doom and gloom, it's celebrating a wealth of different views.' (Bennett 1988)

The popularity of women's writing, and the desire to grow the burgeoning market around female literature, was undoubtedly also what motivated the organizers of the Book Fortnights (they were partly backed by mainstream company WH Smith), but they nevertheless played a part in establishing an alternative to the traditional review culture. The need to continually confront the bias of literary traditions was made manifest in 1987 with the publication of another very important WiP report. *Reviewing the Reviews* gave a damning indictment of the nature and influence of review culture, highlighting the bias that remained and revealing 'a discrepancy between the apparent interest in women's books and the actual notice they receive in the press. A casual glance at the book pages will often show a much larger number of reviews of books by male authors' (Women in Publishing 1987, 1).

The report showed that male authors got more and longer reviews, as well as more prominent positions on the page – both for fiction and non-fiction (in spite of the fact that women wrote more fiction than men). Of the twenty-eight publications studied, women authors only took top billing in the magazines published explicitly for a female audience. 'In all the other twenty-one publications, she is left in the shadows while the male author takes centre stage' (Women in Publishing 1987, 9). In addition, even within the women's magazines, men weren't as overlooked as were women in the mainstream publications. The report also showed that women wrote fewer reviews and mostly reviewed other women writers, 'so the minority female reviewer finds herself linked up with the minority female author' (Women in Publishing 1987, 30). It confirmed what Virago already knew: that it and the other feminist publishers were battling a powerful literary tradition from which women had long been excluded.

The consequence of this sidelining of women's writing on the review page is twofold: first, 'until female authors are given adequate review coverage on the book pages, they will be unable to attain their rightful share of the market' (Women in Publishing 1987, 65); and, second, women's exclusion from the review pages perpetuates a general view of literature as 'male': 'literary editors may claim that their pages reflect society, but people in positions of responsibility who deal with the world of ideas are the best placed to influence changes in attitudes. In producing pages biased against women, they are perpetuating existing prejudices and subtly shaping people's perceptions of reality' (Women in Publishing 1987, 91).

The report figured the work of Virago and other feminist publishers as vital, providing as they did a challenge to this construction of literature as male. Virago writers such as Angela Carter, who was acerbic about the effect of the male reviewing tradition, recognized the discrimination women faced in getting their work a fair hearing:

> Writing fiction is a profession dominated by women; you just wouldn't think it when it comes to reading the posh reviews. It's a question of justice, really. And it's a long haul – and it's a disgrace that Grub Street is in the same position vis-à-vis women as it was when George Eliot was working. (Harron 1984)

Ursula Owen further notes that the exclusion of feminist texts from coverage by reviewing media constitutes 'a powerful form of censorship', having a real effect on the way feminist ideology is presented to a mainstream audience (Owen in Owen 1988, 100).

Feminist critics therefore focused their attention on the review tradition. Dale Spender argued that 'it is not the writing, but the sex which is responsible for the poor ratings given to women's writing in the literary world of men' (Spender 1989, 1). She figured Virago's Modern Classics as an important challenge to this male bias in reviewing and its effect on the English canon: 'when they found and reprinted so many various women from the past, the presses produced the ammunition which could challenge the defences of literary men' (Spender 1989, 52). The Modern Classics, and the reprint series' published by other feminist presses following Virago's example, challenged the notion of 'great' canonical literature (see Chapter 2). They both fuelled and were fuelled by the feminist literary critical scene, which, by the time Spender was writing these words, had become established in the academy and was gaining in influence.

These reprinted books created new avenues for critical study – for example, Antonia White and Dorothy Richardson had long been overlooked by literary scholars, but their inclusion in the Modern Classics list drove feminist critics towards them.[13] In making these texts available, Virago made it possible for feminist critics to theorize them. In addition, it made visible a wealth of historical women's fiction that provoked a reassessment of the literary canon as a whole. Such reprints proved there was literature of worth beyond what had historically been deemed canonical. The Modern Classics also suggested new inclusions for a contemporary canon, for example, by reprinting in 1982 Margaret Atwood's 1979 novel *Life Before Man* (Atwood 1982c). Spicer draws a line of continuity between women's writing from the past and that of the present, underlining the need for a reframing of the canon both in historical and contemporary terms. 'I think they were [all] as political and as reaffirming of women as *Life Before Man* which was one of the first reprints', she says.[14]

In and around the Mainstream: Feminist Publishing Makes Inroads... and is Invaded

At the start of Virago's second decade, it was enjoying the results of ten years of growth. The 1970s had seen a groundswell of feminist activity in the United Kingdom that had created a ready market of readers for Virago's product: female writing. During its second decade, however, Virago and the other feminist presses faced new challenges. Mainstream houses began to figure women's writing as a money-spinner and sought to cash in on its new popularity. Michelene Wandor, a Virago writer and one-time member of its Advisory Group, makes the following point:

> Twenty years ago the word 'feminism' was a term one used with be-leaguered defiance, knowing that, in most spheres of life, to declare oneself a feminist was to unleash a range of responses from vicious hostility through ridicule to simple ignorance. Now the word can be used to blazon sales on book covers. (Wandor 1989)

Having realized there was a profitable market in women's writing, mainstream presses began to encroach on the ground claimed by Virago, The Women's Press and their contemporaries. The feminist presses became, in a sense, victims of their own success. They now had stiff competition: 'in 1988 the first two feminist publishing houses in Britain to address mainstream society, Virago and The Women's Press, came officially of age . . . both these presses now have an annual turnover of over a million pounds. On the back of their success the straight, male-dominated presses began to produce their own feminist lists' (Duncker 1992, 40). This appropriation of women's writing by mainstream publishers angered many in the women's movement, who claimed that 'the straight male presses only produced their feminist lists when women had proved themselves to be profitable. They let women take the risks, then climbed aboard the financial bandwagon' (Duncker 1992, 40).

The greater financial clout of mainstream houses meant they were able to buy off already-established writers from the feminist presses. Virago, The Women's Press and, to a lesser extent, Sheba, Pandora and Onlywomen all recognized, as Gerrard puts it, 'that losing authors, and acting as stepping stones to aid them into the mainstream, was an inevitable part of success' (Gerrard 1989, 29). Gerrard contends that feminist presses were left with only the more 'risky' authors to publish, a point also made by one of Virago's authors. '"They are a springboard for ambitious young writers," says Michele Roberts. "They'll take them on when perhaps nobody else will touch them because they're unknown writers in our Thatcherite, commercial world. Nobody worries if you spend half a million promoting Julie Burchill's newest sex shocker: it sells lots of copies and everyone's very happy. The Women's Press doesn't have that kind of budget"' (Briscoe 1990b). Limited by their size to smaller marketing and distribution budgets, feminist publishers had to gamble more on unknown authors, nurturing them and helping generate their success – and risking that such success might be the catalyst for them to move to a bigger publisher.

The writer Ali Smith admits that she left Virago because it 'paid me almost nothing'.[15] Jeanette Winterson also departed Pandora for greater riches in the mainstream – more women writers followed suit. The relationships between writer, agent and publisher of course complicated these arrangements. Doubtless Callil's close friendship with Carter played a not insubstantial part in Virago keeping the paperback rights to Carter's work. 'Loyalty was an absolute cornerstone of her personality', Callil wrote on her death in 1992. 'About a month ago, in Brompton Hospital, she was fiddling with a manuscript on her bed: the next *Virago Book of Fairy Tales*, to be published in the autumn. "I'm just finishing this off for the girls," she said' (Callil 1992).

This co-option of women's writing by mainstream publishing represented a real dilemma: women's writing was getting a broader readership, but this came at the price of endangering the presses' own livelihoods. Literary commentators wondered what role remained for the feminist presses:

Their role has clearly changed considerably since the rebel-rousing days of their inception. Then they were pioneers, opening the floodgates for a mass of theory and fiction previously left by the wayside and giving voice to women of different creeds and backgrounds. Feminist publishing for the nineties is quite another matter not so much because of our dubious espousal of the term 'post-feminist' as the closing gap between feminist and mainstream houses, the increasing commercial pull of the women's publishers and the realisation that 'women's' writing is a great little money-spinner. (Briscoe 1990b)

This troubling of the role of feminist publishers points to the changing nature of feminism itself as Virago's second decade rolled on. The 'rebel-rousing' of early second-wave politics gave way to more diverse and fragmented formulations of feminism, which had a great impact on the types of books that were written (see Chapter 4). Yet the second-wave feminist publishing phenomenon endured, even while the balance between political impulse and commercial reality became more challenging as feminism itself fractured, at the same time as it also moved into the academy. Callil argues that Virago managed to strike this balance by publishing books of broad appeal: 'we were far less politically correct. Definitely. I mean, I always wanted to reach out to the world, to the woman who wasn't a feminist, and the men who weren't feminists you know. I was never interested in the ghetto'.[16]

The perception of Virago as publishing books of mainstream appeal, alongside its having been situated within the mainstream at CBC, certainly helped it sustain healthy sales. In contrast, The Women's Press was in a more ambivalent position: in some ways it was perceived of as being more radical than Virago as, under de Lanerolle's stewardship, it built up a reputation for championing writing from minority groups: 'under her the Press grew from a small concern to a notable and exciting force in international women's publishing. She was clear in her mind that the role of the Press in the eighties should be to provide a public platform for women who might have no other access to the mainstream media' (Benson and McDermid 1993). Yet de Lanerolle's forced departure from The Women's Press in 1991 was put down to the perception that she published 'mostly unsexy, issue-based books which no-one else will touch' (Steel 1998). This was in spite of The Women's Press being home to big-name authors such as Alice Walker, Marge Piercy, Michele Roberts and Janet Frame.[17] Owner Naim Attallah added to this framing of The Women's Press under de Lanerolle: 'my support began to wane as it became clear that her editorial policy was having a negative effect on the Press and giving everyone involved a cause for concern' (Attallah 2007, 465).

At Pandora, a turbulent series of moves between publishers began in 1985 with its sale by Routledge & Kegan Paul to Associated Book Publishers, who were themselves taken over two years later by International Thomson Publishing. A year after, the Pandora imprint was sold on to Unwin Hyman and then to HarperCollins in 1990. This meant that by 1990, Pandora was part of Rupert Murdoch's empire – further, following a failed attempt to buy it back in 1991, founder Philippa Brewster was sacked, leaving the press without an identifiable feminist director . . . or direction. Inevitably, as Simone Murray argues, this compromised its feminist intent: 'the telling shift from publishing radical treatises to publishing consumables for the professional women of market-rationalised Tory Britain undoubtedly echoes the general tenor of the times' (Murray 2004, 105).

Independent feminist presses such as the collectively run Sheba and Onlywomen continued to publish material that was worked on by all-women editorial and design teams (some of whom would read every manuscript submitted to them in their entirety), produced as well as disseminated through feminist distribution and sales networks. These presses measured their success in terms of the absolute freedom they had to choose what to publish and the consequent symbolic meanings this had for women generally. 'It was the price we paid for having total control over the whole publishing process', says radical publisher Joy Pitman. 'Something which as women we rarely have, and as writers, almost never. It was worth it' (Chester and Neilsen 1987, 106). Yet their collective work practices and separation from mainstream networks meant the scale – and arguably the impact – of these presses was limited. Onlywomen published just twenty-six books between 1983 and 1992, Sheba only slightly more – proof if it were needed of the claim that 'democracy is appallingly time-consuming' (Duncker 1992, 41). Radical publishers such as Gail Chester and Sigrid Neilsen warned that 'feminists need to find a balance between taking the opportunities commercial publishers can offer and maintaining the small feminist presses. For those of us who come from so-called "minority" groups, it is a matter of our very survival' (Chester and Neilsen 1987, 15).

Twenty years after Virago was set up, these 'minority group' women's presses still sat alongside the larger feminist publishers, all maintaining their presence in an industry that had caught on to the profitability of women's writing. By the close of Virago's second decade, the 'London's Women Research and Resources Centre listed twenty-one women's publishing houses and an article in the Times Educational Supplement commented on the "rise of feminist publishing" in the context of the increasingly "dire straits" of publishing generally' (Scanlon and Swindells 1994, 41). In spite of the challenges thrown up by mainstream encroachment into their territory, as well as the perpetuation of sexism in the review press and in the industry itself, feminist publishing was still succeeding in an altered literary landscape.

Reflecting on Virago's twentieth birthday, Lennie Goodings (now in place as its publisher) described a company that had grown from a staff of three to nineteen, publishing almost 1,000 books along the way. 'I strongly believe that being independent has meant survival for us', she said. 'We control our own costs and savings, we decide ourselves where we will compromise and where we won't. We choose the books we want to publish' (Goodings 1993b, 26). Virago's second decade was played out against the boom of Thatcher's Britain, where the icon of the 1980s Power Woman was contradicted by the reality of women's continued containment within prescribed gender roles. It was the decade of Virago's most rapid growth and was to prove its last as an independent publishing house.

Notes

1. Interview with Harriet Spicer, 20 October 2004.
2. Interview with Ursula Owen, 5 February 2009.
3. Interview with Jane Cholmeley, 28 September 2004.
4. Anon. 1991.
5. Interview with Harriet Spicer, 20 October 2004.
6. Editorial 1989.
7. Ibid.
8. Interview with Alexandra Pringle, 28 October 2009.
9. Interview with Ursula Owen, 5 February 2009.
10. Ibid.
11. Interview with Alexandra Pringle, 28 October 2009.
12. Interview with Harriet Spicer, 20 October 2004.
13. Dunn 1998; Hanscombe 1982; Watts 1995.
14. Interview with Harriet Spicer, 20 October 2004.
15. Interview with Ali Smith, 19 July 2004.
16. Interview with Carmen Callil, 10 November 2004.
17. Frame 1984; Piercy 1979; Roberts 1983; Walker 1983.

Chapter 4

Fragmenting Feminism and Diversifying Women's Writing

During Virago's second decade, the feminist movement changed dramatically. The communality and sense of shared purpose that drove it during its formative years gave way in the 1980s to a much more complex, fragmented and often fraught feminism that can be largely defined by its fractures rather than its shared focus. While early second-wavers had sought to collectivize and empower women under the unifying banner of their sex, lobbying together for a common goal, the very symbol 'woman' came under scrutiny. Sheila Rowbotham, whose writing had been used as the 'mission statement' in all Virago texts during the press' first decade, described this changing feminist landscape: 'there is no longer a single women's liberation movement. The context in which ideas have developed is more diffuse' (Rowbotham 1989, xiii).

The issues of race, sexuality and class in particular came to pose challenging questions for feminism during Virago's second decade, as early second-wave formulations of female identity were problematized for their oversimplification of women's histories and experiences – social, psychological, political and economic. A fracturing of feminism as a political movement occurred during the 1980s as black and minority ethnic (BME), working-class, lesbian and disabled women started to give voice to their feelings of disenfranchisement. Arguing that early figurings of female experience within the women's liberation movement had failed to address the specificity of their experiences, they drew attention to the inauthenticity of the unifying figure 'woman'.

This new focus on identity and individual experience provoked an outpouring of critical material on ethnicity, sexuality and class. Black-British and British-Asian women began to voice their feelings of disenfranchisement from feminist spokeswomen who had, up to that point, been predominantly white and middle class. Gay and bisexual women also began to describe their politics as distinct from the 'mainstream' women's movement and its preoccupation with housewifery and motherhood within a heterosexual paradigm. These debates led to the 'identity politics' that came to define 1980s feminism, causing alarm among some women in the movement. Tania Modleski, for example, warned that feminism's reluctance to make generalizations of behalf of the group 'women' left feminism without a sense of purpose: 'The once exhilarating proposition that there is no "essential" female nature has been elaborated to the point where it is now often used to scare "women" away from making any generalisations about or political claims on behalf of a group called "women"' (Modleski 1991, 15). Others argued that the insistence on theorizing difference rather than unifying *as women* disempowered feminists:

> Identity politics, a political ideology that consumed the 1980s, was based on the premise that the more marginal the group the more complete the knowledge. In a literal appropriation of standpoint theory, the claim to authenticity through oppressive subjecthood produced a simplistic hierarchy of oppression. The outcome was the cliché-ridden discourse which embodied the holy trinity of 'race, class, and gender', within which black women, being the victims of 'triple oppression', were keepers of the holy grail. (Mirza 1997, 9)

The specifics of ethnicity, class and sexuality posed new challenges for Virago, although Owen argued that the fragmentation of feminism was useful to an extent, in that it broadened out the subject matter to which women's writing addressed itself: 'the fragmentation of the women's movement has meant feminism has taken up different issues: education, government and so on. There is still a way of looking at things though a feminist lens' (Briscoe 1990b). Towards the end of Virago's second decade, there emerged another important shift in the direction of feminist politics – the rise of queer, beginning in 1990 with the publication of Judith Butler's *Gender Trouble* (Butler 1990). Butler's central thesis – that gender is performative (the repetitious enactment of culturally sanctioned behaviours) and, further, that sexuality and anatomical sex itself are constructions produced in relation to imposed norms – provoked a renewed examination of male and female identity, and arguably redefined the terms of feminist debate. Queer theory turned away from identity politics and the insistence on specifying the difference of female experience, instead problematizing the very categories that define 'woman' (or 'man') in order to destabilize them and therefore diminish their power to organize culture (see Chapter 6).

Butler's postmodern restaging of all identities – male, female or other – also put centre stage the overarching paradigm of consumerism that increasingly came to define culture as the 1980s wore on. Queer ideology shifted the emphasis from a focus on just women to a focus on the ways in which *both* sexes were constructed within a consumerist culture, ideas that were more fully explored during Virago's third decade (see Chapter 6). Negotiating a path between specificity and commonality became a much more urgent challenge for feminist publishers. Virago had always maintained its intention to appeal to as wide an audience as possible and to represent all women's experiences (past and present). Its second decade saw it move more towards the publication of fiction, moving it away from the theoretical arguments (of identity politics and queer) that were occupying feminists in the academy. As Owen explains, 'what happened in the early 1980s is that a lot of feminist ideas got written in the form of fiction'.[1] Virago certainly published a much larger proportion of new fiction between 1983 and 1992 – around 170 new novels – than in its previous ten years (when just twenty new fiction titles were published). Virago's output during its second decade showed its commitment to Callil's idea that reading – and *pleasure* in reading – was the most effective way of communicating ideas. 'I think that's what's interesting about polemics, don't you? I really do believe that thing of Karl Marx: you learn much more, you can cause revolution with the novel much more.'[2] While fierce battles were raging between the proponents of different schools of feminist theory, during its second decade Virago moved more into communicating its politics through fiction.

Including BME Perspectives

Ethnicity emerged as a hugely problematic issue for feminism in the 1980s. The second-wave movement was forced to realize that, as Virago writer Anne Phillips put it, 'feminists have proved no more immune to racism than the society they inhabit, and as they have documented this, black women have challenged many of the preoccupations of the contemporary women's movement' (Phillips 1987, 6). The formulation of a racial perspective within feminist politics challenged not only white patriarchy, but also white women's racism, black men's sexism and the privileged site of literature itself, historically denied to BME women.

bell hooks was an early instigator of this black feminist perspective, arguing at the end of Virago's first decade that 'contemporary black women could not join together to fight for women's rights because we did not see "womanhood" as an important aspect of our identity. Racist, sexist socialisation had conditioned us to devalue our femaleness and to regard race as the only relevant label of identification. In other words, we were asked to deny a part of ourselves – and we did' (hooks 1982, 1). Black feminists argued that the women's movement had privileged – because it was driven by – the needs of middle- and upper-class college-educated white women. For example, Sho-walter – whose influence on Virago I discussed in Chapter 2 – was taken to task by black critics for her lack of attention to race (and class and sexuality) in formulating her theory of gynocritics. Barbara Christian set out to redress Showalter's colour-blindness, undertaking the first black 'gynocritical' project in 1979. Her text *Black Women Novelists* set out to recover the writing of *black* female authors who had been left out of literary history: 'there did not exist, in 1979 . . . a single definitive volume of criticism that made available both traditional and non-traditional analyses and examinations of the works of a representative and significant segment of skilful Black women writers' (Evans 1985, xvii).

It is fair to say that Virago and (some of) the other feminist presses were playing catch-up in terms of representing BME women's writing on its lists. Ursula Owen concedes that Virago was culpable for not addressing the issue of ethnicity head-on earlier on: 'we concentrated too heavily on the experience of white women . . . black women have felt excluded from the account, [but we're] conscious too of the difficulties for a largely white women's press in getting such publishing right' (Owen in Owen 1988, 94). This admission points to another important obstacle in BME women writers' paths: most of the women employed in publishing – feminist or otherwise – were white. There was a need for BME women to enter the industry itself in order to mark out their perspective within the feminist publishing environment. US feminist theorist and publisher Barbara Smith criticized feminist presses for their failure to address ethnicity earlier on: 'too often we were required to fight with the white women, who had begun and/or controlled these publications, in order to get what we believed into print' (Smith in Rush and Allen 1989, 203).

Goodings acknowledges the absence of BME women in the publishing industry: 'publishing *is* pretty middle-class isn't it . . . one thing about publishing that keeps it quite middle-class I suppose is that it's friends of friends, you know'.[3] Since few BME women were part of this middle-class in 1970s and 1980s Britain, they were left out of the account. Virago made an attempt to problematize the constitution of feminist publishing specifically, and the publishing industry more generally, as white with its publication in 1987 of Anne Phillips' *Divided Loyalties*. Phillips describes feminism as a privileged arena, echoing Goodings' assessment of publishing and, like Goodings, advocates greater inclusion of the perspectives of less privileged women (working-class as well as BME): 'middle-class concerns have shaped the priorities of the movement, dictating the demands that have dominated campaigns' (Phillips 1987, 7).

And it was Goodings who, along with Ros de Lanerolle of The Women's Press and writer/publisher Margaret Busby, founded Greater Access to Publishing in an attempt to accelerate this inclusion of BME women in the industry. Virago also took on a BME editor in its second decade in a deliberate attempt to enact the politics it was espousing: 'Melanie Silgardo at Virago is a one-up on The Women's Press' (Rukhsana 1991, 11). Such interventions during the 1980s had some effect: 'black women made increasing inroads into the world of publishing. While still forming a miniscule minority, individual black women began to acquire positions of political influence' (Lovenduski and Randall 1993, 104).

Sheba was set up in 1980 to 'give priority to the work of women writers who continue to be marginalized'.[4] Sheba boasted important BME authors such as Audre Lorde, Barbara Burford and bell hooks, and its output during the 1980s included a broad range of first and third world BME writers. Alongside Sheba, The Women's Press became very much associated with BME women writers during the 1980s, as MD Ros de Lanerolle maintained that the most exciting writing was that emanating from the disempowered and disenfranchised – those who didn't have to defend their position and could thus take risks:

> The collection now includes such impressive black British writers as Joan Riley and Merle Collins, and Ros de Lanerolle is publishing the first novel by a Zimbabwean woman for the [press' tenth] anniversary. There are writings from India, Iran, Algeria, Central America, Canada and China. She says: 'I believe we now have one of the most international lists in publishing. Now it is important to hear what women with different experiences and from different cultures have to say.' (Neustatter 1988)

The association of The Women's Press and a championing of BME women's writing was also thanks in no small part to its publication of Alice Walker's *The Color Purple* (1983). Sales of Walker's novel secured The Women's Press' financial health throughout the 1980s, particularly after the release of Steven Spielberg's film version. 'Alice Walker, famously, has sustained The Women's Press for many years. *The Color Purple* alone enabled them to move from cramped quarters in Shoreditch to a relatively spacious Clerkenwell warehouse' (Steel 1998). It also hugely increased the visibility of The Women's Press – 'the gains for the company have been enormous: *The Color Purple* has given them an entree into many bookshops which formerly would not stock their books' – and this in turn secured greater exposure for future titles, and a more secure financial future (Evans 1986). In addition, it drew publishers' attention to the potential profitability of BME women's writing, helping to open up a market for this fiction in the mainstream.

Walker's book was followed in 1984 by Virago's (UK) publication of Maya Angelou's *I Know Why the Caged Bird Sings*. This text, which was reprinted five times in its first year, secured Virago's fortunes in the mid 1980s in a similar way to what *The Color Purple* did for The Women's Press. Lennie Goodings recalls how it was the selling of this text to a high street bookshop in Northern Ireland that foregrounded, for her, the problems that ethnicity posed for feminism: 'We were trying to sell Maya Angelou to some bookshops in Belfast and they said they didn't have any black readers. Now that was a shock . . . that sense that only black people will read black writing.'[5] This anecdote helps outline why ethnicity was such a huge issue within feminism during the 1980s (and still is to this day) – many women in the second-wave movement simply didn't recognize the double oppression of BME women, who faced prejudice regarding their gender as well as their skin colour. The urgent task for Virago and the other feminist presses, who had already challenged the notion that women-authored texts must be only of interest to women, was to break down the similar racist assumption that BME writing was only a 'minority' genre too.

The profits generated for The Women's Press by Walker's book, as well as Angelou's for Virago, stand as evidence that in spite of Goodings' experiences in Belfast, BME women's writing had huge appeal. Along with these books, Virago also published fiction and poetry from Paule Marshall, Grace Nichols, Audre Lorde and Bharati Mukherjee, as well as fiction from a large number of lesser-known BME women writers. There was a concerted effort by Virago – along with the other feminist presses – to broaden their published output to reflect greater diversity. For example, Virago was the first feminist publisher in the United Kingdom to take up Christian's challenge to trace back the history of black women's writing, publishing Mary Helen Washington's *Invented Lives: Narratives of Black Women 1860–1960*. This was an attempt to 'piece together those "broken and sporadic" continuities that constitute black women's literary tradition' (Washington 1989, xx). Virago also secured the rights to reprint other important historical work, including that of Zora Neale Hurston, credited by critic Gina Wisker as being the literary foremother of Alice Walker.

So although hooks argued at the end of the 1980s that 'it is profoundly disturbing to see how little feminist theory is being written by black women and women of other colour', there was more and more evidence of the emergence of this critical writing (hooks 1989, 38). Virago's nonfiction titles included *The Heart of the Race* by Beverley Bryan, Stella Dadzie and Suzanne Scafe (1985), as well as Scafe's later collection *Teaching Black Literature* (1989). There were many memoirs by BME women that gave voice to women's stories from different cultures around the world: *The Tiger's Milk* by Adriana Angel and Fiona Macintosh (1987) on the women of Nicaragua; *Harem Years* by Huda Shaarawi (1986) and Nayra Atiya's collection *Khul-Khaal* (1988), which both gave voice to Egyptian women's stories; and Lauretta Ngcobo's collection of essays by black British women *Let it Be Told* (1988). Its lists during the 1980s show that Virago 'sustained a commitment to publishing Black and Asian women's writing, both fiction and non-fiction' (Scanlon and Swindells 1994, 43).

The Sex Debates in Identity Politics

While Virago's first decade had seen a feminist expression of anger at the sexual stereotyping of women as passive objects, in the 1980s there appeared much more complex formulations of female sexual identity. Radical feminist ideologies emerged that posited *all* heterosexual sex as inherently oppressive to women, while lesbian feminists began to assert the difference of their own experiences. Conflicts arising from the different – and opposed – positions around sex and sexuality that were articulated created huge rifts between feminists, and stymied the momentum the women's movement had gathered during its early years.

One of the most vociferous and divisive debates, which arose early on in this period, was centred on the issue of pornography. Susan Brownmiller set the terms of this debate in 1975, arguing in *Against Our Will* that the threat of rape is the fundamental means by which male power is maintained. Rape is 'nothing more or less than a conscious process of intimidation by which *all men* keep *all women* in a state of fear' (Brownmiller 1975, 15). Resulting from this, she argues, pornography is a manifestation of the destructive expression of masculine sexuality – consequently, she calls for sanctions against it.

In contrast, Virago published Angela Carter's *The Sadeian Woman* in 1979, her examination of the works of the Marquis de Sade and positing of the notion of 'moral pornography' (Carter 1979). In this text, the first of her works published by Virago, Carter explores de Sade's representation of male and female sexual behaviours, arguing that his writing shows the extent to which *either* sex can be depraved. She troubles the masculine/feminine structure imposed onto sexual roles by revealing the ways in which de Sade's work, which covers the range of sexual behaviour to its very extremes, allows women as well as men expression of an aggressive, active and perverse sexuality. In this, Carter set herself as being at odds with an emerging feminist separatism, which radicalized the debates around women's sexuality, specifically focusing on pornography as the root of female oppression.

Carter condemned attempts to prohibit pornography, pointing out that repression of any kind is always also an attempt to enforce hegemonic ideology: 'when pornography serves . . . to reinforce the prevailing system of values and ideas in a given society, it is tolerated; and when it does not, it is banned' (Carter 1979, 20). Texts such as *Desire: The Politics of Sexuality*, which Virago published in 1984 (it was originally published a year earlier in the United States), took up Carter's idea that censorship could only further disempower women: 'no pornographer has ever been punished for being a women-hater, but not too long ago information about female sexuality, contraception, and abortion was assumed to be obscene. In a male supremacist society the only obscenity law that will not be used against women is no law at all' (Willis in Snitow et al. 1984, 83). Echoing Carter, the essays in this text refute the notion that women and men must be limited to feminine and masculine sexual roles. Instead, they posit the free and authentic expression of *all* human sexuality, rather than censorship, as feminism's goal: 'if feminists define pornography, per se, as the enemy, the result will be to make a lot of women ashamed of their sexual feelings and afraid to be honest about them. And the last thing women need is more sexual shame, guilt, and hypocrisy – this time served up as feminism'.[6]

This differentiation between Virago's sexually libertarian stance and The Women's Press' more radical alignment with anti-pornography (and thus censorship) marks an important point of divergence between the two most 'mainstream' feminist presses. In 1981 The Women's Press published Susan Griffin's *Pornography and Silence* and Andrea Dworkin's *Pornography: Men Possessing Women*, texts that followed Brownmiller to argue that pornography imprisons women psychically as well as physically. Dworkin was to become synonymous with anti-pornography campaigning, alongside feminist lawyer Catharine MacKinnon. For Dworkin and MacKinnon, pornography was a disturbing indicator of the reality of women's oppression: 'we will know that we are free when pornography no longer exists. As long as it does exist, we must understand that we are the women in it: used by the same power, subject to the same valuation, as the vile whores who beg for more' (Dworkin 1981, 224).

In publishing these texts, The Women's Press aligned itself with the radical separatist politics espoused by Griffin, Dworkin and others. Such separatist rhetoric, which figured *all* men as oppressors of women and therefore posited women-only spaces as the ideal, gathered momentum throughout the 1980s, at times creating uneasy alliances between radical feminists and the moral right, whose usurpation of the messages of the anti-pornography movement allowed them to peddle their own version of sexual conservatism. Yet the anti-pornography movement was fuelled by a very real sense of female anger at the sexual dualism of patriarchal culture, in which women were figured as passive objects for male consumption: 'the tendency for male voyeurs to be aroused by characterless and completely sexualised images of women fits directly with the long social history of regarding women as simply extensions of their genitals in a way that men have never been' (Root 1984, 47).

Pornography remained a divisive issue. In 1990, The Women's Press continued the debate with its publication of Sheila Jeffreys' *Anticlimax* (1990), in which the author argued that women are symbolically represented through pornography as a hole, a zero, a nothing, waiting to be filled and given meaning by the active penis. For Jeffreys, 'the demolition of heterosexual desire is a necessary step on the route to women's liberation' (Jeffreys 1990, 312). In a rebuttal of this position, Lynne Segal revisited the issue of pornography in her 1992 text *Sex Exposed,* published at the end of Virago's second decade. Again presenting an ideal of feminism as a politics that *included* men, she expressed her frustration that 'the issue of pornography just won't go away. Its presence has dogged and divided Western feminism like no other' (Segal in Segal and McIntosh 1992, 1). Segal pointed to the anti-pornography movement's alliance with the political right, arguing that 'moral conservatives interested in attacking gays and lesbians, as well as in controlling women's sexuality, have become more successful precisely through focusing on pornography and, especially in the USA, using the rhetoric and tactics of the feminist anti-pornography project' (Segal in Segal and McIntosh 1992, 11).

The pornography debates arose from women's dissatisfaction with their sexual representation, their limitation to a consumed and commodified body. The sexual double standard that had been identified and challenged in Virago's first decade, as reflected in the books it published, remained. Feminist anger at the status quo led to the formulation of a new alternative as the figure of the 'political lesbian' emerged, who chose sex with women as a political rather than sensual act. 'Political lesbianism' was posited as a way in which women might reject their historical construction as mere 'object' in sexual terms and instead attain a more empowered form of sexual expression. Adrienne Rich had argued in 1981 that heterosexuality is socially and psychologically imposed rather than naturally assumed, and thus lesbian separatists defined their sexuality – which could mean anything from a refusal of sexual relations with men, to bisexual activity, to having sex with women – as an act of feminist praxis, an evasion of these imposed norms (Rich 1981).

As the 1980s progressed, the figure of the political lesbian created division, as lesbians objected to the co-optation of their sexual identity as a *political* identity and heterosexual women problematized a politics that structured their sexuality as innately oppressive. Segal again had already posited a positive heterosexuality, which insisted on men's inclusion within, rather than exclusion from, healthy and empowering figurings of sex. In *Slow Motion* (1990) Segal sets out this idea that feminism must look at the way in which *both* sexes are confined to specific sanctioned behaviours and roles – only looking at those imposed on women risks figuring them as the 'troublesome sex'. She calls for new ways of imagining desire and makes that a task that should fall to women and men alike: 'transforming the meanings attaching to sexuality is a political task which men and women can share' (Segal 1990, 216).

The debates over pornography, separatism and political lesbianism also led to a literary exploration of alternative sexualities. Feminist publishers were at the centre of a huge amount of writing that described lesbian lives during the 1980s, both through fiction and nonfiction. During this period, Virago launched a dedicated lesbian series, publishing the work of Sandra Scoppetone, June Jordan and Fiona Cooper, and collections of lesbian writing and poetry, as well as Nancy Garden's exploration of lesbianism for younger readers as part of Virago's Upstarts series.[7] It also reprinted historical fiction by lesbian writers – Radclyffe Hall's novels *The Well of Loneliness* and *The Unlit Lamp*, Pamela Frankau's fiction and Maureen Duffy's lesbian novel of the 1960s *That's How it was*.[8] There was also a range of nonfiction, spanning everything from the nineteenth-century diaries of Anne Lister to lesbian travel guides, psychoanalytical studies and histories of gay communities.[9] The Women's Press also established a dedicated lesbian series (while its bestselling text *The Color Purple* included a lesbian plotline), Pandora published theoretical work on gay parenting and some lesbian biographies, as well as the fiction of Jane Rule and Jeanette Winterson, and Onlywomen continued its dedication to publishing lesbian writing, producing texts of fiction, nonfiction and poetry.

This expanding range of lesbian writing was an important part of the feminist landscape during Virago's second decade. Feminist bookshops such as Silver Moon reflected the trend by not only publishing their own range of 'lesbian pot-boilers' – 'a conscious decision on the part of Silver Moon's publishers, Jane Cholmeley and Sue Butterworth, to "do 'fun' lesbian books"'– but also by making a priority of displaying lesbian writing in their shop (Dunckner 1992, 41). 'Within our display, we particularly highlight lesbian books and black women's writing on the main floor of the shop – not hidden in a discreet or uneconomic corner, but confident and featured', says Jane Cholmeley, who founded the bookshop with Sue Butterworth. 'Publishing and commerce are as white, male, and heterosexist as the rest of society, so we enjoy saying "we're here too"!' (Cholmeley in Redclift and Sinclair 1991, 230). The boom in lesbian writing was also a rebuttal, then, to the silencing of lesbian lives. The outpouring of literary material from and about lesbians was both a result of, and a rejoinder to, the politicization of the figure 'lesbian' by separatist feminists.

Lesbian existence came to be more fully explored and articulated – and represented in literature – during the 1980s as issues of sexuality, and in particular the specificity of lesbian sexual identity, preoccupied the feminist movement. As with BME women, nonheterosexual women who had felt excluded from early formulations of second-wave feminism began to more fully articulate the specificity of their experiences. Ethnicity and sexuality had an electrifying effect on feminism in the 1980s, exposing faultlines between different demographics of women. These would be further revealed with the arrival of queer theory at the start of the next decade (see Chapter 6).

Changing the Formula: New Feminisms and New Feminist Fictions

During the 1970s, there had been a concerted effort to appropriate the genre of life-writing for feminism's purposes as well as to celebrate women's achievements in this field (see Chapter 2) – this was to extend to other literary genres as the 1980s wore on. There emerged a new kind of feminist fiction that drew on the conventions of genre writing, reinventing crime, romance and science fiction for a feminist audience. Critical writing around women's appropriation of generic fiction went alongside these experiments in feminist fiction writing. Part of this project included a deliberate attempt to exploit the popularity of generic fiction in order to disseminate feminist messages to as broad an audience as possible. The profitability of genre fiction made it an ideal vehicle for both female writers and feminist presses. Genre fiction 'sells by the truckload', hence 'as a conscious feminist propagandist it makes sense to use a fictional format which already has a huge market' (Cranny-Francis 1990, 2).

Feminist appropriation of generic fiction was figured by Anne Cranny-Francis as an attempt to rebuff the historical derogation of women's writing by deliberately figuring it within the 'lower' literary forms of genre fiction:

> Generic fiction, characterised as feminine by a masculinist (political, psychological, artistic) establishment, is now being transformed by feminist ideology. Rather than rejecting the mass culture to which they were relegated (and which, as female, was relegated to them),

feminist writers have embraced it, seeing its characteristic popularity as a powerful tool for their own propagandist purposes. (Cranny-Francis 1990, 5)

Angela Carter, whose novels toy with the conventions of both romance and science-fiction writing, notes how problematic the demarcation between high and low literary forms is for writers: 'take that story, "The Juniper Tree", in which a little boy is murdered. You'd get away with that in a horror movie, but you certainly wouldn't get away with that in a novel that was a contender for the Booker prize. It's as if a lot of the real violence of human relations has been consigned to second-order cultural forms' (Mansfield 1990). Carolyn Heilbrun wrote her Kate Fansler crime stories pseudonymously as Amanda Cross until 1972, keeping her identity secret because she felt the profile of 'crime writer' (lowbrow) would hamper her (highbrow) academic career (Cooper-Clark 1983, 187).

Part of the feminist critical engagement with genre fiction included tracing it back to plot out women's role in its development. For example, in examining crime fiction, feminist critics pointed out that women's contribution to the emergence of the genre had itself been overlooked. 'Current women writers of crime fiction belong on a continuum that begins with the writers of female gothic and that occasionally intersects with the continuum that includes Poe and Conan Doyle. A feminist tracing of the history of crime fiction would acknowledge literary foremothers as well as forefathers' (Reddy 1988, 9). Alongside Reddy, other feminist critics undertook the task of excavating early female crime writing. 'Linda Semple, speaking at the ICA in 1988, identified the first female crime novel as being *The Dead Letter* by Seeley Regester (1866), and reported that she has discovered a further 400 writers between then and 1950' (Munt 1994, 5). In a later article, Semple and Ros Coward identified two earlier works: *East Lynne* by Mrs Henry Wood (1861) and *Lady Audley's Secret* by Mary Braddon (1862). The latter text had already been reprinted by Virago as a Modern Classic in 1985.

The Women's Press, Virago, Onlywomen and Pandora all launched their own crime series, and between 1983 and 1992, Virago published twenty-five crime titles, constituting 14 per cent of its total fiction output (excluding the Modern Classics): 'in July [1989] Virago will rejacket its individual titles, including the popular Kate Fansler mysteries, in a flurry of ads and dump bins and launch its first cohesive crime list. For women, crime is starting to pay' (Briscoe 1989). At Pandora, Semple worked with Coward on the press' 'Women Crime Writers' series, which republished some of the out-of-print texts the two critics had identified in their article. It was also noted that the most prolific and successful 'Golden Age' crime writers of the interwar period were women – Agatha Christie, Dorothy Sayers and Ngaio Marsh – and it was to their work that contemporary writers could trace their literary inheritance.

Feminist literary critics similarly rewrote the history of science fiction. Cranny-Francis referenced Mary Shelley's *Frankenstein* in her discussion of the genre's beginnings, before moving on to identify female successors, including Alice Sheldon, who wrote under the pseudonym James Tiptree Jr. Sheldon's work was widely respected by her contemporaries – because they believed it to be penned by a male hand. Even her feminist short story 'The Women Don't See' was credited by her editor as exhibiting strong 'male' language: 'Tiptree simulates an "entirely masculine manner" in the story by constructing a narrative voice from a number of sexist discourses which are so effectively naturalised that even the editor, Silverberg, did not suspect that the narrative voice was part of, not simply the authoritative medium for, the "feminist story"' (Cranny-Francis 1990, 31).

In spite of the problems arising from a misogynist review press, genre fiction had a powerful trick up its sleeve: 'genre readers are not only devoted to a genre, they become devoted to an author and are despondent unless there is a new book forthcoming each year. Once this following is established, it ensures the success of every book the author writes, however unequal in quality' (Rosenberg 1982, 17). Writing within the conventions of a genre guarantees an author a loyal readership eager to consume successive texts. Crime writer Val McDermid explains: 'whenever they [crime-fiction readers] encounter a writer they enjoy, they immediately rush out and grab everything else that person has ever written, regardless of whether it's the kind of mystery they normally buy' (McDermid in Windrath 1999, 20–21). For the feminist presses, this meant that authors who published generic fictions could generate a degree of loyalty among fans of that genre that translated into sales and success, as well as exploit the genre itself for feminism's ends.

'Precisely because of the set structure, women writers were able to move into and utilise the same icons and patterns that made the genre familiar and at the same time change some of the expectations', explained Barbara Wilson, who published two crime novels with Virago (Wilson in Gibbs 1994, 219). For example, McDermid's established success as a crime writer allowed her to introduce lesbian sleuth Lindsay Gordon to a mainstream readership. Genre fiction thus creates a 'safe space' to introduce more challenging themes: 'the feminist discourse which many readers might be totally unfamiliar with is presented within a familiar and much-loved format' (Cranny-Francis 1990, 3). Employing the apparently conventional narratives and form of crime writing allowed feminist writers to present *un*conventional characters and concepts to their readership.

This appropriation of genre fiction would not have been possible without the intervention of the feminist presses through Virago's second decade: 'from modest beginnings when The Women's Press brought out their first titles in 1982, crime fiction has stealthily nosed its way to bill-topping status, with hefty promotional backing from the major women's publishers and a host of new titles' (Briscoe 1989). And the same went for romance and science fiction. The inclusion of all this genre fiction on the lists of the feminist presses attracted a mainstream readership of fans of these kinds of books, while simultaneously allowing women writers new opportunities to invest genre fiction with feminist meaning. This combination was to prove hugely attractive:

> There's a large middle market to be tapped of intelligent, broadly feminist women who resent having to suspend their political views for the sake of a rollicking read, yet who are addicted to the traditional blockbuster. Who has not, be they the staunchest hardliner, plunged into a sex and shopping saga between chapters of *Sexual Politics*? Says Alexandra Pringle, 'I've always enjoyed reading Celia Brayfield, Shirley Conran, Jilly Cooper and so on, and there are a lot of intelligent women in demanding jobs who go home at night and watch Dallas or read something completely relaxing. It's like an anaesthetic. From that came the idea that a novel of that sort can be a vehicle for all kinds of ideas about the world, politics, life and so on, and can have a serious undercurrent'. (Briscoe 1990a)

As Pringle makes explicit, Virago's intention is to both push the boundaries of what genre fiction constitutes and reinvest the genres of crime, romance, sci-fi and fantasy with value.

Feminist appropriation of genre fiction also meant a refiguring of its motifs and characters. The female sleuth, for example, represented a challenge to the traditional categorization of rationality and logicality as male. Feminist crime fiction set up new relations between the sexes by allocating a female figure control and command. 'Feminist crime novels, far from being mere escapist literature or isolated, peculiar experiments in an essentially masculine preserve, participate in the larger feminist project of redefining and redistributing power, joining a long and valuable tradition of women's fiction' (Reddy 1988, 149). The 'hard-boiled' female private investigator of 1980s and 1990s feminist crime fiction was the most obvious example of this challenge to existing gender roles, and the eagerness with which readers engaged with this female 'tough-guy' was evidenced in sales: 'the gradual acceptance of hard-boiled female investigators is supported by the bestseller status of the works of Grafton, Muller and others' (Betz 2006, 5). Readers were exhilarated by the chance to see a woman call the shots:

> Julia MacPherson of Virago says: 'you can get completely wrapped up in the excitement and pace, yet you're not being thrown these very male Raymond Chandlerisms. I actually like Chandler but I find his sexual politics offensive, whereas with feminist crime fiction I don't feel torn'. But perhaps crime fiction's greatest pull is that it provides the sleuth or narrator with an automatic pretext for examining society. (Briscoe 1989)

Virago's Barbara Wilson similarly theorized crime fiction as an attempt by both writer and reader to see justice done for women: 'the appeal of the investigator novel to women writers and readers would seem obvious. For to be a woman is to have been silenced and socialised into passivity. To be a woman is to have been the victim or bystander of many nameless and hidden crimes: battery, rape, sexual abuse, harassment' (Wilson in Gibbs 1994, 222). To take on the role of investigator, then, either by writing a character or by vicarious enjoyment through the act of reading, is to become empowered. 'Crime novels are about society and power. What changed when women began to write crime novels in the 1980s was that traditional notions of authority and justice were called into question' (Wilson in Gibbs 1994, 222).

The figure of the lesbian sleuth also emerged, first in the character of Val McDermid's Lindsay Gordon – The Women's Press published three novels featuring this character during Virago's second decade. Gordon was soon followed by a growing number of lesbian detectives: 'in the last fifteen years the number of professional lesbian detectives on the literary marketplace has more than tripled from fourteen in 1986 to forty-three in 1995' (Plain 2001, 201). Just as lesbian identity was being brought to the fore in the sexuality debates that marked 1980s feminism, the lesbian sleuth took centre stage in crime fiction.

Feminist writers also appropriated the science-fiction genre, as Dale Spender notes in her assessment of the literary scene in 1985:

> Whether strong women come first and are called science fiction, or vice-versa (and we could do with some order here), there can be no doubt that there is some exciting women's fiction being written. And there's a growing demand for it, which is why The Women's Press launches its new (cheap) science fiction list this year. Women want strong, independent characters they can identify with – and

creative solutions for world problems – and if this is labelled science fiction, so be it. (Spender 1985)

Just as with crime writing, feminist science fiction challenged the male dominance of the genre: 'feminist science fiction has brought the politics of feminism into a genre with a solid tradition of ignoring or excluding women writers, and in so doing it has politicised our understanding of the fantasies of science fiction' (Wolmark 1993, 2).

Feminist critics explored the ways in which sci-fi motifs and conventions could be appropriated to expose the biases of patriarchal culture: 'at its best science fiction must shake us from our complacencies. For women this is no luxury' (Armitt 1991, 136). The monstrosities and dystopias of feminist fiction were used to jolt readers into seeing their own, everyday realities in new ways: 'what the narratives of feminist science fiction can do is to test the limits of the dominant ideology of gender by proposing alternative possibilities for social and sexual relations which conflict with the dominant representations' (Wolmark 1993, 35). Sci-fi became another way for women writers to explore gender structures and to subvert them.

Accordingly, the women's presses published a range of sci-fi fiction. The Women's Press' science fiction series included writers such as Joanna Russ, Sarah Lefanu and Rhoda Lerman (Lefanu 1985). The Women's Press also published polemical texts, including Sarah Lefanu's *In the Chinks of the World Machine* (1988) and Ursula le Guin's *The Language of the Night* (1989). Virago, in turn, published work from Naomi Mitchison, Ursula le Guin and others, as well as Atwood and Carter, whose writing was figured by some as being 'one of the critical influences on a whole generation of British SF writers' (Kavaney in Sage 1994, 171). Carter's novels are rich with fantastical creations that defy the boundaries and limitations of reality, imagining new possibilities for women. She uses the conventions of the sci-fi genre to play with identity and morality, creating new, fluid identities for women. 'Carter was keen on expressing the mutability of individuality' and accordingly her characters change their minds, change their appearance and even change their gender (Kavaney in Sage 1994, 172). Atwood's 1985 novel *The Handmaid's Tale* also plays with the characteristics of the science-fiction genre (Atwood 1987). Atwood usurps traditional sci-fi narratives and employs the conventional imagery and structure of sci-fi storytelling to put across her explicitly feminist messages – about male control of culture, women's control of their bodies and humankind's control of nature.

The romance genre also came in for feminist reappraisal. Critics like Janice Radway and Tania Modleski reassessed the worth and significance of generic romance novels such as the Mills and Boon series or its US equivalent Harlequin, especially for female readers. Alongside this, female novelists took on the conventions of the romance narrative to write new, feminist versions of the love story. In her important study of generic romance fiction, Modleski argues that such literature offers women an escape from their reality into a world of fantasy: they impose their own agendas and desires onto the characters they read, and are allowed to assume a position of superiority over both the male 'hero' of the story and the female protagonist: 'since she knows the formula, she is superior in wisdom to the heroine and thus detached from her' (Modleski 1988, 41). Modleski argues that women's satisfaction in romance reading is derived from a revenge fantasy: the woman reader shares the satisfaction enjoyed by the woman in the text in bringing the man to his knees. This satisfaction is heightened by the reader's command of a narrative that, in contrast, the female character in the book is without authority to control.

Janice Radway similarly argues that romance fiction acts as a means by which women are able to fulfil their psychic and emotional needs – needs that are not met in their everyday lives: 'Romance reading, it appeared, addressed needs, desires, and wishes that a male partner could not' (Radway 1994, 13). Radway regards the consumption of generic romances as a means of private, self-focused pleasure for women, 'the opportunity to experience the kind of care and attention they commonly give to others' (Radway 1994, 100). Female readers of romantic fiction use literature as a means of escape – a literal denial of the present through their absorption in the text – as well as a way of identifying with a female protagonist whose life is very different from theirs. Radway concludes that romance reading is a way of producing feminist community.

Women writers began to use the conventions of the romance genre to portray strong, independent images of women and new, empowering kinds of (sexual) relationships. This is evidenced in the fiction of Atwood, Carter and Michèle Roberts at Virago (Roberts also published with The Women's Press during this period), Alice Walker and Janet Frame at The Women's Press, and Jeanette Winterson at Pandora – all recast the conventions of romantic fiction to present new, empowered versions of the – female – romantic hero. As Owen argued: 'if love, friendship, birth, death, work, travel, affection comprise a limited world, it is a ghetto many of us would choose to live in' (Owen in Owen 1988, 92).

This development of genre fiction was in large part enabled by the feminist publishing houses of the 1980s and early 1990s. They helped reshape the literary landscape, introducing these new forms of women's writing as well as new critical formulations of the notion of 'women's writing' itself. During Virago's second decade, the shift within feminism – away from the notion of a unifying figure of 'woman' and towards an 'identity politics' that insisted on women's differences – brought new challenges and saw Virago focus more on fiction as a way of engaging its readership with feminism outside of the complex and often heated debates happening in critical writing. As Virago marked its twentieth birthday, commentators were happy to pay tribute:

> Virago remains buoyant financially and emotionally. Its writers suggest why they remain so attractive. Janette Turner Hospital says: 'I didn't seek them out because they're a women's publisher, but because they make extremely handsome books. And I like the fact that they're prepared to keep one in print.' Michele Roberts agrees: 'The reason I went to them was quite simply that they seemed to be coming up with the best at that time. Best marketing, best editing, best financial offer.' Both of them still feel positive about it being a women's house: 'It gives back one's tarnished faith in sisterhood.' (Walter 1993)

Notes

1. Interview with Ursula Owen, 5 February 2009.
2. Interview with Carmen Callil, 10 November 2004.
3. Interview with Lennie Goodings, 8 November 2004.
4. Anon., 'About Sheba Feminist Press' *Maryland Institute for Technology in the Humanities,* retrieved 21 September 2017 from http://www.mith2.umd.edu/Womens Studies/ReferenceRoom/Publications/about-sheba-press.html (para. 4 of 10).
5. Interview with Lennie Goodings, 8 November 2004.
6. ibid.
7. Garden 1988; McEwen 1988; McEwen and O'Sullivan 1988.
8. Duffy 1983; Hall 1981, 1982; Whitbread 1988.
9. Gelder and Brandt 1992; Healey and Mason 1994; O'Connor and Ryan 1993.

Part III

1994–2004

Chapter 5

Working Women and the Changing Face(s) of the Book Industry

At the start of its third decade, Virago was operating as an independent once again, headed by Spicer as managing director and Goodings as editorial director – Owen and Callil remained on its board, but no longer had a say in its day-to-day running. The years 1993–2002 were to prove tumultuous: Virago itself was to change radically, as was the industry in which it operated as the effects of book price wars, new literary prizes and aggressive marketing strategies took hold.

Virago would be fundamentally changed by its sale in 1995 to Little, Brown, part of a multinational publishing conglomerate. Virago's move from an independent to an imprint once again problematizes its description as a 'feminist publisher', becoming as it did part of the corporate mainstream. The establishment in 1996 of a literary prize for female writers generated controversy and plenty of headlines, and discussion of its value (or other- wise) continues today. The Women's – formerly the Orange – Prize for Fic- tion offers one of the largest financial rewards for its winner and, like Virago, is predicated on the idea that to challenge a fundamentally biased culture (either publishing or literary prize-giving), one can set up an alternative, par- allel culture rather than work from within the original. Arguably, it is during the 1990s that the second-wave feminist publishing phenomenon came to an end, an end accelerated by the rise of 'star authorship' and the effect of celebrity culture on publishing – but this did not mark the end of feminist publishing itself. Rather, it marked the start of another chapter in its history.

Virago's 1995 Sale: The End of a 'Feminist Dream'?

At the end its second decade Virago was enjoying financial solidity and rep- utational strength. But as the press readied itself for its twenty-first birthday, things began to go awry. Early on in 1994, Lennie Goodings was forced to acknowledge that a more challenging economy was having an impact: 'we are responding to some quite tough conditions in the trade at the moment and we are not the only ones. We are a medium-sized independent publisher, and our cushion is very thin' (Ward 1994). Virago had already responded to the changing economic climate, trimming back its output from one hundred new titles in 1993 to half that number in 1994. In addition, and for the first time in its history, Virago also had to trim back its staff: the team of nineteen women was reduced to nine full-time and four part-time members. Rothschild Ventures, which had helped finance the press' buyout in 1987, sold off its shares to the directors and to Bob Gavron, who became the largest single shareholder.

Goodings and, in particular, Spicer as MD came under increasing pressure as business continued to do badly. 'I remember there were very difficult times, and difficult board meetings which Harriet . . . she felt very under siege I think', says Owen. 'All sorts of things going wrong.'[1] Declining sales were blamed by some critics on a perceived lack of ambition or imagination, who argued that Virago was losing its edge and prioritizing style over substance: 'now that it can no longer beguile the public with a list which is interesting because it is different, Virago concentrates on having an unusual image' (Bennett 1993). As a consequence, Bob Gavron invited Callil to return to hands-on action at Virago as a 'company doctor', working on a successful relaunch of the Virago Modern Classics series (this return was made possible by Callil's resignation from her job at Chatto). Callil does not hold back in expressing her opinion of the press' output and direction: 'the list was going down the sewers, no question', she recalls.[2] Somewhat unsurprisingly, her reinstatement to the fold proved disruptive and provoked a series of events that would culminate, dramatically, in the sale of the press in 1995.

Callil admits now that her blunt expressions of opinion were a big factor in the breakdown of relations between Virago's key women – and is clearly still disturbed by her memories of events. 'I think you can say there were differences, personal differences that made it very difficult. You see, let's put it like this . . . I was a complete monomaniac you know, because the books came first.'[3] The situation very soon came to a head, prompting Callil to renounce Virago entirely and decide, instead, to sell it. 'Life was very, very tense between her and Harriet and Lennie, and in something like the February of either 1994 or 1995, she resigned.'[4]

As a result, Virago's board had to vote on who the company would be sold to, with the casting vote dramatically falling to Callil herself. Of the two shortlisted buyers – Bloomsbury and Little, Brown – Callil opted for the latter and the deal was done. The sale was met with both resignation and regret by all of Virago's key women, and Callil now expresses great sadness about the outcome: 'I loved Virago, you know. I didn't want it to end like that.'[5] Whatever the details of the 1995 sale – and there have certainly been allegations of blame and bad behaviour on all sides in the years since – the event itself marked a critical moment in Virago's history. Once again, the press moved from being independently owned to part of a mainstream publishing group. But this time the change took place in a culture that was markedly different from that of 1983, when Virago was sold to Chatto.

In 1995, all three of the publishers linked to the Virago buy-out were headed by female MDs: Liz Calder at Bloomsbury, Philippa Harrison at Little, Brown and Gail Rebuck at Random House. It is a little ironic, then, that Virago's sale was interpreted in media and industry circles as evidence that feminism was dead: 'when Virago was sold last month, it was the end of a feminist dream' (Pitman 1995). Yet in spite of the obvious progress women had made in advancing through the ranks of the publishing industry, as evidenced by the buyers in the running to acquire Virago, there remained deep-rooted prejudice and a continuing devaluation of women within publishing and within wider culture. Comment on the Virago sale is useful in illustrating this.

In the press coverage of the events of 1995, Virago's women were demonized as egotistical mismanagers who would rather see their company torn apart than lose their influence over it. Such negative representations of Virago's businesswomen, with Callil in particular 'caricatured as a steely harridan', points to the fact that powerful women were still viewed as anomalous (Fowler and Thomas 1995). Comment on the sale was telling: 'the publicity has concentrated on the personalities but it is not only in all-women companies that personality conflicts have proved destructive' (Dalley 1995). The media sought to return these powerful women to the confining stereotypes of 'feminine' behaviours by structuring their actions as personality clashes and squabbles. Callil, Goodings and Spicer were depicted as egotistical, hysterical and incompetent, with commentators insinuating that the 'sisterhood is too fragile for strong individuals'.[6] This image of the troublesome woman is evidenced in media reportage that figures the sale as evidence of the company 'imploding in a thousand recriminations' (Hattenstone 2001). Callil's walkout was an 'end fitting of a virago heroic and tempestuous', while the fallout was 'something more like *Dallas* crossed with *Absolutely Fabulous*' (Freely 1998). In all these descriptions, it is not the business but the *women* that form the focus of attention.

It is hard to imagine such descriptions being made of a change in personnel and structure within a male company: 'the mergers and buy-outs of largely male-run multinational publishing companies are read as auguries of market trends; those of feminist publishing companies betoken nothing more significant than the hysteria of the wandering womb' (Murray 2004, 30). Just as tellingly, there was a notable silence on the fact that a woman had won out in such high-level negotiations for control of a powerful all-female company. Bloomsbury's Liz Calder and Little Brown's Philippa Harrison vied with one another to buy Virago, yet there was no sign 'of the headline that runs: "female moguls battle for women's dream"' (Dalley 1995). Similarly, when Gail Rebuck was promoted in 1991 to chair and chief executive of Random House, one of the major players in UK publishing, industry commentators couched the appointment in terms of her gender: '*The Times* felt it necessary to report her promotion with the headline "Woman takes top publishing job"' (Wroe 1999).

After the sale, Goodings was installed as Virago's publisher (she and Spicer had resigned as events progressed through 1995, but Harrison invited Goodings back), and from January 1996 Virago ran as an imprint of Little, Brown.[7] There followed a 'relaunch' of Virago in 1997 that was heralded as a great success – the Virago 'V' series, edited by Sally Abbey, was launched to foreground new women's writing targeted at twenty- to thirty-five-year-olds (Sarah Waters' *Tipping the Velvet* launched the list) and 1997 marked the highest turnover in the company's history up to that point (Murray 2004, 63). Virago's output during its third decade mirrors that of the previous ten years when it ran as an independent, in terms of the proportion of fiction and nonfiction published. From 1993 to 2002, Virago published 472 books, around three hundred of which were fiction (a third of these were Modern Classics) and two hundred of which were nonfiction (the vast majority of which was new material).

There was a marked reduction, however, in the number of titles printed overall during the latter half of Virago's third decade: from 1996 to 2002, there were 282 books published, compared to the 190 that were published in just two years between 1993 and 1995. While Virago published a lower *number* of books, its profit margins increased considerably: 'Goodings' results speak for themselves. In six years with Time Warner [the conglomerate who then owned Little, Brown], Virago has doubled its turnover to a gross of nearly £4 million, with six hundred titles in print. Talk to any of her authors, and one quickly gains an impression of a kind of individual who's now all too rare in modern publishing: the committed editor' (Bostridge 2003).

This drop in the overall number of titles published would continue. The changing nature of the book industry meant that Virago had to adapt, and its new position within a conglomerate meant new methods. As one commentator wrote of the 1995 sale: 'Virago was always going to date; it belonged to a specific feminist moment. Its future may be in doubt, but it has a part in history' (Baxter 1995). Virago's task during its third decade was to ensure its continuing relevance within the changed landscape of contemporary book publishing, and changing feminist debates.

The End of Feminist Publishing?
Women's Role in a Changing Industry

Natasha Walter used the occasion of Virago's twentieth birthday in 1993 to point out 'the cultural myth British feminism finds it so hard to overcome – that women in power are a bizarre anomaly' (Walter 1993). She argues that the publishing industry remains, on the whole, an old boys' network: 'it is still true that women enter at a lower level than men and tend to hit a glass ceiling early in their careers'.[8] Virago's example thus constituted an important challenge to men's dominance, as Goodings pointed out: 'even if Virago is now part of the literary establishment, a feminist perspective on the world is not as firmly established' (Goodings 1993a). Feminist publishing may have made vital inroads into the literary firmament, but women still had a long way to go.

The continuing gender-bias in publishing was brought into sharp focus with the publication of a report from the Bentinck Group in 1995. The Bentinck Group was formed in 1993 by Paula Kahn and six other senior managers in mainstream publishing to find out what was happening within corporate organizational cultures to work against women's promotion to top management positions. Kahn's experience at Longman, where she had risen to chief executive and chair, had taught her that the ratio of women to men was roughly equal until it got to board level (a fact that remains true today). Bentinck's paper, 'A Case of Covert Discrimination', revealed the continued existence of a culture of long hours and low pay in publishing, prohibitive of women's entry to the higher ranks of the industry – with the predictable effect that women remained significantly underrepresented at board level (Walsh and Cassell 1995). 'The report turned out to be about exclusion, limiting people's ambition, and failure to reward staff of potential unless they shouted out their message of self-importance. It clearly shows that most of the people who feel uncomfortable with this culture are women, and they compose over fifty per cent of the workforce' (Walsh and Cassell 1995).

The Bentinck paper crucially showed that women in the industry were as ambitious as men, but were simply unable to sidestep the culturally ingrained practices that had historically denied them equality of opportunity. 'The researchers exploded the myth that women are not interested in moving up to senior management positions; they had the same aspirations as their male colleagues. The study was carried out in companies where equal opportunities policies were already in place. However, even in such companies, there were numerous covert barriers to women's success, and considerable gaps between policy and reality' (Aitchison 1995).

As the Bentinck group was reporting this, Virago was making the move from independence to imprint under the umbrella of the Time Warner Group, owner of Little, Brown. During this period of the mid 1990s, the publishing environment was turbulent – the collapse of the Net Book Agreement in 1995 meant that publishers could no longer set a book's price, marking the start of the price wars (Clark 2001). With Waterstones and Dillons soon coming to monopolize the bookshop market, and the internet offering consumers ever-cheaper ways to buy books, publishers were increasingly pressed on ways to cut production costs in order to increase profits. Many smaller ventures that could not absorb large losses went under or were swallowed up by larger media conglomerates:

> The recent transformation of the publishing industry from a large number of family-run houses to a small number of major publishers owned by giant, multimedia parent companies has completely transformed the nature of authorship and publishing . . . There are now few areas of book publishing which do not, either directly or indirectly, come under the control of seven main conglomerates: Bertelsmann, Pearson, Viacom, Rupert Murdoch's News Corporation, Time Warner, Hearst and Holtzbrinck. (Moran 2000, 36)

The effects of this conglomeration of the publishing industry became more obvious during Virago's fourth decade (see Chapter 7). But Virago's acquisition by Time Warner was testament to its strong reputation, sound financial history and impressive roster of respected authors – it was thus sought-after. For the other feminist presses set up in the 1970s, their position in the changing marketplace of the mid 1990s was much less straightforward.

During Virago's third decade, Sheba, Pandora, The Women's Press and many other feminist imprints all ran into serious trouble. By 1995, Pandora had gone from an imprint of Routledge to assimilation under a multinational to a failed buy-out attempt by founder Philippa Brewster. Eventually, it was sold to the independent Rivers Oram Press in 1998, where it continues to run as an imprint (see Chapter 3). Sheba, similarly, had ceased to publish new literary material – its last publication was dated 1993. Initially it sought to stave off closure by shifting its focus away from the book industry to run as a web-based enterprise, 'turning its attention to the exciting possibilities opened up by new technology, particularly multimedia and computer-mediated communications . . . Sheba's dedication to openness, fluidity, and the absence of boundaries finds a natural home on the Internet'. This 'natural home' ultimately failed to revive the press' fortunes and Sheba ceased operations in 1994. A year later, it donated its records to be archived at the Women's Library in east London (itself now also closed down).

Throughout Virago's third decade, its nearest rival The Women's Press floundered and, ultimately, failed. On her appointment as managing director of The Women's Press in 1991, Kathy Gale stated the importance of it being an independent (in spite of the press' position within the Namara group):

> Kathy Gale, publisher of The Women's Press, believes that, in some ways, this is a good time to be an independent publisher because the conglomerates daren't take a risk with new authors in such a difficult economic climate. 'Because the big companies are all producing books in such large numbers, they have to take on writers who they think are going to deliver a sure-fire commercial success', she says. 'Otherwise, they are going to have hundreds of thousands of copies sitting around in the warehouse. And I think that this is creating a gap, a lack of writing, which the independents are able to fill.' (Wolff 1994)

Gale's belief that The Women's Press could benefit from remaining small in scale (albeit not 'independent' as she erroneously describes it) was to prove misguided. Continuing financial difficulties prompted owner Naim Attallah to seek a new buyer for the press, or a new partner to run it with him, in 2003. The solutions proposed included a daring attempt by the feminist review magazine *Mslexia* to buy a controlling share in the press by drumming up funds through its readership:

> 'We calculated that if each of our subscribers contributed £25, the Press could be ours', says Debbie Taylor, *Mslexia*'s editor. 'If we can make £50,000 to £100,000 then we'll contact Pat Barker and Fay Weldon and see if we can finish off the rest in big chunks. It started as a mad idea and then we thought, why not?' (Byrnes 2003)

Sadly, what would have made a remarkable feminist success story was not to be – *Mslexia*'s staff couldn't drum up the required £250,000 and the project failed to come to fruition. The Press' last published book came out in 2003, although David Elliott, who has been on its board since the 1980s, insists that it is still an ongoing proposition, and The Women's Press continues to reprint its back catalogue while looking out for future opportunities. Even this has brought problems: its star author Alice Walker defected to Weidenfeld & Nicolson in 2004 for a five-figure sum – a deal rumoured to be due to late royalty payments (Teeman 2004).

Of all Virago's contemporaries, only one, Onlywomen, survives. However, in marked contrast to Virago, it is essentially a one-woman project, with Lillian Mohin's decision to retain total control of her press meaning that it publishes just a handful of titles each year. As Harriet Spicer acknowledges, there is value in this style of publishing: 'I'm sure Lillian Mohin of Onlywomen would say "I wished to make choices about my business that were going to limit its size, because I would raise money that way, and not that way, and therefore I'd be able to get *that* much money and therefore I'd be able to do *that* much publishing".'9 But of course while Mohin has total control and editorial freedom, her style of publishing lacks the reach and thus the potential influence of a larger press like Virago – and while Onlywomen's politics are uncompromised by a need to operate within the mainstream, the dissemination of those politics is severely limited by the press' scale.

But of course it could be argued (and indeed it has) that Virago's assimilation by a mainstream conglomerate is limiting of its feminist politicking in different but just as critical ways. Virago's sale in 1995 meant its staff now operated as part of the mainstream publishing industry, with all its attendant limitations and prejudices. Goodings claimed that Virago would retain its feminist principles, continuing to publish politically important titles that might not generate a good return: 'I sort of feel a certain duty to do things as a women's publisher, a feminist publisher . . . there's a sort of citizenship job that we do.'10 She insisted that Virago's status as an imprint constituted an ideal combination of corporate muscle and feminist intent: 'the combination now of having the might, the money, and the identity makes us a really attractive publishing house for people to come to.'11 She further argued that Virago's position within a conglomerate meant it was more able to lure established writers to the press: 'the other reason we're doing better is we have more money. I mean someone like Sarah Dunant for example, we didn't publish before – she was published by Penguin'.12 And even for writers with whom the press had long enjoyed a mutually beneficial relationship, the effect of Virago's new status was advantageous: 'even Margaret Atwood we've sold better since we got here'.13

Gooding's *intentions* are clear: that Virago would continue to be a feminist publishing house and she a feminist publisher. She argued that changing conditions in the publishing industry couldn't be ignored and that there was of course ever-greater pressure to hunt out those books that would generate profit – but she insisted, nonetheless, that Virago retained its commitment to political principle: 'There's a very great anxiety not just from this publishing house but from all publishing houses about "small" books because of the way bookselling is going now – the big books sell so much better and the little ones just disappear. [But I will publish even if the book is] small because I think it's an important book to do.'[14]

Inevitably, though, Virago couldn't escape some of the conformity demanded by absorption into the umbrella group. Virago's famous green spines, which had long served as an important identifier and helped in generating a loyal readership with a strong sense of feminist purpose, were one of the first casualties. Goodings explains:

> Our sales people who sell into [WH] Smiths and other places said they discovered that people thought you had to be really smart to read Virago, because it looks serious, and it had these green spines, you know. So we took them off, we took them off all the books. We kept them on the Classics for a long time but they're not even on the Classics now. So we kept the apple [logo], and I don't know what I think really . . . I mean one thing I do know is that you do have to keep reinventing yourself. If you hang on to stuff forever, you go down – so you have to listen to people like that, you have to listen when they tell you.[15]

Goodings suggests some reservations about the change, but sees it as an unavoidable aspect of Virago's situation as a *business* with a need to generate profit. Its books are now packaged in a way that makes them less easily distinguishable on the shelf – and thus one could argue that the famous Virago 'brand' is diminished. Yet if it is true that 'the design of a book's jacket can make a difference in sales of several hundred per cent', then innovation is inevitable in order to keep up with changing consumer tastes (Todd 2006, 25).

The excising of the green spines may have come about anyway had Virago remained independent. Virago's creation of a strong 'brand' identity resonated during the years of second-wave feminism when collectivity and the unifying emblem of 'woman' had a galvanizing and politically important significance. By Virago's third decade, and thanks in great part to Virago itself, this had changed, diminishing the need for strong identifiers: 'women who would have been considered too feminist by mainstream publishers in 1973 are now bankable. Roger Bratchell, marketing manager of Waterstone's book chain, points out that Jeanette Winterson is now published by Jonathan Cape and Helen Zahavi by Macmillan' (Ward 1994).

By the end of the millennium, many important nonfiction feminist texts also came from the stable of mainstream houses: writing by Naomi Wolf, Germaine Greer, Judith Butler and many others were published by mainstream publishers in the United Kingdom, and former Virago writers such as Lynne Segal and Natasha Walter published their work with other presses in the 1990s. Walter intentionally allied her 1998 text *The New Feminism* with the Little, Brown imprint rather than Virago's (which came under their umbrella) 'because I wanted the book to hit a mainstream audience – and with its title, I felt I already had the Virago readership' (Griffey 1998). This is an interesting manipulation on Walter's part: she clearly wishes to address a feminist audience (the 'Virago readership') while also exploiting the possibility of a better return and wider circulation by publishing with a more generalized imprint.

A year later, Walter seems to reverse her position in discussion of her text *On the Move,* which Virago published in 1999. '"I'm editing a collection of essays by young women writers about aspects of feminism," she says. "I can't imagine the idea having come from a mainstream publisher." And the company bringing it out next year? Virago' (Griffey 1998). This encapsulates the ambivalent position in which Virago found itself during its third decade. On the one hand, feminism had become somewhat incorporated in the mainstream, reducing the importance of a women-only publisher, while on the other hand, feminism's targets were still often sidestepped or overlooked by mainstream editors, leaving a space in which an avowedly feminist enterprise would continue to have meaning.

As Virago progressed through its third decade, then, there was discussion of this ambivalence and the extent to which the publishing industry could be figured as a feminist success story. Critics noted that 'in 1973 there were few women in important roles in publishing. Today they thrive, and dominate some major publishing houses', and so the argument followed that the publishing environment was one in which women were positively advantaged (Ward 1994). Callil herself argued that part of Virago's legacy – and that of the other feminist presses – was precisely that women were now more able to shatter the glass ceiling that once prohibited their progression to the top of the publishing industry: 'Virago's greatest success, apart from the writers that we served, has been the fact that every single trade publishing house in Britain today now has a thriving list of women writers. Many of these are looked after by editors who are themselves remarkable young women, for publishing is a business where women can flourish' (Simons 1998, 187).

Callil was not alone in crediting feminist publishing with effecting women's incursion into the higher echelons of the mainstream industry, in spite of the institutionalized disadvantages described in the Bentinck research. In spite of the findings of this group in 1995, by the end of Virago's third decade, Goodings also claimed that things had changed and that women were making headway into the most powerful areas of the industry: 'if you look at other industries you do not find women on the board. So yes, I would say it is a women-friendly environment'.[16] Certainly, many more women were now in place at the top of mainstream publishing houses. Goodings herself answered to a woman, Ursula Mackenzie, the overall publisher for Little, Brown, and within the industry as a whole there was a growing coterie of powerful female executives.[17] By the turn of the millennium, Gail Rebuck was 'routinely described as the most powerful figure in British publishing' (Wroe 1999). Note Rebuck's depiction as a powerful *figure*, not woman. And in a 'digital dialogue' on Bookseller.com in February 2003, the question 'are women now the dominant force in UK publishing?' took up the idea that the industry now presented women with no barriers to their success. Publisher-turned-literary agent Clare Alexander argued that the appointment of Caroline Michel as MD of Harper Press signalled the shattering, at last, of the glass ceiling: 'In the past, high profile female publishers would have reported to male managers (or suits), but Michel was hired by the MD of HarperCollins's general division, Amanda Ridout, who reports to chief executive officer and publisher of the UK company, Victoria Barnsley, who in turn reports to the American head of HarperCollins publishing worldwide, Jane Friedman.'[18] As Callil put it: 'I think they [women] run things now in a way that they never did in my day. It's fabulous. I'm happy about it.'[19]

Callil herself has been hailed as 'the most significant editor of her generation in Britain, who virtually single-handedly proved that women's publishing is not only a viable enterprise but one that recognises the importance of the niche market of women readers and writers in a stunningly successful way' (Simons and Fullbrook 1998, 5). She was cited as inspirational by fellow female publishers such as Liz Calder: '"Carmen galvanised my political education and my interest in feminism", Calder says. "I was tremendously admiring of Virago but felt I could do something for women from within an established company"' (Jaggi 2005). Calder, whose 'judgment has made her a key figure in momentous changes in British publishing since the early 1970s, reflecting feminism and the internationalisation of literary fiction', went on to become one of the most important publishers in UK literary history.[20] 'For fellow publisher and friend Carmen Callil, she is "probably the most magnificent of the generation of women who changed things; who moved the centre of the universe, of vision, and gave it a jolt".'[21]

In contrast to the apparent success story of female publishers – and, as I've described, women's advances in the book business were hard-won and even harder to retain – the broader situation of women in the workplace was far more problematic. Examination of women's status at work reveals a depressing picture, in spite of great optimism at the start of Virago's third decade that, as more and more women formed part of the UK workforce, there would be a 'feminisation of the economy' (Wilkinson 1994, 12). Yet despite this apparently successful incursion of women into the workplace, analysis of women's actual working conditions and financial reparations continually revealed a 'persistent gap between women's wages and those of men. On average, women still earn only seventy per cent of men's full-time hourly earnings. When comparing women in full-time manual occupations with men, the gap widens with women earning only sixty-three per cent of men's average weekly earnings' (Truman in Cosslett et al. 1996, 37). This research at the start of Virago's third decade also revealed that the job market was further segregated by ethnicity, with BME women receiving only 75 per cent of white women's hourly pay.[22] Success in material terms was limited to a very specific female demographic: 'for the first time in history, amongst a strictly limited category – young, childless and educated professionals – a pay differential in men's favour no longer exists. According to very recent figures, women in this age group are now earning 104 per cent of the equivalent male wage' (Franks 2000, 24).

This example was an anomaly. The wage gap persists (see Chapter 7) and through the 1990s and 2000s, mainstream workplace cultures and expectations continued to benefit men, to women's detriment. Feminist writers pointed out that 'not only is the glass ceiling still firmly in place in Britain, but so too are powerful gendered cultures which underpin organisations and approaches to change and management' (Maddock 1999, 192). This gendering of the workplace continued to direct women's lived, material realities: they prevented women from ascending to top jobs and they prevented women from being paid the same as men. Even after thirty years of feminist activity, two of the fundamental aims of the second wave – parity of pay and equal access to work for women – remained pressing.

In light of this, Virago's women, along with others like Ros de Lanerolle, Gail Rebuck, Liz Calder, Philippa Harrison and others in the book industry, were important exceptions to the rule. Publishing seemed to have more than its fair share of powerful women and at Virago, even after the sale in 1995, the company remained an important example of a female-run business that allowed women agency at every level of its operations. Figuring women as active negotiators and agents was important – it was a rare thing. Goodings insisted that although Virago now sat within a larger, mainstream group, its female staff still called the shots: 'Now I go to an acquisition meeting which is huge, absolutely the entire boardroom is full. There's our finance director, our CEO, the publicity, the marketing, the sales, the export sales, the oh . . . there's, like, ten people making the decision. And do you know, mostly I get my way. I do, mostly I do.'[23] In this changed landscape at the turn of the millennium, Virago's example continued to be important, with Goodings and her team exemplifying that still-rare figure: the female executive. More than that, Virago's work in creating and distributing literature that shone a light on women's continued disadvantages in culture and commerce was as pressing as ever.

Sharing the Fruits of the Prize Industry

Virago's sale in 1995 constituted a critical shift for women's publishing – and it was not the only significant event to occur at this juncture. The creation of the Orange Prize for Women's Fiction and the proliferation of the literary prize industry more generally during Virago's third decade of operations were to fundamentally alter the way in which publishing houses conducted their business. It is difficult to overstate the influence book prize lists now have on sales and consequently on the way in which books are contracted, produced and marketed. Authors nominated for the Man Booker Prize or the Costa Book Awards longlists, for example, can expect huge uplifts in sales. Titles that make the Booker shortlist are guaranteed thousands of extra hardback sales – though many consider this a very conservative estimate (Todd 1996). During the 1990s, as competition over book pricing became ever-more cut-throat, garnering the extra sales that come with longlisting and shortlisting grew increasingly vital to a publishing house's profit margins and thus its viability.

The literary press, and consequently the world of literary prize-giving, has historically been dominated by men (see Chapters 2 and 3) who, as many feminist critics have pointed out, 'have found the contributions of their own sex immeasurably superior' (Spender 1989, 1). This resulted, unsurprisingly, in many more men than women being awarded literary prizes – the Booker Prize, for example, was instituted in 1969 (as second-wave feminism itself began to take hold) and since then has had twice as many male winners as female. The feminist writer Natasha Walter was invited to form part of the Booker Prize jury one year and discovered for herself the arrogance and innate misogyny of this review culture when fellow judge John Sutherland 'startlingly discounted one book because it was "so much a woman's novel"' (Walter 2006a). This culture of privileging male writing led women writers, readers and publishers to think about ways of challenging the status quo, leading to the instigation of the Orange Prize for women's fiction.

The Orange Prize, an annual award for fiction established specifically to reward women writers, was catalysed by the exclusion of Virago writer Angela Carter from the 1991 Booker Prize shortlist, an omission that was widely condemned in literary critical circles. Kate Mosse, one of the driving forces behind the first Orange Prize, had long noted a tendency among literary critics to view any Booker-shortlisted woman writer as somehow representative of her sex, so that a female-authored text constituted a 'woman's entry', whereas male-authored texts were assessed on merit alone: 'writing by women is always "women's writing", to be understood and evaluated in terms of the special case of their gender. Writing by men is just writing' (Morris 1993, 46). Mosse and others thought the only way to address this was to institute a prize for which only women could be considered: 'paradoxically, the way to take gender out of the equation was for all the entrants to be women' (Bedell 2005). Goodings was on the prize's organizing committee, involved in early meetings to help get it established. It was originally to have been called Uni, with Mitsubishi agreeing to sponsor the award, but the company pulled its backing in 1994 after derisory press coverage provoked anxiety among its directors (Todd 1996).

A new sponsor was found and the renamed Orange Prize was launched in January 1996. Mosse was shocked by the vitriol that surrounded its inception: 'I thought everybody who was concerned about reading books would be happy that there was a new prize. The first question anyone asked was, "Are you a lesbian?"' (Bedell 2005). Literary media comment questioned the need for a women-only prize, yet 'in the week of the Orange launch, one broadsheet newspaper carried twenty reviews, nineteen of them on books by men. Women publish about seventy per cent of novels in Britain'.[24] Almost a decade after Women in Publishing's 'Reviewing the Reviews' had identified the extent of women's exclusion from the review pages, the launch of the Orange Prize showed how little things had changed.

The importance of the Orange Prize, then, was not so much in attributing 'greatness' to a select group of writers or texts, but in the effect it had on sales of women's writing, allocating a similar boost in profile and sales as the Booker had long afforded (mostly) men's work. The effect of the Orange can be clearly discerned in the rising sales of women's literature – five years after the award's inception, women writers outnumbered men in *The Guardian*'s Fastseller list, the definitive guide to the year's hottest paperbacks, for the first time (Gibbons 2001b).

In this sense, the Orange Prize began to democratize the literary prize industry, awarding a fair share of the fame and reputation generated by mainstream book prizes, and their attendant sales, back to women writers. There was of course discomfort – among women writers themselves as much as anyone else – that there should be a dedicated women's prize: 'Anita Brookner, a Booker winner, has no mixed feelings. "I'm against positive discrimination. If women want equality, which they do, and which they have largely achieved, they shouldn't ask for separate treatment. Publishing is an open

forum. If a book is good, it will get published. If it is good, it will get reviewed. The whole idea of an award just for women fills me with horror." She
has backed her words with deed, refusing to allow her latest book to be put
in for the award' (Jeffreys 1996).

Brookner has stuck by her position, but the reality was – and still is –
that mainstream review and prize cultures are biased in favour of men. Even
when women writers have triumphed in mainstream prize competitions,
their work has simultaneously been derogated, as examination of the coverage of Margaret Atwood's (long-awaited) Booker Prize win in 2000 shows:
"'I feel reading Margaret Atwood is rather like eating Bran Flakes," says
writer Alain de Botton. "You know it is good for you, but it's not much fun."
His view is often shared by men' (Jardine 2000). Even in the moment of her
win, Atwood's value as a writer is undermined and her work is judged on
the criterion of gender, not art. The chairman of the Booker judges was even
forced to insist 'this was not a lifetime achievement award, but a prize for this
book' (Gerard 2000). The insinuation that the work *itself* didn't warrant the
prize is difficult to miss.

Atwood's win is useful, too, as evidence of the sales boost generated by
Booker success: 'Bloomsbury, the publishing group, yesterday basked in the
success of writer Margaret Atwood, pictured, whose novel *The Blind Assassin*
won the Booker prize at the start of the month. A trading statement from
Bloomsbury said sales of the book had soared since Ms Atwood took the prize
at her fourth attempt. Around 120,000 copies of the hardback have been
sold' (Teather 2000). Bloomsbury publish Atwood's work in hardback before
Virago publish the paperback versions – for both, Atwood's Booker Prize was
expected to lead to a more than doubling of sales. Goodings notes the effect
of a Booker nomination for another of Virago's authors: 'Carol Birch was
long-listed for the Booker and we sold something like 2,000 hardbacks in that
space between the long-list and the short-list being announced.'[25]

The Rise of the Star Author

The shape of the book business began to alter significantly during Virago's
third decade as a result of this focus on literary prize-giving. And alongside it there also came another new phenomenon: the star author. Cultural
reification of the individual came to define late 1990s and early 2000s culture – certainly in the United Kingdom – with the result that a focus on
celebrity and 'personalities' made fame the new currency in an increasingly
consumer-led culture. The construction of a cult of celebrity in which the
singular self is celebrated came to be tied in to an increasingly commodified

and commodity-obsessed culture. In literary terms, this meant that as well as the books themselves, literary 'personalities' were also desirable, consumable commodities. For publishers, the writer as well as their work became something to be promoted and pushed.

Increasingly, details of authors' personalities, their private lives and their love lives were brought into discussion of their work since within a celebrity culture, it is these aspects of identity that are the most 'sellable'. The effect for publishers was that they began to market their authors as much as their books, since 'an established literary publisher can make use of a "totemic" author as a strong marketing asset. It will be no surprise to learn that publishers aggressively promote "lead" authors and titles at the expense of those lower down a seasonal list' (Todd 1996, 25). The focus on individual 'names' meant that publishing houses marketed authors as commodities in order to secure sales and thus longevity.

In 2001 there was a debate at the London Book Fair over how women writers' looks were being used to sell their work. 'Publishers were now judging writers on how many features they might generate in newspaper lifestyle sections, rather than promoting the older "gargoyles" who count themselves lucky if they make it onto the review pages' (Gibbons 2001). Virago writer Sarah Waters describes her discomfort with this culture, recounting an occasion when the *Evening Standard* contacted her for an interview: 'I hadn't realised that it wasn't really for their book page, it was for their lifestyle page and so it was just this piece about me, you know, not about the books. And it was about where I lived and what I was wearing, you know. And it felt really unpleasant and really exposing.'[26] Literary agent Clare Alexander directly links the 'celebrification' of authors to their success in the marketplace: 'there has been a drive to get authors into the features pages and the glossy magazines. Obviously if they are young and gorgeous they have got a head start' (Gibbons 2001).

This rise of the celebrity author has important repercussions for women writers: while it can be figured as detracting from literary worth, focusing on personalities rather than the writing itself, in a sense it also levels the playing field, since writers of both genders are subject to its standards of judgement. Further, as Moran argues, star authors 'have the potential to be commercially successful and penetrate into mainstream media, but are also perceived of as in some sense culturally "authoritative"' (Moran 2000, 6). One effect of this is that the parameters of judgement are no longer set by the literary establishment that has long excluded or devalued women's work, but rather by a kind of publicly ordained system of popularity and merit. Moran cites the example of a female BME author to show how celebrity culture can advance writers and the themes in their work that might not necessarily gain widespread cultural currency: 'the celebritization of African-American women authors like Toni Morrison shows how questions of simple market appeal can merge with broader social, cultural and racially inflected issues'.[27]

For Virago, survival has of course meant an engagement with this celebrity culture, marketing big-name authors such as Waters and others in order to ensure their books' success in the marketplace. It has also developed a growing list of celebrity memoirs, selecting a range of 'bad girls' who refused the feminine role for publication – in its third decade there were books about or by Janis Joplin, Gloria Steinem, Dolly Wilde, Mae West and Mary Wollstonecraft, to name but a few. As Spicer says, 'the individual authors are now the way that Virago succeeds. It's more like other publishers'.[28] The celebrity figure has in fact always been tied up with the ways in which feminism itself has been constructed in mainstream culture. As witnessed by the focus on writers such as Germaine Greer, Gloria Steinem, Camille Paglia and Naomi Wolf, identifying individuals and examining their work in the context of their 'personalities' has defined the women's movement as it is understood in the mainstream: 'the media historically have focused on the fascinating protagonists who populate the women's movement rather than the collective change or cultural critique that feminism has created' (Farrell 1995, 643).

To a degree, this 'celebrification' of feminism has been utilized to convey messages to a wider audience, as Amy Erdman Farrell argues. She posits that feminists' engagement with celebrity culture constitutes 'the experimental and daring attempt by a number of women's movement activists to engage a mass audience using the commercial media as their vehicle' (Farrell 1998, 2). Her concept of 'popular' feminism legitimates Virago's selling of their 'star' authors: feminism must make use of all the tools at its disposal in order to further its cause. But this focus on the individual can also reinstate old gendered stereotypes, with celebrity culture facilitating images of the famous to reinstate patriarchal norms. As McRobbie argues, 'the commercial domain (rather than the welfare state) has established itself as the primary public space in which the parameters are set for what constitutes acceptable codes of femininity' (McRobbie 2006). If women – famous or otherwise – diverge from this 'acceptable' feminine model, the celebrity icon can be (ab)used to direct censure their way. So, 'the female celebrity has become a focus of condemnation. This is especially the case when such young women are seen to be unapologetic in their pursuit of those same goals that are being relentlessly advocated in popular culture – a glamorous career, sexual freedom and an independent income allowing full participation in the consumer culture'.[29] The inexorable rise of the cult of celebrity continued into Virago's fourth decade (see Chapter 7) and continues to fracture the ways in which feminism is constructed and received.

The concept of celebrity and the ever-increasing cultural currency conveyed by fame has complicated repercussions for women, for feminism and for feminist publishing. For Virago during its third decade, these changing cultural norms were coupled with a shift in the structure of the company, following its incorporation into a mainstream conglomerate. All of this made the press a very different proposition in 2002 than it had been in 1993. By the end of its third decade of business, Virago constituted a rather singular voice in the landscape of feminist publishing. Yet Goodings remained an important driver of the press' politics and, appropriately enough in a culture that increasingly valorized the individual, it was she alone who represented the 'new' Virago. Her former mentor Callil credited her with being a critical factor in the press' ongoing success: 'it's my experience (and I've been in publishing all my life) that a lot of the best publishing, the real publishing comes from an individual'.[30]

Goodings oversaw the transition of the 'old' Virago into its new form within a conglomerate, carrying with her Virago's history, personal experience of Callil's original vision and a clear idea that despite now operating as an imprint Virago should remain a feminist concern. The result was year-on-year increases in profitability as well as a growing and diverse list of lauded names. Her authors spoke extremely highly of her, with Ali Smith for example saying she was 'a great and spirited editor for Virago in the new era'.[31] In spite of the changes that transformed Virago during its tumultuous third decade, as well as the changed cultural and literary world within which it sat, Goodings remained at the helm of a publisher that seemed to still carry with it a strong sense of feminist purpose. Callil credits Goodings with perpetuating the press' politics in this way, in the face of an ever-more challenging publishing scene: 'Lennie has a magic way of getting what she wants.'[32]

Notes

1. Interview with Ursula Owen, 5 February 2009.
2. Interview with Carmen Callil, 10 November 2004.
3. Ibid.
4. Interview with Ursula Owen, 5 February 2009.
5. Interview with Carmen Callil, 10 November 2004.
6. Ibid.
7. Anon., 'About Virago Press', *Virago Press*, retrieved 21 September 2017 from http://www.virago.co.uk/about_virago.asp?TAG=&CID=&PGE=&LANG=EN (para. 49 of 70).
8. Ibid.
9. Interview with Harriet Spicer, 20 October 2004.
10. Interview with Lennie Goodings, 8 November 2004.

11. Ibid.
12. Ibid.
13. Ibid.
14. Ibid.
15. Ibid.
16. Interview with Lennie Goodings, 8 November 2004.
17. Ibid.
18. Anon, 'Are Women Now the Dominant Force in UK Publishing?', *The Bookseller*, retrieved 17 February 2003 from http://www.thebookseller.com.
19. Interview with Carmen Callil, 10 November 2004.
20. Ibid.
21. Ibid.
22. Ibid., 39.
23. Interview with Lennie Goodings, 8 November 2004.
24. Ibid.
25. Ibid.
26. Interview with Sarah Waters, 12 July 2004.
27. Ibid., 50.
28. Interview with Harriet Spicer, 20 October 2004.
29. Ibid.
30. Interview with Carmen Callil, 10 November 2004.
31. Interview with Ali Smith, 19 July 2004.
32. Interview with Carmen Callil, 10 November 2004.

Chapter 6

Third Waves and Disconnections

Virago's third decade was a complex and difficult one for feminism. The years 1993–2002 are defined, in part, by the United Kingdom's political emergence from Conservative rule with the election of Tony Blair's New Labour in 1997, which brought with it a kind of optimistic liberalism – at least in the early years of Blair's premiership. Against the soundtrack of 'Things Can Only Get Better', the new government promised to create a fairer society, bringing in new opportunities for women.[1] The 1997 election saw the influx of 'Blair's babes' into the House of Commons and with them the hope that – at last – the theoretical formulations of a fairer society for women might finally be transformed into lived realities.

The shift in the United Kingdom's political and cultural climate had an effect on the literary and feminist environments within which women writers were working. The 1990s, which began with the publication of Judith Butler's seminal *Gender Trouble* (1990), was an ambivalent decade for feminism: on the one hand, the emergence of popular cultural interpretations of Butlerian 'queerness' broke down the binary gender divide, as manifested in cultural artefacts such as music, fashion, film and TV (see the section entitled 'Gender Roles and the "Queering" of Culture' later on in this chapter). On the other hand, as a limited demographic of white, Western, privileged women began to attain parity with men in terms of pay and status at work, there began in earnest a feminist backlash and a widespread campaign to disavow the 'f-word' itself.

As the 1990s progressed, the Butlerian shift in focus to foreground the ways in which *both* sexes were a construction within cultural discourses put centre stage the overarching paradigm of consumerism that increasingly came to define cultural constructions of all identities – male, female or other. The second wave gave way to the third, with its understanding of the concept 'gender' incorporating both the second-wave critique of the mother/housewife/sex object triad as well as a more nuanced understanding of the ways that all identities were in some way culturally contingent and potentially fluid. This was reflected in the books that were written, the songs that were sung, the images that were on display and the language that was used in both literary and popular cultural texts.

Third-Wave and Post-feminisms: Things Can Only Get Better

As Virago moved into its third decade, feminism went through another kind of shift, arising from the fractures caused by the identity politics debates of the 1980s. Some women felt that these arguments had put women too far into the position of 'othered' victim: limited not only by sex but also by ethnicity, class, sexuality, disability and others. During the 1990s and 2000s, a 'third wave' emerged, originating in the United States as feminist writers negotiated a politics that contained elements of second-wave feminism as well as critiques of it. Third-wave feminism, a description first coined in 1995 by Rebecca Walker in her edited collection *To Be Real*, sought to escape the traps of identity politics, separatism and essentialism that had divided second-wave feminists, as well as re-energize a feminist movement that had lost its way through internal conflict and diverting energy on combating negative media representation (Walker 1995).

Alongside this new formulation of feminism, there also emerged a new category: 'power feminists' similarly distanced themselves from the figurings of identity politics, while also arguing that feminism problematized rather than celebrated too many aspects of female identity. 'Power feminists' such as Camille Paglia (1990), Katie Roiphe (1993) and Christine Hoff Sommers (1994) – all American writers, but whose work was published and critiqued in the United Kingdom – claimed that women now had no need to demand change. These 'post-feminist' messages were presented by a sexist media as evidence that feminism had gone out of date, or just too far. The subsequent feminist 'backlash' that ensued forms an important part of the cultural context of Virago's third decade. Susan Faludi examined the phenomenon in her 1992 text of the same name that proved to be a catalyst for many of the ideas of third-wave feminism that were to follow. She wrote:

> By the end of the 1980s many women had absorbed the teaching of the media and were bitterly familiar with various 'statistical' developments, most notably a 'man shortage'; a 'devastating' plunge in economic status for women divorcing [. . .] an 'infertility epidemic'; and a 'great emotional depression' and 'burn-out' attacking, respectively, single and career women. (Faludi 1992, 21)

This backlash was to stymie the women's movement, leaving especially younger women ambivalent about identifying themselves as feminist. This disavowal of the f-word was borne out by surveys of women's attitudes to feminism in the 1990s and 2000s – these showed that up to three-quarters of young women did not identify as feminist. As one put it: 'the twenty-something women I know don't care about old-style feminism. Partly this is because they already see themselves as equal to men: they can work, they can vote, they can bonk on the first date' (Taylor 2006).[2] It was also partly because anti-feminist rhetoric had succeeded in constructing an image of feminists as man-hating, separatist and 'unattractive'. 'Most young women are feminists, but we're too afraid to say it – or even to recognise it', writes Jessica Valenti. 'And why not? Feminists are supposed to be ugly. And fat. And hairy!' (Valenti 2007, 8). The renouncement of feminism was the result of a complex interplay between right-wing rhetoric (the predictable cry that women had won more than their fair share economically, politically and socially – in spite of consistent evidence belying this – or simply that they should 'return to the kitchen') and a more real sense that women had in fact gained some ground. The confused rejection of the 'f-word' also reveals the pernicious influence of consumer messages that 'sold' women the idea of emancipation while simultaneously reinforcing sexist images of the 'ideal' female type.

Certainly culture had altered since 1973, the year of Virago's birth, and within that women's status had changed – to an extent. But the battles set out at the start of the second wave continued into the third, and the same issues were explored during the 1990s as had been during the 1970s. Gender roles, sexual behaviours, women's role in the workplace and in the home remained sites of contestation – all were explored, too, in the fiction and poetry of feminist writers during this period. Women remained systematically disadvantaged in economic terms as the twentieth century came to an end. They continued to be unfairly remunerated at work, to bear the brunt of responsibility for childcare and to be sexually objectified. The depressing recurrence of these themes meant that third-wave feminism continued to organize around the same issues, although some new topics were added to the feminist agenda. Alongside naturalized gender roles and sexual objectification, there also emerged a new feminist emphasis on global issues such as ecology, poverty, the environment and technology alongside the ongoing engagement with second-wave feminism's original goals.

The idea of 'ecofeminism' was not new – the term had been coined in the 1970s and events like the Greenham women's peace camp merged concerns for the environment and ecology with the politics of the women's movement. But during the 1990s it gathered momentum as scientific dialogues about global warming and ecological disaster began to preoccupy the mainstream. Issues such as global warming and the depletion of the ozone layer, the finite reserve of carbon fuels, the push towards deforestation and the destruction of natural environments, and potential technological disasters such as the much-discussed 'Y2K' bug meant that ecofeminist approaches began to develop into a more holistic 'global feminism' that looked beyond the privileged Western perspective to include consideration of how these issues impacted in particular on third world women: 'when we consider that we are fast approaching the day when eighty per cent of the world's women will live in the third world, it becomes an urgent task for feminists to think about how women's lives can become more visible while minimising the conceptual biases of race, class, and caste' (Curtin in Warren 1997, 83). Theorists such as Karen Warren (1997), Mary Mellor (1997) and Carolyn Merchant (1992) theorized women's relationship to the planet and the ways in which they could play a role in combating these threats to its health and viability. Virago played its part in disseminating these ideas, publishing its own ecofeminist nonfiction that took up these arguments (Garrett 1995; Steingraber 1998).

There was a growing sense that third-wave UK feminism must include global perspectives. While Western women rejected the label 'feminist', women in developing nations remained systematically disadvantaged in terms of their education, health, safety, and social and sexual freedoms. In the academy, there emerged new 'postcolonial' theoretical positions, arising from critic Edward Said's observation that developing nations and former colonies of the British Empire were represented as 'other', as different-from-Western culture (Said 1973 and 1993). There was a new interest in and focus on representing different national and cultural contexts, particularly through literature, although also in music, art and drama. As these postcolonial theories and postcolonial artforms were explored in the academy and beyond, feminism was required to think about who it spoke for when it spoke of 'woman' or 'women', and to figure race not just in terms of BME women's position in the Western world, but also in terms of the status of nonwhite, non-Western women globally. In a collection of feminist essays published by Virago at the end of the millennium, Oona King articulated this tension: 'women today make up half the world's population, yet do two thirds of its work, receive only one tenth of its income, and own less than one per cent of world property. To say that women have achieved equality, even on paper, is to dabble in fiction' (King in Walter 1999, 41).

Third-wave feminist critics pointed out that the privilege of a first-world perspective and its apathy about feminism was in fact partly predicated on a system that served to maintain the poverty and inequality of women in the developing world. 'This is a question that feminism must face: if individual rights come at the price of the negative aspects of globalisation, to what extent should that concept of rights define feminist praxis?' (Heywood and Drake in Gillis et al. 2004, 18). A more global feminism, which paid attention to the history, politics and cultures of the developing world, was now required. The articulation of postcolonial identities and its ramifications for feminism was more fully developed in Virago's fourth decade, and was reflected in fiction writing by women, including Virago's Margaret Atwood and Barbara Kingsolver, as well as Andrea Levy, Chimamanda Ngozi Adichie and Kiran Desai, all of whom demonstrate this global feminist perspective in their writing (see Chapter 8). At Virago, efforts were made to diversify the editorial staff as well as support more BME women into and upwards through the publishing industry itself via a diversity network called GAP: 'GAP was set up by Ros de Lanerolle – it was her idea. She was South African, so she had more experience of us here of putting structures in place', recalls Goodings.[3]

Gender Roles and the 'Queering' of Culture

The radical new formulation of gender put forward by Butler in her 1990 text *Gender Trouble* posited that both gender and the body were 'created' through a process of repetitious re-enactments of culturally sanctioned behaviours: 'Gender is not to culture as sex is to nature; gender is also the discursive/ cultural means by which "sexed nature" or "a natural sex" is produced and established as "prediscursive", prior to culture, a politically neutral surface *on which* culture acts' (Butler 1990, 11). Butler's queering of gender shifted the emphasis from a focus on women to a focus on the ways in which *both* sexes are constructed within cultural discourses – in this queer theory turns away from 1980s identity politics and the insistence on specifying the difference of *female* experience.

Many of the new formulations of female identity expressed during the years 1993–2002 arose from a kind of Butlerian queerness, a blurring of the boundaries between male and female. While Butlerian performativity was not a straightforward co-option of consumption as a means to reinventing the self, outside of the academy the gender-benders of the 1990s embraced consumption of fashion, art, media and music as modes of self-expression. Following on from Butler's central proposition that gender and sex were culturally contingent, during Virago's third decade one of the most notable shifts in culture was the emergence of new identities that queered the divide between male and female, playing with the limits of masculine and feminine norms. There was the 'girl power'-spouting ladette (as well as the lesbian 'boi') who enacted historically masculine behaviours, being sexually boastful, brash and crass. In addition, the 'metrosexual' man emerged, portrayed in magazines and books as a *desirable* blend of feminine and masculine stereotypes:

'ever more ambiguous homo-het, man-woman pictures of "men" in both mainstream and alternative media' were emerging (Hearn 1998). For a time, this troubling of the gender order generated a sense of freedom and optimism that anticipated, and then proliferated within, Blair's new post-1997 Britain.

The incorporation of these subversive identities into mainstream culture is evidenced in such cultural phenomena as fashion, music and art – the emergence of popular cultural icons such as the Spice Girls, Marilyn Manson, Eddie Izzard, models Kate Moss and Agyness Deyn and even David Beckham, all of whom transgressed the boundaries between masculine and feminine, showed a shift towards a more androgynous, queer figuring of identity. Popular culture in the mid to late 1990s was manifesting 'queer': 'in many respects through figures like Sigourney Weaver and Madonna, kd lang and Sharon Stone, popular culture has been far ahead of politics in thinking through the blurring of the boundaries of male and female identity, and the potency of female sexuality' (Wilkinson 1994, 9).

The mainstream appropriation of previously taboo enactments of transvestism and drag is, in a sense, hugely radical. Butler had argued that trans communities serve effectively to mock 'both the expressive models of gender and the notion of a true gender identity' (Butler 1990, 174). She explored transvestism and drag to argue that it effectively parodies the notion of an 'original' or primary gender identity: '*in imitating gender, drag implicitly reveals the imitative structure of gender itself – as well as its contingency*' (Butler 1990, 174, original emphasis). This was an important step in the attempt to denaturalize masculine and feminine behaviours: 'clothing as an artefact, with its clear gender divisions, illustrates, as few other things can, the socially constructed nature of gender which goes beyond biological sex' (Suthrell 2004, 14). Playful and *positive* engagement with queer identities showed that there had been a shift in cultural attitudes to previously rigidly imagined and enforced gender roles. There was a freer expression of identity that was less tightly bound to binaried conceptions of masculine and feminine.

In literary terms, texts such as Sarah Waters' *Tipping the Velvet* (1998) explored such transgressions of gender norms. *Tipping the Velvet* launched Virago's V series in 1998 and portrays the liberatory potential for women of donning a male appearance and garb. Waters depicts the cross-dressing rituals of Victorian music hall culture to reveal, through her character Nan, how transgressing gender-prescribed dress codes allows the experience of new freedoms. Disguised as a man, Nan enjoys acting in ways forbidden to her when coded female by her garb:

London, for all my weeping, could never wash dim; and to walk freely about in it at last – to walk as a boy, as a handsome boy in a well-sewn suit, whom the people stared after only to envy, never to mock – well, it has a brittle kind of glamour to it, that was all I knew, just then, of satisfaction. (Waters 1998, 195)

Nan's cross-dressing resonated with contemporary readers, making Waters' novel a smash hit – although set in the past, it was very much a product of its time.

In Virago's nonfiction, too, there were texts that engaged with queer ideas such as performativity, transgressive sexualities and nongendered realities. Texts such as Dianne Hales' *Just Like a Woman* (1999) troubled the link between biology and gender, exploring new constructions of the individual that discarded gender entirely (Hales 1999). Historical depictions such as *Suits Me* (1998), the biography of female-bodied jazz performer Billy Tipton who lived as a man, as well as the fantastical imaginings contained in *Women Who Wear the Breeches* (1995) are also evidence of Virago's engagement with the ideas of 'queer' (Middlebrook 1998; Shahrukh 1995).

The intersection of queerer formulations of identity and feminist publishing was, however, somewhat limited. Virago's fiction and nonfiction certainly reflected some of the ways in which queer ideas had permeated culture, but it didn't publish any of the more radical, theoretical queer texts written and discussed during the 1990s. The Women's Press made an explicit stand *against* queer politics, with publisher Kathy Gale expressing cynicism about what she perceived to be an obfuscation of the continuing exploitation of women in consumer culture, and a simplistic conflation of sex and emancipation. She explained:

We've taken a pretty clear stance against queer politics, for example, because I think that women who've adopted queer politics in many ways have just been seduced into it by the old patterns of self-destructive behaviour. You know, the whole kind of S&M thing. I think it's all deeply unfortunate. Part of what we mean by the line 'books of integrity' in our publicity is that we've stayed close to a politic of integrity. (Steel 1998, 28)

The disengagement of The Women's Press points to one of third-wave feminism's conflicts – between 'old-fashioned' feminism and its rigidity in defining women and men as separate, and a (naïve) third-wave feminist position that denied the line of inheritance owed to second-wave politics and based its concept of female empowerment on playful androgyny and sexual ambiguity. There was something of a generational divide opening up, with second-wave publishers like The Women's Press being criticized as being outdated and out of step: 'it is possible to be anti-sexist, anti-racist, sexy as hell and queer as fuck all at the same time. Many others have proved it since' (Steel 1998, 28).

As feminism entered a new wave and became increasingly multigenerational, a new demographic of young women had different ideas about what it should prioritize. Goodings says that Virago responded by publishing books (like that by Waters) that chimed with cultural and feminist debates, but didn't demand identification with any particular political position. 'What we've always had and is part of why Virago survived', she says, 'is that you don't have to identify as a feminist to read our books, or want to read our books, and actually I think that's part of why some of the other presses didn't last. You had to be sort of card-carrying, and we just . . . like it says here, "books by women, for everyone". That really matters.'[4]

At the turn of the millennium, the inculcation of queer politics into popular culture seemed to have made the desirable androgyny first articulated by Virginia Woolf and then taken up by many second-wave feminist critics to be an imminent reality: 'a report on relationships in the UK showed that young people under twenty-five had less conforming gender strategies and were moving towards a more androgynous ideal' (Maddock 1999, 47). The 1990s were marked by this queering of appearances, a superficial androgyny, and a playful engagement with political ideas. What underlies this, however, is not simply a re-alignment of gender roles along more feminist principles. This apparent 'queering' of culture, while undoubtedly owing some of its effect to feminism, was also driven by a much less woman-centred and increasingly powerful force: consumerism.

The Limits of Girl Power: Conflating Consumption with Liberation

While Virago's third decade saw the emergence of new, more plural and transgressive images of women and men in popular culture, many of the images of this 'queerer' culture prioritized style over substance (as Kathy Gale had argued). The emphasis on the body and modification of the self emerged within and from a culture that was increasingly defined by consumption, so that while women and men alike were encouraged to fashion their own self-stylings, they did so by buying into a capitalist consumer paradigm that had profit rather than politics as its motivating factor. Examining these queerer cultural constructions of gender reveals as much about patterns of consumption and marketing as it does about sexual politics.

The 'queering' of sex and gender through the 1990s was inextricably linked to a new cultural climate that foregrounded the consumption of goods as 'part of a newly legitimate – politically acceptable – "postmodern" interest in pleasure and fantasy. Those days are gone when consumerism could be comfortably identified as oppressive or regressive without more ado, and from some safely assumed position of exteriority' (Bowlby in de Grazia 1996, 382). Queer politics troubled the second-wave corollary between consumer culture and women's oppression – it gave the act of consumption political meaning, formulating a way of constructing identity through display, exteriority and the consumption and subversion of 'straight' styles to give new meanings: '*consumption is always a cultural as well as an economic process*' (Lury 1996, 51, original emphasis). The incorporation of men into consumer culture was figured, for example, as a way of disrupting traditional formulations of the 'masculine'. As Frank Mort argued, men are also made targets within a commercialized style culture, with the result that the concept of masculinity itself is destabilized – the effect should be 'a positive contribution to men's social roles' (Mort 1996, 83).

But feminist appraisal of consumer culture figured it as another paradigm within which women – and, increasingly, men – were figured as manipulable dupes, influenced by market forces that overrode any commitment to political ideology and cultural change. Susan J. Douglas, for example, identified a culture in which 'women's liberation metamorphosed into female narcissism unchained as political concepts and goals like liberation and equality were collapsed into distinctly personal, private desires' (Douglas 2000, 267). She argues that this focus on consumption and individual pleasures travesties the 'personal is political' slogans of the 1970s: 'women's liberation became equated with women's ability to do whatever they wanted for themselves, whenever they wanted, no matter what the expense' (Douglas 2000, 268).

It can be further argued that the 'queer' female identities represented by, for example, the girl band the Spice Girls – female sexual agency, outspokenness, sporty/punky attire alongside more traditional garb – was in fact a valorization of masculine attributes in female form. Ladette-style girl power, then, was nothing more than an aping of male behaviours, pointing to the fact that characteristics defined as masculine continued to be those deemed most desirable. Simply assuming masculine behaviours did not mean that women interrogated why those behaviours held most cultural authority – accordingly, they didn't make meaningful inroads into changing the status quo.

Following the emergence of the gender-bending ladette and the metrosexual man, there swiftly followed a restatement of gendered norms in figures such as the 'new lad' and the rise of a hyperfeminine 'girlyness'. Laddism valorized unreconstructed masculinity, employing sexist stereotypes of men and women to present an 'ironic' version of gender relations. Its focus on 'useless' men who don't understand their female partners, or women who are 'gagging for it' sexually, peddled easy ideas of masculinity and femininity as a 'joke'. Its effects are rife in today's 'rape culture' and the continued efforts of the right-wing media to make comedy out of women's oppression (see Chapter 8).

The emergence of laddism came as a rebuttal to feminism, an attempt to retake the ground women were perceived as having advanced into. Men who were uncomfortable with the idea that women might break out of their traditional 'feminine' roles embraced laddism since it allowed them to continue to embody an unreconstructed masculinity, as long as they explained their behaviour as 'ironic'. Alongside laddism, there also emerged representations of a kind of extreme femininity: 'femininity, then, with all its most retrogressive trappings, seemed to experience a mini-revival in the 1990s through to the present day, witnessed by a surge of interest in fashion, lifestyle and beauty' (Whelehan 2005, 177). Hyperfemininity's most insidious expression has come in the form of the 'Barbie' body ideal, as the 1990s saw the emergence of a toned, tanned, hairless torso that represented a literal embodiment of female success. The new female beauty ideal was slimmer, harder and younger, a testament to the emergence of a diet and exercise industry that had much to gain from exploiting women's bodies, as well as a 'symbolic statement about the value our society attaches to youth' (Romaine 1999, 253). This reification of an eternally youthful, trim and taut body had direct consequences for female self-image and identity, and marked the convergence of a sexist view of woman-as-object with a consumer culture in which women's insecurities could be exploited for financial gain.

In addition to the diet and exercise industries, the 1990s saw the normalization of plastic surgery procedures. Germaine Greer addressed the growing popularity of all these artificial manipulations of the body – everything from make-up and dress to plastic surgery, dieting and even exercise – in her 1999 text *The Whole Woman,* a revisiting of the ground she first covered with her 1970 polemic *The Female Eunuch.* She argued that 'women have been deliberately infected with B[ody] D[ysmorphic] D[isorder]' through the imposition of an unattainable ideal body type in popular culture (Greer 1999, 21). Women, and to a lesser extent men, were being aggressively targeted by a body industry that had much to gain from creating images of them that required consumer input. Julie Burchill described the pressure this put women under, arguing that those who refused to ascribe to this ideal type 'have committed one of the most heinous modern crimes a woman can: they do not care whether or not they are physically attractive. Whereas a woman might once have been disapproved of merely as sloppy, today her appearance calls into question her sexual orientation, morals and even sanity' (Burchill 2000).

The tyranny of this idealized body type was examined in Virago's published output. Natasha Walter's 1999 collection of feminist essays focuses on critiques of the body. In *On the Move,* Katherine Viner acknowledges that although the imposition of ideal body types onto women has long been a focus of feminist attention, 'the images we see of women, on billboards, in magazines, are more uniform than ever. You really will not see the hint of a bulge anywhere – that would be too much like real life' (Viner in Walter 1999, 20). Virago also published texts such as Emily Jenkins' *Tongue First* (1999) and Betsy Lerner's *Food and Loathing* (2003) that examined women's attempts to assimilate the uniform physical images of themselves seen around them, as well as to break out of these confining ideals. The Women's Press (the only second-wave feminist press still publishing alongside Virago at this point) similarly engaged with these debates during the late 1990s and early 2000s, publishing Charlotte Cooper's *Fat and Proud: The Politics of Size* (1998), Shelley Bovey's *Sizeable Reflections* (2000) and *What Have You Got to Lose?* (2002) as well as Helen Hines' *Perfect* (2002), which examines younger women's attitudes to body image.

This emphasis on women's bodies and an idealized version of the female form was depressingly reminiscent of the sexist culture of 1970s Britain. While the 1990s certainly threw up new and arguably 'queerer' manifestations of gender, these were based in a commodity culture that made such manifestations as much the product of consumption as of political or cultural change. Women's status at work and in the home, as well as within sexual and commercial tropes, was still (for most) curtailed by the same inequalities that were the focus of second-wave feminism.

Same Old Stereotypes: Mothers and Sex Objects

While more women were in work at the start of the 1990s than had been at the beginning of the 1970s, the glass ceiling that limited them to the lower echelons of most industries was still in place, due in no large part to the continued assumption that childcare was mainly a woman's duty. The issue of parenting and caregiving was tackled in Lynne Segal's *Slow Motion: Changing Masculinities, Changing Men,* published by Virago in 1997. Segal argues that an insistence on men's participation in childrearing is fundamental to women's more equal status. The outcomes are manifold: women are freer to concentrate on their careers; they are paid more as the cultural assumption that their wages are mere supplements to their partner's is erased; male parenting will reinvest the concept of childcare with dignity and authority; and relations between the sexes will alter as 'men are changed by greater involvement in childcare' (Segal 1997, 309).

Women's ability to work is restricted by the unequal distribution of childcare responsibilities within a heterosexual paradigm. This is complicated by the structural inequalities of working culture: for example, the brevity of the paternity leave granted to new fathers denies them the opportunity to be stay-at-home-dads, even if they so wished. Accordingly, third-wave feminism tackled the still-pressing issue of motherhood and its corollary, housewifery. Virago's lists during its third decade evidence these themes in terms of both its fiction and nonfiction, which explored alternative figurings of motherhood as well as alternatives *to* motherhood. There were texts by Jane Bartlett and Janet Hadley that addressed women's right to choose not to have children (Bartlett 1994; Hadley 1996). There were texts that explored women's ambivalence towards being a mother (Parker 1995; Shaw 2001). There were texts about women who chose to parent alone (McNeil 1994). And there were feminist explorations of what it meant to become a mother, live within a family unit, and create relationships with both sons and daughters within a cultural and political paradigm in which girls and boys were treated differently (Mosse 1993; Payne 1994; Goldsworthy 1995; Glendinning and Glendinning 1996; Roiphe 1997; McFerran 1998; Freely 2000). In addition, motherhood was a theme that cropped up in Virago's fiction in novels such as A.M. Homes' *In a Country of Mothers* and Michéle Roberts' *During Mother's Absence* (Homes 1994; Roberts 1994).

That motherhood continued to occupy feminism as the third wave took shape evidences the lack of real progress made in interrogating the assignation of the role of primary caregiver for children as 'feminine', in spite of the gender-bending in evidence in some areas of popular culture. In fact, it could be argued that the same women who were held up as empowering examples because of their transgression of gender norms in their clothes and attitude were conversely utilized by a sexist media to become totemic of 'fashionable' maternity. Baby bumps boomed in the 1990s, as the exposure and exploitation of women's bodies extended to those who were expecting children – a lucrative market – as evidenced in media coverage of the pregnancies of pop stars (some members of the girl band the Spice Girls, alongside Madonna and P!nk) for example. Within the new consumerism, for all its promise of 'selling' women empowerment, motherhood became just another marketing niche in a culture 'where images of women for sale litter every billboard, every street corner, and every newspaper' (Simonton in Lont 1995, 144).

Similarly, the second-wave attempt to counter the depiction of women as passive sexual objects continued into the third wave – and has done into the fourth (see Chapter 8). At the start of Virago's third decade, Lynne Segal explored the potential of sexuality and the act of sex itself to change gender norms. She reasoned that since women's sexuality is so fluid and multiplicitous, sexual play allows women the freedom to explore all kinds of identities in a way that can lead to a re-alignment of how we figure men and women: 'at the heart of the problem lies the polarity of "active" and "passive" which, roped to "masculinity" and "femininity" via the existing conception of heterosexuality, must itself be challenged if we are ever to turn around the oppressive cultural hierarchies of gender and sexuality' (Segal 1994, xiv). Segal moves from a second-wave articulation of straight sex as emancipatory (an idea put forward by Greer, for example – see Chapter 2) to a third-wave, 'queerer' figuring of sex as not only confronting of the binary masculine/feminine or gay/straight, but actually destabilizing of the very concept of these binaries:

> Sex is often the most troubling of all social encounters just because it so easily threatens rather than confirms gender polarity. The merest glimpse of the complexity of women's and men's actual activities suggests that straight sex may be no more affirmative of normative gender positions (and in that sense no less 'perverse') than its gay and lesbian alternatives. In consensual sex, when bodies meet, the epiphany of that meeting – its threat and excitement – is surely that all the great dichotomies (activity/passivity, subject/object, heterosexual/homosexual) slide away. (Segal 1997, 86)

Segal echoes Butler's argument that heterosexuality and homosexuality alike are enactments, repetitions of given behaviours. For Butler, both are parodies of a false idea of natural/original sexuality: 'The repetition of heterosexual constructs in non-heterosexual frames brings into relief the utterly constructed status of the so-called heterosexual original. Thus, gay is to straight *not* as copy is to original, but, rather, as copy is to copy' (Butler 1990, 41).

In this context, homosexual identities were, to a degree, mainstreamed during the 1990s. The publication – and popularity – of lesbian fiction such as Waters' *Tipping the Velvet*, *Affinity* and *Fingersmith* (see above) went alongside the reinvention of the lesbian image – 'lipstick' lesbianism and 'lesbian chic' arrived. Lesbian iconography and enactments were suddenly fashionable, a confident performance of female sexuality, in defiance of historical presentations of lesbians as 'unfeminine' and undesirable. Largely played out in the arena of popular culture – in pop music, fashion and performance – lesbian chic can be described as a moment of cultural 'queering', achieved at the intersection of consumer culture and gay politics. Equally, it can be figured as a salacious co-optation of female sexuality – albeit an alternative sexuality – to serve the ends of a leering, heterosexual male audience. *Plus ça change.*

In the 1990s Virago continued to publish a wide range of fiction that took on lesbian themes and characters, including the novels of Ali Smith, Emma Donoghue, Stella Duffy and Sarah Waters. There was also nonfiction that examined lesbian existence past and present, helping queer historical as well as contemporary formulations of female sexuality (Healey 1996; Eisenbach 1997). Other Virago books explored ideas about female sexuality and sexual agency in a heterosexual context. There were polemic works such as Jennifer Berman's *For Women Only* and Jenny Diski's *View from the Bed and Other Observations* that encouraged women (and men) to consider the ways in which they could enact their sexuality authentically, resisting cultural formulations that rely on gender binaries (Berman 2001; Diski 2003). Diski and other fiction writers such as Carol Anshaw and Gaby Hauptmann, and in particular the Virago V series' writers, also presented female characters who transgressed the divide between passive 'feminine' sexuality and active 'masculine' sexuality. Their heterosexual encounters allowed for a depiction of women as active agents in sex – continuing into the third wave the ideas of second-wave feminist fiction writers such as Atwood and Carter.

But in spite of the examples contained in some of Virago's published output, and the apparently liberatory potential of lesbian chic and its corollary, the 'manly' gay man, the imposition of a limited female sexuality and the sexual objectification of women remained an issue for third-wave feminism. Thirty years of feminist lobbying against the construction and naturalization of woman-as-sex-object had had only a limited effect as women continued to be defined by – indeed, *as* – their sexuality during Virago's third decade. Within an increasingly consumerist culture, the acceptance of a more open approach to sexuality led to greater commodification of sex than ever: 'Commodified sex in all its forms, targeted at most sexual communities with the resources to indulge their preferences, is of major economic significance in the cultural capitalism of the twenty-first century' (McNair 2002, 6). By the end of the twentieth century, feminist critics were refocusing their attention on the problem of female sexuality. Greer argued in 1999 that women's sexuality had come to be all that defines them: 'to deny a woman's sexuality is certainly to oppress her, but to portray her as nothing but a sexual being is equally to oppress her' (Greer 1999, 319). The portrayal of women's bodies as sexed and sexual was reinforced by powerful consumerist influences that succeeded in making desirable, even empowering, the strip club, the sex toy and the topless model image. The sex-positive messages of third-wave feminism failed to counter the *sexism* endemic in the messages themselves. In spite of all the feminist work done to redefine female sexuality, 'girls are still taught by mass culture that they need above all to be desirable' (Connell 2002, 2).

Notes

1. The song 'Things Can Only Get Better' by D:Ream was adopted as an anthem for New Labour in the run-up to the 1997 election.
2. The survey data is cited in France and Wiseman 2007.
3. Interview with Lennie Goodings, 8 May 2008.
4. Ibid.

Part IV

2004–17

Chapter 7

Virago's Place in the New Millennium's Literary Marketplace

Virago's fourth decade saw it become the world's largest women's imprint and command a significant share of the UK literary fiction market. It retains this position in the first years of its fifth decade of operations, still under the umbrella of Little, Brown. Its status as the only feminist publisher remaining from the glut of companies that were set up at the start of the second wave means that although it can legitimately be criticized for losing some of its feminist credentials, sitting as it does within the structure of a mainstream multinational conglomerate, it must also be recognized as a vital outlet for writing that conveys feminist ideas and themes. The decision to sell Virago in 1995 – although one arrived at acrimoniously – helped secure the company's future. Rather than marking the death of feminist publishing (as was stated in media comment at the time), the 1995 sale saved Virago and thus preserved a (lone) feminist voice in UK publishing.

Virago's move into Little, Brown, coinciding with the rise of an increasingly commodified consumer culture, the conglomeration of the book industry and more pluralized expressions of feminism, allowed it to continue to work as a publisher of feminist writing while none of its contemporaries survived. Important changes in the ways in which books, and even authors, are sold as 'commodities' means that Virago has had to innovate in order to survive, engaging with new technologies and new audiences as it moved into the twenty-first century and a changed literary landscape that includes new and niche publishing enterprises and a rise in online writing and self-publishing. The new millennium has seen new challenges for Virago, but it has also had to navigate the ongoing sexist bias of the mainstream book industry and the increasingly cut-throat marketplace emerging from the corporatisation of publishing more broadly. Virago has flourished in the twenty-first century in terms of its profit and its reputation – what remains at issue is the extent to which it remains an avowedly *feminist* publisher.

Continuing the Virago Story

At the start of its fourth decade, Virago was in good shape. Being under the umbrella of Time Warner was proving profitable: Virago's turnover had doubled between 1997 and 2003, and it had a catalogue of over six hundred titles in print as its thirty-year anniversary was celebrated, with Goodings still at the helm. Since 2003, Virago's structure has changed very little. Little, Brown, with Virago still on board, was sold by the Time Warner Book Group to Hachette Livre, a French conglomerate, in 2006 – the stable within which Virago now resides. Virago's ownership by one conglomerate and then another is symptomatic of the way in which the UK book industry has come to be dominated by multinationals, containing the more distinct imprint names of smaller operations like Virago (and Little, Brown) within them.

In practical terms, for Virago this meant a move (of a mere few hundred metres) from offices on Waterloo Bridge to a new home in the Unilever building on Victoria Embankment in London. Virago's slick new corporate home was described by a *Bookseller* journalist as a 'limpid metropolis', but for Goodings it is simply a new gloss on an old format: 'when I look at this open plan, it's a glamorous version of what we had earlier. We've come full circle' (Allen 2010). Virago's current home in Carmelite House is a little further down the Victoria Embankment. Its rooftop garden boasts what is undoubtedly one of the best views of the city of London.

Virago now describes itself as 'the outstanding international publisher of books by women', a statement that (intentionally?) avoids use of the word 'feminist' – a word, as previously discussed, that has become highly problematic (see Chapter 6).[1] Goodings defends this choice: 'if you're going to say feminism and all the shutters are going to come down, then you don't say that. We'll talk about women, we'll talk about a particular book'.[2] The fine line she – and Virago – treads, then, is in negotiating a way of expressing feminist ideas without alienating readers who would automatically disassociate with the f-word. The result, according to Virago's website, is a tangential referencing to the political term that dare not speak its name:

> The cultural, political and economic landscape has changed dramatically in the last four decades, but Virago has remained true to its original aims: to put women centre stage; to explore the untold stories of their lives and histories; to break the silence around many women's experiences; to publish breathtaking new fiction alongside a rich list of rediscovered classics; and above all to champion women's talent. Sometimes we publish to entertain, sometimes we

publish to give readers the sheer pleasure of beautiful writing, sometimes we publish to change the world.[3]

This sidestepping of the term 'feminist' indicates the extent to which the
word has been co-opted by a powerful right-wing media agenda that rid-
icules strong women and alienates people of all genders from the politics
of equality. Virago's nuanced description of its political intent fits with the
times: avoiding the f-word needn't mean a dilution of principle, but is rather
a way of communicating messages about strong, independent (read: feminist!) female writers that fits with cultural and literary trends. Goodings is
canny in understanding Virago's audience and has been able to retain the
loyalty of older readers while attracting new audiences – evidenced in Virago's rising sales and profits – from within the slick corporate environment in
which she now operates. As she says:

> Rarely has there been such a close and intimate relationship between
> publisher and reader. And, like any familial relationship, it isn't al-
> ways harmonious! You tell us when you don't think the jacket image
> is right, when an introducer gives away the plot, when titles are out
> of print, when there are too many typos – but you have also poured
> in your praise and pleasure and thoughts, and Virago has become a
> brand name.[4]

This kind of marketing/communications cleverly emphasizes the relationship
between Virago and its readers, evoking the structure of family to produce
a sense of intimacy and reciprocity that persists in spite of Virago's status
within a huge conglomerate machine. It is also necessary in the changed
literary marketplace of this millennium, where 'women's' texts containing
messages of equality or empowerment are no longer the exclusive preserve
of feminist publishers, as Jane Cholmeley points out: 'Now, if you look at
women's reading: I'm reading Anne Tyler's *The Amateur Marriage,* a perfect
Virago book except it's published by Vintage. It's subtle, it's clever, it's intel-
ligent, it's human . . . the whole women's market.'[5]

Virago's incorporation into Hachette Livre brought further penetration
into the book-buying market as well as greater visibility in the review media,
and in a literary marketplace vastly changed from that of 1973, there is no
doubt that this financial clout plays a big a part in its continuing success.
Goodings is clear about it: 'the problem with publishing, and that's why
Virago foundered too actually [before the 1995 sale], is that it's a gamble, so
you've got to have money up front all the time, because you're investing in

projects you might not see a return for a long time or at all.'[6] Being part of Hachette means that money is much more readily available.

Virago sealed its position at the pinnacle of the industry when Little, Brown and Goodings were nominated for *The Bookseller*'s Imprint and Editor of the Year awards respectively in 2010:

> Virago has had its most successful year in terms of turnover and profit and in 2009 its share in the literary fiction market grew from fourth to third biggest. It remains the largest women's imprint in the world. Marilynne Robinson's book *Home* won the 2009 Orange Prize for Fiction and has sold over 100,000 copies in the UK alone. Sarah Waters's *The Little Stranger* was shortlisted for the Man Booker Prize 2009 and has now topped 133,000 paperbacks as well as 51,000 hardback copies. Titles from the backlist by Nina Bawden and Shirley Hazzard have been nominated in the six-strong shortlist for the Lost Booker Prize. Virago titles did well among TV book clubs, with Frances Osbourne's debut, *The Bolter*, chosen for 'Richard & Judy', and *The Little Stranger* and Sarah Dunant's *Sacred Hearts* chosen for Channel 4's 'TV Book Club'. (Broughton 2010)

The trend towards conglomeration continued through Virago's fourth decade. As Claire Squires notes, 'the actual number of independent literary fiction publishers housed in different premises, usually in the Bloomsbury area of London, has halved in the past ten years' (Squires 2007, 25). Remaining outside of the 'big four' – Penguin Random House, Hachette Livre, HarperCollins and Simon & Schuster – that have come to dominate the UK publishing scene means that it is very hard to compete across different platforms in the way that they can or to afford aggressive and expensive marketing campaigns. Squires explains that 'while supporters of the conglomeration of the industry often maintain that the blockbusters help to subsidise the loss-making books, and it is certainly true that the ratio of books produced to those which actually make a profit is extremely high, this argument does not take account of the headstart given to a small number of books by the hugely varying sums spent on publicity' (Squires 2007, 38).

Goodings, however, believes Virago's move into Hachette has ensured its future success. This is a sentiment echoed by another powerful female publisher, Victoria Barnsley. Having founded Fourth Estate, she has overseen its transition to become part of HarperCollins and defended the move as in the best interests of the company: 'she rejects the idea that the publishing industry is pursuing a "bigger and fewer is better" strategy, pointing out that there are many more books published today than there were 10 years ago'

(Martinson 2005). Barnsley here highlights the two fundamental shifts in the publishing industry that have occurred since the 1990s: the shift towards domination by a few very powerful conglomerates (such as Hachette) and the rise in number of the titles that are published each year. Book industry expert Eric de Bellaigue confirms that 'any investigation into the distinctiveness or otherwise of trade imprints has to confront the phenomenon of the explosion in titles published', going on to say: 'on the one hand it is an encouraging sign of creative vitality. On the other it threatens the whole trade with submersion' (de Bellaigue 2004, 17). This disagreement about what the rising numbers of books represents has not been resolved. Richard Curtis, another industry expert, argues that it indicates 'the emergence of a system for producing literature that might best be likened to dairy farming, with authors forced into the role of domesticated cattle resignedly allowing themselves to be milked to satisfy the thirst of a mass market. That the product will inevitably become homogenized goes without saying' (Curtis 1998, ix).

De Bellaigue is more ambivalent: 'while many *a priori* judgements assume homogenization, these are not supported by much of the available evidence. What have emerged as threads running through the discussion are the advantages of scale and a build-up of pressures on both publishing and retailing that could well pose a threat to diversity and individuality in publishing in the next few years' (de Bellaigue 2004, 27). The shift towards conglomeration, and the resultant rise in published titles, is driven by economics – it has become harder to make publishing profitable: 'the fact that a hardback title in 2004 is probably five times cheaper in real terms than it was half a century ago is a remarkable statistic' (Todd in English 2006, 23). With books-as-objects getting cheaper, larger scales of manufacturing, distribution and marketing are required to return a profit – hence the gradual incursion of publishing conglomerates.

Goodings is ambivalent about the charge of short-termism made against conglomerate companies and the idea that a focus on profit is antithetical to the necessarily slow process of developing a book for market: 'the way it works is, I have to get the sales and marketing people to agree with me on how many it will sell, and then I work out an advance – so it's not as simple as just "I'd like to publish that". But on the whole, I do publish what I want'.[7] Virago is, she states, still very much a women's publisher: 'it's still women taking the decisions about which books are published. How we get them out there, and what they look like and all that stuff – that's a joint enterprise'.[8] And the women taking the editorial decisions, she also argues, are doing so to further a feminist perspective of the world.

She also points out that having more financial security means that Virago can offer to pay its writers more – a feminist act in itself: 'we got a lot of offers at the beginning, you know people like Angela Carter, who came for very little money because they believed very firmly in it', she admits. 'And that was great and that was appropriate but it's not appropriate thirty years on that people should still be selling you their books cheaper.'[9] Virago thus seeks to tackle the issue of equal pay – an ongoing feminist battle – by fairly remunerating its authors. And Goodings is very clear that Virago retains its feminism and is still publishing literature by avowedly feminist writers, and on themes and subject matters that offer a female, and feminist, perspective of the world.

Literary experts assert that, as the publishing world comes to be dominated by conglomerates, 'perhaps the worst by-product of all is the loss of corporate memory that accompanies the dismissal of senior staff members of publishing companies. No matter how much data is storable in computer memories today, the knowledge of how to do things, of what works and what doesn't, of house history and tradition, of where skeletons are buried and dirty linen stored – all this knowledge and more resides in the hearts and hands, minds and souls of employees who have worked for publishers for a long time' (Curtis 1998, 64). Yet Goodings' retention as publisher at Virago means that it has not suffered this loss. Indeed, Virago's success is surely at least as much predicated on the retention of its most vital employee, and while Goodings remains at the helm, the imprint thrives financially while retaining the feminist principles she has always championed:

> Virago is still up and running almost 35 years after its inception, and running (pretty much) according to its founding ideals. Still publishing only female authors, Virago continues to play an invaluable role in a profession that boasts a very tough glass ceiling. For many women writers (as Coe says) 'that indefinable sense of being taken seriously' can still seem to dangle 'tantalisingly out of reach'. While it does, it's good to know that there's a company out there rooting for my team. (Millar 2007)

Goodings is lauded by her readers, authors and peers as the reason for Virago's continued success – and relevance. And she in turn argues that Virago retains that relevance – as a publisher dedicated to women's writing – in a popular and literary culture in which women continue to be sidelined, devalued or underrepresented. "'I'm not going to feel defensive about Virago until the *Today* programme changes", she says, referring to the fact that just 18% of contributors to the flagship news show are female. "It's a tougher and more uneven world, and there's a certain level of contradictoriness that we just to have live with"" (Rustin 2013). In this uneven world, Goodings is happy with the balance she has struck.

Books-as-Commodities: Sales Tactics in the New Millennium

Virago's fourth decade has thus been played out from within the structure of a multinational conglomerate – and its fifth decade looks set to continue in this way. This, coupled with the changing nature of the publishing industry itself, has brought much greater emphasis on marketing and publicity, and Goodings herself often references the Virago 'brand': 'you know one of the reasons Virago survived is that people recognise it as a brand with a genuine philosophy. A brand is something people recognise whether they like it or not' (Rustin 2013). This is significant: presenting Virago's books in a distinct way, as well as creating a 'brand' identity that, through avoiding the word 'feminist', remains as inclusive as possible has helped Virago gain sales year-on-year. As Imelda Whelehan argues, 'fiction, more freely than political writings, can take opposing sides and study conflicted opinions and ambiguity, and is therefore far more likely to chime with the uncertainties of women attracted to feminism but confused by the mess of emotions generated by their own personal lives' (Whelehan 2005, 12). Creating its woman-centred twenty-first-century brand has helped Virago promulgate feminism by stealth.

In the current literary marketplace, the look of a book and the way in which it is promoted increasingly dictates its chances of success. During the 1980s and 1990s, distinct visual shorthands emerged for women's literature, evidenced in the conformity of its appearance – the thick, glossy metallic colours that defined 1980s design were replaced with 'sweetie-coloured' covers in pastel shades that identified a book as a 'woman's text' (Colgan 2001). The packaging of women's writing in 'feminine' tones spread from 'chick lit' right through to canonical classics: 'earlier this year Penguin brought forward the publication of its Red Classics editions of Jane Austen to get ahead of Headline, which has since given *Pride and Prejudice* a horrible chick-lit-style cover in pretty pastels' (Cooke 2006). Now, 'there are gazillions of books available and something has to help you decide. Loud shades of pink seem to help and increasingly chick-lit books sparkle with sequins and gemstones on the cover' (Groskop 2011).

Virago's image is different, avoiding the pink and shimmer that wraps around so many works of popular fiction. Having excised the green spines and classic portraits from its covers – which helped create its distinct 'brand' in the 1970s and 1980s – Virago's books retain their apple logo that helps to quickly identify them on the shelf, but the focus now, much more, is on marketing campaigns rather than cover design, with Virago having the financial clout to compete for publicity (and sales) in the mainstream marketplace. For example, the 2009 launch of Sarah Waters' novel *The Little Stranger* was supported by a huge publicity campaign:

> Virago is planning to spend £100,000 on publicity for Sarah Waters' latest book, which will include shop promotions and a consumer-facing poster campaign. The publisher is 'in negotiations' over front page coverage in the national press, and is hoping to secure radio airtime for *The Little Stranger*, due to be published in June. (Jones 2009)

The campaign kicked off with a mailout of 2,500 proofs of the first chapter to reviewers and booksellers, with the aim of generating excitement around the title. This red hardback sampler was followed by limited-edition bound proofs and the launch of a new website, www.sarahwaters.com. Goodings was confident that the campaign, and the book, would be a success, saying that Waters 'seems to be one of those very few writers who people want to read in hardback – so much so that we have the confidence of sending out [the proofs] called 'The New Sarah Waters' – it is rare that you can do that. And it's rare that [readers] don't wait for the paperback. That is why we have all this energy behind it' (Jones 2009). The investment paid off: *The Little Stranger* was shortlisted for the Man Booker Prize 2009 and a year after its launch had topped 133,000 paperback sales as well as 51,000 hardback transactions (Broughton 2010).

There have been other marketing innovations: 'designers including Cath Kidston and Orla Kiely are creating new cover artwork for a series of eight Virago Modern Classics, which will celebrate the imprint's 30th anniversary next year' (Flood 2007). This marketing ploy harnessed the contemporary trend for retro textiles in order to increase the desirability of the book-as-commodity – and it was very well received. 'There's been a lot of discussion around here recently about the value of books as physical objects versus their value as text alone, divorced from medium. There's no question, of course, that the words are the thing – but when the medium and the message combine as attractively as they do here, what's not to celebrate?' (Crown 2011). As Claire Squires points out, specific imprints offer their books to readers in specific ways, and this coupling of tasteful design with Virago's classics is a continuation of the press' effective use of a specific aesthetic to appeal to its particular demographic of readers (Squires 2007, 93). This revamping of the Classics' design was followed by an expansion of the Classics list itself at the end of 2011, with the announcement of a Virago Modern Classics young adult list, including four works by Rumer Godden. It is all part of maintaining the list's distinctive look and feel, in order to continue to engage a readership who recognize the series as a shorthand for Virago's 'brand' of quality, women-focused writing: 'the world that surrounds us is a shallow world surrounded by brand names', says Goodings. 'I think one of the reasons Virago is still necessary and is also really powerful is that it has become a brand name that has come to really mean something to people.'[10]

Virago's position within Hachette gives it the corporate muscle to compete in these ways in a heavily commercialized literary marketplace. As journalist Viv Groskop notes, it's 'important to recognise the power of the shorthand of marketing', thus Goodings' exploitation of Virago's position within an international conglomerate is key to its remaining competitive (Groskop 2011). There are further examples, as *The Bookseller* reported in June 2010: 'The tough UK market means publishing with export territories in mind is more important than ever. Virago publisher Lennie Goodings said: "Export is terribly important – Australia has a lot of independents who are very keen on literary fiction, for example. So you think more globally"' (Page 2010). UK publishing's more global scope in the twenty-first century has also seen Virago engage with its readership online, across the world. In 2010 a new 'News and Blog' website was set up, introduced by Goodings as a natural progression of Virago's long history of close allegiance with its readers: 'I am convinced that one of the reasons Virago has flourished is because of our relationship with our readers. And now conducted via emails, websites, networking sites, tweeting – it's a relationship still very much alive and still very active. And still, just like family . . . Welcome to the Virago news and blogging site. Keep 'em coming!'[11]

Virago's online activity is now central to its maintaining this familial bond with its readership. Innovations such as print-on-demand via its website, social media profiles, podcasts and an online book club bring Virago closer to its audience, as readers of all ages are more and more connected online:

> Virago has launched an online book club, with 549 members signing up within the first 24 hours. A new Virago title will be discussed on the affiliated forum every two months; the titles will initially be chosen by the Virago team, but will eventually also be chosen by club members. Stephen Dumughn, Virago marketing manager, said: 'We had always known that Virago is a little bit special – it does have a distinct and engaged readership. We want to get their opin-

ion and feedback. I think there has always been a feeling that Virago is a bit of a club, and we are always very passionate about books that we publish here.' (Williams 2010)

Feminist blogs, websites, digital magazines and online forums have proliferated in the past decade, evidence of the new ways in which feminist writers are now exchanging ideas and organising action. Kat Banyard, author and founder of UK Feminista, describes the phenomenon: 'over the past five years hundreds of feminist blogs have appeared online, new feminist magazines have started up, and grassroots activist groups have been forming' (Banyard 2010, 10). Its growing online presence allows Virago to be part of this exchange.

Virago has also developed links with literary websites such as webzine For Books' Sake, which focuses on the work of female writers: 'More mainstream publishing houses have mostly ignored us so far (with a couple of exceptions such as Virago)', writes the website's founder Jane Bradbury (Allen 2010). Supporting small-scale web-based initiatives such as For Books' Sake is also good business since, as detailed in a report in *The Bookseller* citing Andrew Gallix, editor of *3:AM*, independent literary websites are gaining in influence: 'When we started out, webzines were looked down upon in Britain as being second-rate. We're now assiduously courted by publishers, big and small, especially since the credit crunch (which led them to look for cheaper ways to promote their books)' (Allen 2010).

Virago's use of the internet in these ways fosters a kind of intimacy and immediacy of exchange with its readership reminiscent of its early years when it used alternative magazines and newspapers such as *City Limits* and *Spare Rib* to market its books, discover new authors and spread its feminist messages (see Chapter 1). And just as then, they also offer a way of circumnavigating the mainstream review tradition that continues to privilege men – as both writers and reviewers. A Virago blog posting in 2010 pointed to research by US organization VIDA showing that women remained vastly underrepresented at the review level. VIDA's report analysed data from a range of literary publications to show how much space in each was devoted to the work of male and female authors. Their scan of the *London Review of Publishing* showed that 168 reviewers were men compared to 47 women – less than a third. And of the authors reviewed, 68 were women and 195 were men. In the *Times Literary Supplement,* male reviewers outnumbered female by 900 to 341, and while 330 women writers were reviewed, the number of male writers' work was more than three times this, at 1,036. VIDA's report concluded: 'We know women write. We know women read. It's time to begin asking why the 2010 numbers don't reflect those facts with any equity.'[12]

Coming more than twenty years after Women in Publishing's *Reviewing the Reviews,* VIDA's report makes for very depressing reading – as a blogger on Virago's website pointed out:

> We often get people asking whether the aims of Virago are still relevant in a society which claims equality. Well, take a look at this fascinating (depressing!) bit of research from Vida (an American website). It shows that in (mainly American publications but I wonder what the tally would be for UK publications . . .) the majority of books reviewed in 2010 were overwhelmingly those written by men. In most cases more than 75 per cent. There is only one example of female writers being reviewed more than men, and that is for poetry. Women buy more books than men do and represent between 60 and 70 per cent of the readership, so why the disparity at review level?[13]

Men continue to dominate the review press, with the depressing inevitability that they continue to favour the work of other men. Goodings recognizes this: "'I have to say that there is a sense that when a man publishes a book, it is an event," says Lennie Goodings, Virago's publisher. "Women write more fiction, women read more fiction, but the good male novelist is regarded as more noteworthy." It frustrates her that recent Virago authors such as Marilynne Robinson and Shirley Hazzard, whose books sell – Robinson's *Gilead* has sold more than 100,000 copies – and are acclaimed, are still not mentioned in the quite same hushed tones as that of their male contemporaries' (Cooke 2008). Virago's attempt to promote its female writers through innovative marketing tactics, coupled with an engagement with alternative (online) literary media, is an act of feminist praxis, a continuation of the project that has run since 1973. Virago's sales tactics have altered, but the challenge to counter male domination of the publishing mainstream remains the same.

Alongside Virago's own marketing and publicity, the influence of book prizes has had a huge – and growing – effect on sales during the last decade. Of more importance, arguably, than the review press, the book prize industry directs sales and consequently has a huge impact on publishing decisions: 'the process of consecration and sanctification of certain literary texts through the awarding of prestigious international literary prizes has made the old-fashioned distinction between aesthetic and commercial value rather blurred' (Ponzanesi in Görtschacher et al. 2006, 116). In other words, books are judged today – in part – by the sales they generate, which enhances the sense of their 'literary' qualities, and book prizes are a huge influence in driving these sales. This means straightforward material benefits for writers, not only in the cash award that comes with the prize itself, but also with the extra sales guaranteed by longlisting and shortlisting. The effect of the Man Booker nominations in 2009, for example, was profound: 'Sales of the titles on the Man Booker longlist increased by sixty per cent following its announcement' (Stone and Allen 2009). That year, Sarah Waters' *The Little Stranger* was the sales leader – it achieved 133,000 paperback sales as well as 51,000 hardback sales in a year thanks to the 'Booker effect' (Broughton 2010).

This 'reshaping of the relationship between journalistic and cultural capital, celebrity and canonicity', as publishing analyst James F. English puts it, means that women writers are less automatically disadvantaged by the review culture than they were in the past (English 2006, 207). But, as with mainstream reviewing, women are disproportionately absent from the longlists and shortlists of mainstream literary prizes. 'I cannot help thinking that some of that bias, subtle and unspoken, remains', writes author Jonathan Coe. 'If we take the Booker prize (for want of anything else) as being indicative of what the British literary establishment has considered most attention-worthy over the past 40 years, a clear preference emerges. In the first 30 years of its history, 108 of those shortlisted for the prize (63.5 per cent) were male, only 62 (36.5 per cent) were female' (Coe 2007).

Novelist Linda Grant places the blame for this squarely at the feet of publishers:

> 70% of fiction is read by women, yet prize shortlists are dominated by men. Why? The answer is not that women are writing inferior fiction, it is that their books are not being submitted. When I was shortlisted for the Booker in 2008, I was the only woman on the shortlist, one of only three on the longlist of 13. Challenging one of the judges about this I was told that this happened to be the ratio of female writers whose work was submitted by their publishers, who are limited to two titles plus previously shortlisted authors. (Grant 2012)

With the exception of Virago, of course, whose books are *all* written by women, publishers prefer to submit the writing of their male authors to book prize judges, which makes commercial sense when men disproportionately come out winners. It is for these reasons, then, that the Women's Prize for Fiction (formerly the Orange Prize) remains an important platform for women writers, going some way towards levelling the playing field by giving women a stage of their own. In a discussion about the validity of this prize in 2012, just prior to its change of sponsor, Grant was candid about the necessity of a women-only award: 'prizes mean seeing a novel that has sold 700 copies go on to sell 100,000. Unliterary facts, but the truth about why prizes matter and why the Orange prize matters' (Grant 2012).

Since its inception in 1996, the Women's Prize for Fiction has flourished, marking its ten-year anniversary in 2005 with an 'Orange of Oranges' prize – partly a quiet riposte to the pomp surrounding the 'Booker of Bookers'. The award's director, Pippa Dunn, 'described the event as a milestone. "Ten years ago the prize shook up the literary world when we launched one of the most controversial literary prizes. Today, it is recognised as one of the UK's most powerful and prestigious awards"' (Ezard 2005). Alexandra Pringle, formerly of Virago and now head of Bloomsbury, is clear that the prize has had a positive effect for women's writing: 'now there's more variety of prizes that have an effect whereas it used to just be the Booker and nothing else. But now the Whitbread does, and the Orange prize – massively, actually. In some ways I think the Orange prize drives sales more than the Booker'.[14]

In 2012 Orange withdrew its sponsorship of the UK prize, with founder Kate Mosse commenting that 'the prize is in such a strong position that it's a sponsorship peach; I imagine there'll be a lot of competition to pick up the baton' (Crown 2012). In the event, that year's prize money was donated collectively by prominent women including Cherie Blair, Martha Lane Fox and Joanna Trollope, before Bailey's was announced as the new sponsor in 2013. And in spite of continued debate over the prize's validity, it is needed now more than ever: 'despite women being the main consumers of books, both reading and buying more fiction than our male friends and relations, as well as writing more novels, we continue to be sidelined and, despite our equal or majority (in population terms) status in the world, treated as a minority and a rarity by the literary establishment' (Battersby 2015). Battersby cites research by novelist Nicola Griffith, which shows that 'only two Man Booker-winning novels had been written by women from a female perspective between 2000 and 2014, compared to nine Booker winners written by men about men or boys' (Battersby 2015). The Women's Prize for fiction serves to democratize women's status as writers in an industry that remains rooted in patterns of misogyny.

Twenty-First-Century Publishing: A Woman's World?

As Virago's fourth decade got underway, there was some sense that the publishing industry was coming to be dominated by women. Goodings was clear that women were progressing further in publishing than they were able to in other areas of business: 'if you look at other industries you do not find women on the board. So yes, I would say it is a women-friendly environment'.[15] And Callil went further still: 'I think they [women] run things now in a way that they never did in my day. It's fabulous. I'm happy about it.'[16] Although it was (predictably) one of the two men shortlisted for the 2003 Booker Prize who won (four women also made the shortlist, but were overlooked for first place), five of the six nominees were published by companies headed up by women: 'Five of this year's six nominated authors have women to thank for taking on, editing, publishing and promoting their novels. These women are now the driving force in the publishing industry and, though still paid less on average than men, are the true power brokers behind the bestsellers. Two of Britain's three leading publishing houses are also headed by women' (Smith 2003).

One of these companies, HarperCollins, was in 2004 run by three female executives: 'they [Caroline Michel, Amanda Ridout and Victoria Barnsley] are the women who decide what you will be reading next year, and they dominate British publishing. Handing over advances of tens of thousands of pounds and bidding for books in hundreds of thousands, this handful of female players control the fate of the British book industry' (Thorpe 2004). By 2006, The Observer's assessment of the top fifty players in the British book trade noted that 'significantly, compared to any previous generation, there are many more women in key positions. The top three slots are occupied by women' (McCrum 2006). This assessment was itself made by a panel of judges comprising three powerful publishing and media women alongside three men.

In 2007 Penguin's MD Helen Fraser took stock of her position in the industry, having spent forty years in publishing, giving birth to two daughters and gaining two more stepdaughters over the course of her career:

> 'When I had my first baby, 25 years ago, I was the first person in living memory at Collins to have a baby and come back to work. Now, at Penguin, babies and maternity leave are the norm; with an 88% female workforce [at the Penguin General division] you have to deal with it.' The Penguin Group as a whole is 75% female, said Fraser. Kate Hyde, senior editor at HarperCollins' Press Books, said the split is very similar at HC: 'It's probably about 70% women and 30% men in most sectors across the company, and probably across publishing as a whole.'[17]

Women have certainly made some progress into the boardrooms that were dominated by 'gentlemen in trousers' when Callil set about creating her own publishing venture in 1973 (see Chapter 1). But by 2013, the year in which Virago celebrated its fortieth birthday, Helen Fraser had been pushed out at

Penguin and Victoria Barnsley had been replaced at HarperCollins – both by men. Men led three of the four major groups in the UK – PRH, Hachette, HarperCollins, and PanMacmillan – and although Gail Rebuck was Chair of PRH, this was a non-executive position.

The current situation with leadership of the 'big four' also serves as a reminder of the precariousness of women's status as leaders and men's continued domination of big business. As Alexandra Pringle says, 'people have always thought it's been great for women because we've been the visible ones, but we're not necessarily the *powerful* ones'.[18] Women might dominate the publishing industry in terms of numbers, but they are still being outnumbered and outpaced by men at the top of the corporate ladder. Doubleday's publishing director Marianne Velmans makes a further point, arguing that a tolerance for poor pay is what helps women succeed in the book world: 'London publishing is full of women. It's been a great profession for them to go into and has been very receptive. It's badly paid compared with other professions and women are more prepared to accept lower salaries. A love of books and reading seems more important than making a lot of money' (Smith 2003). The old equation of money with power has meant that publishing, because of its smaller financial rewards compared to other businesses, has allowed women to creep in through the back door to reach the boardroom (see also Chapter 8).

While Virago has prospered under the umbrella of a publishing conglomerate – and none of its contemporaries from the feminist publishing scene of the 1970s has survived – other women have attempted to carve out their place in the publishing industry by establishing their own niche independents and imprints. These small-scale publishers have sprung up in the gaps that have appeared where conglomerate publishers do (or dare) not tread: 'bookshops still stock good books, publishers still print them. The failings of the larger corporations, meanwhile, continue to be redressed by independent publishers (Serpent's Tail, Canongate) and the recent – marvellous – blossoming of other small presses'.[19] Not in spite of, but rather *because* of the conglomeration of the publishing industry, small publishing enterprises have been able to find a niche, exploiting the market to establish their own distinct specialisms.

So while the landscape of feminist publishing has changed dramatically since the 1970s and many of those pioneering women-only presses are now defunct, new small-scale concerns have launched, filling the gap in the market opened up by conglomeration. This is a positive step: 'women's writing' is not a single genre, but rather an umbrella for many, multiple subgenres of writing. It is therefore appropriate and useful that there is a new set of publishers that cater for the different types of female fiction now on the market.

Raw Nerve Books, for example, was launched in 1999 to 'publish innovative and controversial books in the fields of gender and women's studies'.[20] It set out its point of difference from mainstream publishers by stating an intention to publish books 'quickly and cheaply . . . favouring unusual publications – short monographs, edited collections and experimental works'.[21] Raw Nerve published a range of theoretical work during its decade in business, basing itself in the Women's Studies department of the University of York, but ceasing to publish new material following the discrediting of a book on campaigner Peter Tatchell in 2009.

Raw Nerve was followed by other examples of female-run independent presses. Persephone was set up by Nicola Beauman in 2000 to publish long-out-of-print or unpublished 'woman's novels', a niche area whose popularity is attributable, in large part, to Virago's Modern Classics series. Beauman's point of difference from the mainstream is in the way she packages her books very beautifully, generating an identity that is highly 'literary'. She pays tribute to her publishing forbears: 'What Persephone does have in common with Virago is a love of aesthetics, and a hunger to create books that are not just a good read, but a mixture of style and substance' (Cooper 2008). Virago author Sarah Waters is among Persephone's many fans who have helped secure it a growing readership in the years since its launch.

Additionally, Transita was established in April 2005 to publish books for women aged over forty-five, with its founder Nikki Read claiming that 'until now there hasn't been an identifiable body of fiction that mirrors the experiences of today's 45+ woman – and yet we make up almost forty per cent of the female population in the UK'.[22] Her intention with Transita was, again, to capture a niche area of the market not being catered for by mainstream publishers. The venture generated a considerable amount of press on its launch, with critics questioning the need for older women to have a dedicated publisher – echoing the criticisms levelled at Virago on its launch in 1973. Around the same time as Transita was launched, Sigrid Rausing was unveiling her response to the conglomeration of the publishing industry: 'Portobello Books Ltd was founded at the beginning of 2005 in London at a time when the dynamics of conglomerate publishing in the English-speaking world mean that fewer and fewer literary works of singularity and significance are being published vigorously and with due respect for the author as creator and for the book as durable transmitter of wisdom and wonder.'[23] Rausing believed that conglomeration was having a negative effect on book publishing, arguing that smaller presses such as Portobello allowed their writers an artistic freedom and integrity unavailable in larger firms. Unlike Transita, which has now wound up its operations, Portobello continues to flourish as part of the small but important scene of independent UK publishing houses.

All these women in publishing have continued the work begun by Callil and her colleagues in 1973, carving out a space for women in the book industry. Women writers remain systematically disadvantaged by their gender – even forty years after Virago began its project to put them on an equal footing – in the publishing world, because of the ongoing bias of the review and literary prize industries and the disproportionate number of men at the top. Virago's mission of foregrounding women's writing, and making great female fiction and nonfiction of all kinds available, remains important, as does its retention of a distinct identity as a women-run company. As Goodings says, as long as women are unfairly represented in literary terms as well as cultural, political and material terms, the Virago project continues to be necessary and vital.

Notes

1. Editorial, 'About Virago', retrieved 21 September 2017 from http://www.virago books.net/about.
2. See interview with Lennie Goodings, 8 November 2004
3. Anon., 'About Virago Press', retrieved 21 September 2017 from http://www.virago .co.uk/about_virago.asp?TAG=&CID=&PGE=&LANG=EN.
4. Goodings, Lennie, 'Welcome to the Virago News and Blog Website', retrieved 21 September 2017 from http://www.viragobooks.net/welcome-readers-to-the-new-virago-news-and-blog-website.
5. See interview with Jane Cholmeley, 28 September 2004.
6. See interview with Lennie Goodings, 8 May 2008.
7. Ibid.
8. Ibid.
9. Interview with Lennie Goodings, 8 November 2004.
10. Ibid.
11. Goodings, Lennie, 'Welcome to the Virago News and Blog Website', retrieved 21 September 2017 from http://www.viragobooks.net/welcome-readers-to-the-new-virago-news-and-blog-website.
12. http://www.vidaweb.org/the-count-2010.
13. Pepe, Victoria, 'Review the Reviews', retrieved 21 September 2017 from http://www.viragobooks.net/review-the-reviews.
14. Interview with Alexandra Pringle, 28 October 2009.
15. Interview with Lennie Goodings, 8 November 2004.
16. Interview with Carmen Callil, 10 November 2004.
17. Editorial, 'Men: An Endangered Species?', *The Bookseller*, 21 May 2007.
18. Interview with Alexandra Pringle, 28 October 2009.
19. Millar 2007.

20. Anon., 'Feminist Publishing House Launched', *University of York,* retrieved 21 September 2017 from http://www.york.ac.uk/admin/presspr/pressreleases/rawnerve.htm (para. 2 of 6).
21. Ibid.
22. Anon., 'Welcome to Transita', retrieved 21 September 2017 from http://www.transita.co.uk/index_about.htm (para. 2 of 9).
23. Anon., 'Portobello Books', retrieved 21 September 2017 from http://www.portobellobooks.com (para. 1 of 5).

Chapter 8

Twenty-First-Century Feminism(s)
and Virago's Role
for Women's Writing

Virago's incorporation into a mainstream conglomerate has had an effect not only on its business practices but also on the books it now publishes. At the start of its fourth decade, Goodings was clear that Virago's mission continued to be the publication of empowered and empowering women's writing: 'the heart of the list is still the same: championing women's talent, opening the silences in some women's lives . . . Virago is books and literature, and literature and books can change peoples' lives'.[1] But does Virago, the largest women's imprint in the world, retain its vitality as a 'feminist publisher'? Goodings would say that the power and potential it still holds – to change minds, cultures and lives through exposing its wide readership to women's different perspectives – means that its feminist credentials are assured.

Virago's last ten years have been vibrant for feminism, marked by a re-engagement with some of the issues first set out in the years around Virago's birth: women in the workplace, motherhood and sexual stereotyping. Following the disavowal of the f-word in the 1990s, women have returned to the issues that first energized the women's movement almost fifty years ago, realizing that the battles set out then have still not been won. There has sprung up a sustained new feminist 'wave' and this has been reflected in a wealth of new feminist writing as well as other moments of praxis including marches, workshops, conferences and, in 2015, the establishment of the United Kingdom's first feminist political party, the Women's Equality Party.[2]

As Callil and Goodings have argued, Virago's 'brand' of feminism is to use literature to convey messages that empower women or illuminate their lives (past and present) – as Goodings neatly sums it up: 'I've always said the message is in the book.'[3] Recalling a meeting with Canadian writer Shana Lambert, Goodings explains her belief that Virago will remain necessary as long as the idea of feminism is frightening 'it's really true, isn't it? As long as the idea of a powerful woman (and I'm sure you know Virago means "heroic woman"), as long as that is a scary prospect or a scary concept then we're needed'.[4] Virago continues to have a role in ensuring women's writing has an outlet, making it relevant to feminism in the twenty-first century. As Goodings says, 'books continue to matter . . . good writing will move and nourish us. That essential fact is not going to change' (Tonkin 2011).

Changing Feminist Discourses

The last ten years have undoubtedly seen a resurgence of feminist politicking and writing. Recent critical texts describe this shift: 'against the backdrop of the widely documented phenomenon of young women's repudiations of feminism, it is notable that since 2006, the emergence of a "new feminism" has been proclaimed' (Scharff 2012, 19). Former Virago Ursula Owen herself noted the shift as the fortieth anniversary of the inaugural meeting of the National Women's Liberation Conference at Ruskin College, Oxford, came around: 'people are starting to talk about the women's movement again, aren't they? . . . It's unbelievable. 2010 – it will be forty years since. So hopefully. . .'[5] She wasn't alone in noting the significance of this anniversary:

> 2010 marked the 40th anniversary both of the publication of Germaine Greer's still controversial *The Female Eunuch* and of Kate Millett's landmark *Sexual Politics*. It was also four decades since the agenda-changing first ever National Women's Liberation conference. This killer combination of events galvanised campaigning groups everywhere and if anything our predictions of a feminist bonanza in 2010 underestimated the resurgence of grassroots activism. The first ever Feminism Summer School, hosted by UK Feminista in July, was a major success, picking up international coverage. And the Reclaim the Night movement was invigorated in force, with more than 2,000 women attending candlelit vigils in central London in November, where DJs kept the crowds going until 2am. Meanwhile more than 1,000 people attended London Feminism Network's October conference. (Groskop 2010)

These twenty-first-century incarnations of feminism included revivals of activist events such as Reclaim the Night and their contemporary manifestations 'slutwalks', as well as Ladyfest and FEM collaborations and the recent Million Women Rise events. There is also a contemporary flourishing of feminism online, with websites like Everyday Sexism, UK Feminista and the F-word drawing (especially young) women to feminist ideas and activism. Writers like Kat Banyard, Laurie Penny, Catherine Redfern and Caitlin Moran have, in recent years, emerged to voice their dismay at the virulent strain of misogyny that still especially taints popular culture (Angier 1999; Negra 2009; Banyard 2010; Cochrane 2010; Redfern and Aune 2010; Moran 2011). Virago itself is reaching out to its readers online (see Chapter 7) and has also published new work by established feminist writers, including Natasha Walter, Naomi Wolf and Kate Figes (see the section entitled 'New Feminist Waves – Old Feminist Issues' later on in this chapter).

All these manifestations of feminist activity 'underline the fact that feminism is blooming' (McCabe 2007). In the last ten years, there has been much discussion of the emergence of this new 'wave' of feminism: 'women, and especially younger women (hopefully some young men too), are waking up to what a big journey is still to come. We really are at the beginning of a new wave' (Cochrane 2007). This contemporary feminism has sought to encompass the original aims inherited from second-wave politics alongside the third-wave repositioning of women's freedoms, in particular around their bodies and sexualities. As Kath and Sophie Woodward put it: 'it is our intention to revisit what can be found, reclaimed and reconstituted while still retaining all the creativities of postmodernist and poststructuralist feminism' (Woodward and Woodward 2009, 2). Kat Banyard, who initiated the FEM conferences in 2004, writes: 'the equality that so many people see existing between men and women is an illusion. Proclamations that we are "there" now, that equality has been achieved, have chased feminism from the mainstream. It is time to find the way back – to recognise feminism for what it is: one of the most vital social justice movements of our age' (Banyard 2010, 2).

This new blossoming of feminism has been described as a 'fourth wave'. It is mindful of the intersections with ethnicity, class, disability, sexuality and other specificities of identity, as well as being more critical of the sexualization of culture under the auspices of commercialization. Fourth-wavers like Kristin Anderson argue that the small advances made by a specific demographic of women have been used to justify the broad statement that feminism has succeeded or, rather, that it is 'dead'. She articulates a 'modern misogyny' whereby 'ostensible empowerment in the marketplace through consumerism and in lifestyle choice has replaced the earlier political and intellectual work of feminism' (Anderson 2015, 1). She further points out that this 'post-feminism' fits with contemporary neoliberal politics since it eschews public battles for private self-stylings. 'In the context of post-feminism', she continues, 'an era in which feminism is taken into account but then swiftly dismissed and debased, women's sexual freedom manifests in porn culture and the hypersexualisation of women and girls. The sexually affirming woman of the 1960s and 1970s has turned into a sexually objectified woman of post-feminism. Embedded feminism, enlightened sexism, and the lack of a collective and cohesive women's liberation movement all contribute to this climate' (Anderson 2015, 14).

Susan Douglas has also written about this 'enlightened sexism', whereby culture encourages/enforces the idea 'that it is precisely through women's calculated deployment of their faces, bodies, attire, and sexuality that they gain and enjoy true power – power that is fun, that men will not resent, and indeed will embrace' (Douglas 2010, 10). The conflation of consumer culture's proposition of 'choice' with actual freedom, intersected with a neoliberal political landscape that valorizes the individual above all, has become a major obstacle for contemporary feminism. Evans and Riley recently set out this problem, arguing that 'neoliberal subjectivity is thus inherently contradictory; one must understand oneself as making free choices, while choosing only "appropriate" choices. Freedom thus becomes compulsory' (Evans and Riley 2015, 7).

In light of this, the ongoing disavowal of feminism by (especially) women in contemporary UK culture seems confused. Feminism has an image problem, as articulated by Geri Halliwell, former member of the band the Spice Girls and originator of the expression 'girl power': "'It's about labelling. For me feminism is bra-burning lesbianism. It's very unglamorous. I'd like to see it rebranded. We need to see a celebration of our femininity and softness"' (Moorhead 2007). In a culture in which women are relentlessly marketed images of themselves – and within which desirable 'femininity' is incommensurate with strident 'femaleness' – feminism has been effectively miscast. Halliwell's reductive conflation of feminism with a lack of glamour, and as antithetical to 'femininity', is simplistic, but it nevertheless continues to hold sway. Katherine Rake, former CEO of the Fawcett Society, notes its effect:

> The stereotype of the mythological feminist, while ridiculous, is dangerous in that it gives the impression that feminism is first and foremost about how women should dress or whether they should wear make-up. It belittles feminists' true legitimate and serious concerns – that the pay gap still exists, that violence against women is at crisis levels, that women's caring roles are so undervalued, that women are still woefully underrepresented in positions of power. Add to this the fact that there is no one organisation or definition of feminism, and it makes it all the easier for people to indulge in a spot of feminist-bashing; they can pick and choose and exaggerate the elements they want and then knock them down. (Rake 2006a)

The disavowal of the 'f-word' is also in part predicated on the perception that British women in the 2000s are more empowered, more equal and more free than their mothers and grandmothers had been. And it is not only younger women who no longer identify as feminist: 'in surveys, around three-quarters of women regularly say that they would not call themselves feminist' (France and Wiseman 2007). This does not mean that these women do not believe in women's equality, or even that they would not identify with feminist politics – it is the word that is the problem, not the principle. So 'the time is long overdue for us to reclaim the F-word and ridicule this stereotype, because it is this caricature of the feminist as ugly, aggrieved, anti-sex, anti-men, and anti-fun that keeps women in their place and strikes to ensure that nothing resembling a women's movement will ever regain the momentum of the late 1960s and early 1970s' (Douglas 2010, 305).

New Feminist Waves – Old Feminist Issues

As Gloria Steinem once stated, having it all never meant *doing* it all. In Virago's fourth decade, many women's options in the workplace had greatly changed since the years when the burgeoning feminist movement had made tackling the lack of employment opportunities a key goal, but this hadn't resulted in any fairer share of division of childcare or domestic duties. Betty Freidan's frustrated housewife is no longer the norm – in her place is a beleaguered working mum juggling childcare, housework and a job (or jobs). There also remains further segregation for women in the workplace according to ethnicity, class and disability.

The stereotype of the housewife nonetheless persists, in spite of women's incursion into all areas of industry, from engineering to medicine to finance to law (and of course publishing – see Chapter 7). Partly this is down to a powerful and traditionalist media: 'when women are seen [in the media], they are more likely to be portrayed as homemakers, as sexual objects, and as young. Men, on the other hand, are more likely to be portrayed in a range of professional fields; they are more active, and they are older and portrayed with more power and influence' (Anderson 2015, 79). It is also because women are being forced out of working life by the expectation that they will be caregivers for children and/or parents – the structuring of the workplace (for example, the lack of provision of affordable childcare, the gender pay gap and unequal parental leave arrangements for men and women) ensures that this is so: 'many women are leaving work due to the cuts in child tax credit and child benefit. Unable to pay for childcare, they cannot afford to work, which is senseless and destructive, and will keep alive the dogma that women should not work into the next generation and beyond' (Gold 2012). This has given rise to the contemporary phenomenon of the 'new traditionalist' women who leave high-powered jobs for a homemaker role not as an acquiescence to intrinsic drives, but as a response to the fact that women still bear the brunt of the parenting and housework even if they are in full-time work, and they're exhausted (Fine 2010).

More than forty-five years after the Equal Pay Act, women working full time in the United Kingdom are still paid on average 19.1 per cent less per hour than men.[6] Taking this figure from the Office of National Statistics, Fawcett cites the undervaluing of 'women's work', the lack of flexible working opportunities – or the 'motherhood penalty' – and sheer discrimination for the continuing discrepancy between the pay of men and women. In addition to the wage gap, women remain underrepresented in the top tiers of all areas of work: 'women's progress into positions of power has not only been glacially slow, in some areas it has been going backwards', says Kat Banyard. 'In an analysis of companies of all sizes across the UK a research team found that the total proportion of female directors had decreased from 43 per cent in 1991 to 35 per cent in 2007' (Banyard 2010, 94). In 2015, only 24% of FTSE board directors and just 8.6% of executive directors were women. Women make up a third of MPs sitting in the House of Commons and just a quarter of Peers sitting in the House of Lords.

So while 'women have made significant incursions into the workplace . . . their progress is at a stalemate. Feminism has alerted us to many of the problems and why they occur, but this knowledge cannot resolve the many challenges women face' (Caro and Fox 2008, 120). Women remain disproportionately stuck in low-paid jobs, are less well remunerated than men and continue to be held back at work upon becoming parents in ways that men are not. Notions of 'appropriate' male and female behaviour are partly to blame. Analysis has shown that stereotypes around gendered behaviour continue to direct the way work is done so that, for example, men and women get very different responses when they initiate negotiations. 'Both men and women were more likely to subtly penalise a woman who asked for more. The perception was that women who asked for more were "less nice"' (Vedantam 2007). Cultural assumptions of what constitutes 'appropriate' – and thus approved – gendered behaviour continue to play their part in directing women's lived, material realities. They prevent women from ascending to the top jobs: 'unlike men in the same position, women leaders have to continue to walk the fine line between appearing incompetent and nice and competent but cold' (Fine 2010, 62).

Feminist historian and Virago author Joanne Bourke traces a long line of inheritance for this treatment of uncompromising women:

Aggressive women have always provoked anxiety. We have tradition-
ally invested a vast amount of energy into socialising women to be
thoughtful of others, gentle in disposition, and dependent – or, as
John Ruskin once put it, 'pure womanhood' was 'enduringly, incor-
ruptibly good, instinctively, infallibly wise – wise, not for self-devel-
opment, but for self-renunciation' – traits that don't come naturally
to anyone. Consequently, belligerent women are regarded as far
worse than their male comrades. (Bourke 2009)

Alongside this, the issue of motherhood remains as relevant to feminism now as it was when Virago launched in 1973. Women's ability to
work is restricted by the unequal distribution of childcare responsibilities
within a heterosexual paradigm. This issue is, of course, complicated by the
structural inequalities of working culture: for example, the lack of provision of paternity leave granted to new fathers denies them the opportunity
to be stay-at-home-dads, even if they wished to do so. Tellingly, the wage
gap persists, even for those women who opt not to parent, with research
showing that 'women who work full time and have never taken time off
to have children still earn about eleven per cent less than men with equivalent education and experience' (Vedantam 2007). The cultural imperative
that assumes women will take on most parental responsibilities continues to
restrict *all* women's opportunities in the workplace. The twin assumptions
that breadwinning is for men and childrearing is for women remain deeply
entrenched.

The effect of parenthood on women is, in career terms, disastrous:
'mothers working full-time with two dependent children earn 21.6 per cent
less than men . . . no one should pay such a high employment penalty for
caring for children – women or men' (Banyard 2010, 94). But it's not only
women's pay that is an issue – it's also their career progression. Across all
industries, there is still a dearth of women at the top: 'women are only nine
per cent of directors of the UK's top companies, seven per cent of top police
officers, 23 per cent of civil service top management, and nine per cent of
editors of national newspapers' (Redfern and Aune 2010, 116).

Motherhood continues to have an enormous impact on (heterosexual)
women's careers in ways that simply don't apply to men. Sarah Waters describes the problem as it applies to women writers: 'the one big difference
I can see, I can see women writer friends with families, which has this devastating impact on the time that they get to work, and with male writers I
think it's still true that men just don't have that. That is really actually quite
significant . . . thinking about the writers I know and lots of the women. . .
there's been much more serious disruption of their work from things like

families, that's true.'[7] Shared parenting is fundamental to gender equality, and while there is some evidence that women's campaigning in this area is having an effect – figures from the Office of National Statistics show that the number of stay-at-home dads doubled between 1993 and 2014, so that 2 per cent of British men are the primary carer for their children – there is a long way to go before this number of stay-at-home dads equals the number of stay-at-home mums (McVeigh 2012). In spite of the introduction in 2016 of a new UK system of shared parental leave, allowing couples to split forty available weeks of leave between them as they choose, just two per cent of families have so far used this benefit. Lack of flexible working, the gender pay gap and the fear of a new 'fatherhood' penalty are all helping to perpetuate old structures of work and parenting.

So, as Douglas rightly argues, 'there is so much that the women's movement accomplished and changed for the better, but there is serious work to do. In particular, motherhood, pay equity, female poverty, violence against women, and the acceptability, even celebration of sexism: this is the unfinished business of the women's movement' (Douglas 2010, 306). Along with the housewife and mother stereotypes, the issue of women-as-sexobjects continues to occupy fourth-wave feminism. In the past ten years, the 'hypersexualization' of culture has become a central point of discussion for women of all ages and has driven a new generation of young women towards feminism.

The 1990s/'third-wave' formulations of a pro-sex feminism coincided and intersected with consumer culture's co-opting of female sexuality to 'sell' sex all its forms. Even women who identified as feminist came to claim as empowering the strip club, the sex toy and the topless selfie: 'while retaining the critique of the beauty culture and sexual abuse from the second-wave, young women have complicated the older feminist critique of the male gaze as a weapon to put women in their place, and instead exploit the spotlight as a source of power and energy. Thus girls do not see a contradiction between female power and assertive sexuality' (Rowe in Hollows and Moseley 2006, 64). Ariel Levy was one of the first feminist critics to attack this claiming of empowerment through sex. *Female Chauvinist Pigs* (2006) examined and critiqued the commodification of women's bodies and their sexuality, and the rise of what Levy described as a 'raunch' culture, which sold women an idea of freedom while constraining them to age-old tropes of disempowered display for male pleasure, as well as a dysfunctional emphasis on youth and money within consumer culture.

As sexualized images of women came to be increasingly normalized in UK culture – as evidenced in the pole dancing phenomenon, highly sexual pop music videos and the endemic rise of online pornography – Levy began the fightback against these ubiquitous images of insatiable, pneumatic female sexuality: 'We have simply adopted a new norm, a new role to play: lusty, busty exhibitionist. There are other choices. If we are really going to be sexually liberated, we need to make room for a range of options as wide as the variety of human desire. We need to allow ourselves the freedom to figure out what we internally want from sex instead of mimicking whatever popular culture holds up to us as sexy. That would be sexual liberation' (Levy 2006, 200). Her problematization of 'raunch' was welcomed by feminist critics and young women alike, who were tired of the (re)turn in culture to sexist depictions and sexualized stereotypes: '"what's really interesting," says [director of the Fawcett Society Katherine] Rake, "is that a younger generation of women are really reclaiming the word [feminism]. They're coming to traditional feminist issues via various routes – reacting to the hypersexualisation of culture, for instance"' (Cochrane 2007).

The rise of raunch evidenced a consumer culture that profited enormously from women's (and men's) insecurity about their appearance and desire to accede to powerful social messages about sexual display: 'the apparent freedom to lap dance masks structural inequalities that neoliberal governance seems unable to address, despite its commitment to social inclusion, cohesion and diversity' (Woodward and Woodward 2009, 107). The pressure to conform to a prescriptive body ideal is greater than ever, and more and more extreme forms of body modification have now become the norm, so that plastic surgery, laser surgery and chemical fillers are now part of mainstream 'beauty' regimes – and are sold as desirable 'choices' by a global beauty industry that insists that a woman's value lies in her appearance. Angela McRobbie argues that the very act of assuming femininity makes women unhappy since it *requires* physical and mental ill-health. The ideal feminine body type is thin, hairless, chemically enhanced and sculpted by the surgeon's knife, and 'fashion images occupy a special place in this process of normalization of feminine melancholia' (McRobbie 2009, 112).

In response, there has been a revival of feminist anger at this contemporary construction of woman-as-sex-object: 'the rise of a hypersexual culture is not proof that we have reached full equality; rather, it has reflected and exaggerated the deeper imbalances of power in our society. Without thoroughgoing economic and political change, what we see when we look around us is not the equality we once sought; it is a stalled revolution' (Walter 2010, 8–9). Walter goes on to critique the increasing acceptance of normative ideas of innate gender difference and how these are being used to justify not just the construction of woman-as-sex-object, but also a whole range of cultural, political and psychological inequalities. This is a point also made by Cordelia Fine in her 2010 rearticulation of gender, in which she highlights anew the emphasis still placed on 'natural' differences between the sexes and how these continue to be used as evidence to support the idea that fundamental gender differences exist. 'The sheer audacity of the over-interpretations and misinformation is startling', she asserts (Fine 2010, 237).

Fourth-wave feminist writers including Laura Bates, Caroline Criado-Perez and Emer O'Toole have also written about this ongoing structuring of gender in and by culture, and the effect it has on the construction of women as sex objects and the reification of ideal 'femininity' in contemporary culture (Bates 2014; Criado-Perez 2015; O'Toole 2015). O'Toole articulates the problem: 'we exaggerate [biological] differences, and then place sexual taboos on the female body, defining female nakedness differently and declaring it inherently erotic and/or shameful. This is a gendered use of the fact of biological sex: a social use that allows slut shaming, commodification and curtailing of female freedom' (O'Toole 2015, 121). The objectification of women's bodies continues to trouble feminism. Along with the images of women as housewives and mothers, these three stereotypes of femininity remain unresolved.

The Personal – and beyond – in Contemporary Feminism

Linked to the problematization of women's figuring as sexual objects, feminism has also continued to interrogate female sexuality and the enactment of sexual relationships in contemporary culture. Levy's, Walter's and Banyard's exploration of 'raunch' concluded that the rise of the strip club and the increasing 'pornification' of culture were evidence of continued inequalities in sexual relations between women and men: 'it eroticises the dominance of masculinity over femininity, of men over women' (Banyard 2010, 160). There has been continued examination of the heterosexual matrix, with sexual double standards, female objectification, restrictions on leaving relationships and raunch all posited as issues that hinder women from making their own choices about sex and relationships (Redfern and Aune 2010). But there is also a new recognition that heterosexual men are also victims (as well as beneficiaries) of sexist culture: 'men are boxed in by restrictive stereotypes and pressured to demonstrate how "manly" they are. As long as this culture of sexism continues, some men will prove their masculinity through violence, sexually "conquering" women, and treating them as dehumanised objects. That is why feminism must target men for change' (Banyard 2010, 230).

In the twenty-first century, there has been a shift towards extolling, for men, the virtues of pleasurable involvement in their children's lives, better sex through relationships with sexually emancipated – and happy! – partners, a better work/life balance and the exploration and expression of emotion. This is a mirroring of the original calls of feminism, except now the focus is on *men* adopting these changes, not women. It is a not unremarkable shift: 'the goal of the feminism we swear by is for women to inhabit the full spectrum of human behaviour and endeavour. The new feminism says that men should be able to do so too' (Caro and Fox 2008, 238). Contemporary feminists are reframing (hetero)sexuality as a tool in not only building positive sexual relationships but also driving towards gender equality itself.

Virago has played its part in this, publishing, for example, Naomi Wolf's explosive *Vagina: A New Biography* (Wolf 2012). In this, Wolf continues the exaltation of sex as a means to personal and feminist liberation, focusing on the vagina to offer a very personal explication of female sexuality and the limitations that current constructions of gender pose to women's health, both physical and mental. Wolf has been accused of being provocative rather than challenging in this text, and it certainly lacks the rigour of her earlier writing; as Suzanne Moore put it, 'it's like lesbianism never happened, nor class, nor vast swaths of feminist theory' (Moore 2012). Nonetheless, it succeeded in getting Wolf (and Virago) into the public eye and onto the public stage. It also provided evidence of the contemporary corollary between feminism and a happy and satisfying sex life, and the repercussions of this for women's status in culture generally: 'researchers found that feminist women are generally more sexually assertive, better able to negotiate pleasurable and safe sex, and experience more equality in their personal relationships' (Redfern and Aune 2010, 74)

Moore makes a good point, however, about the heterosexist bias of works like Wolf's. Perhaps one of the most notable shifts in UK culture since the turn of the millennium has been the mainstreaming of gay and trans 'lifestyles' and identities, with trans celebrities now part of everyday discourse and gay marriage made legal. In the years in which Virago was establishing itself, lesbian identity was nowhere near as visible – or as accepted – as it now is. Writer Val McDermid explored this in an interview she gave to *The Independent* in 2010, noting that both her books and those written by Sarah Waters were no longer considered 'lesbian fiction', but simply 'fiction': 'I think there's been an opening up of British culture and a relaxing of British society. Our novels have done well at the same time as we've made legal gains; civil partnerships have come along. There's been a bit of a sea change that would have been unimaginable even 10 years ago' (McDermid 2010). She notes the contrast with her earlier experiences of publishing novels featuring 'the UK's first openly lesbian detective, Lindsay Gordon', arguing that these novels were only considered publishable by a feminist press (she was initially published by The Women's Press): 'Something has changed in the past seven years. My latest novel, *Trick of the Dark,* is probably the most lesbian book I've ever written in terms of the number of its gay female characters. And not an eyebrow has been raised at my publisher, Little, Brown. The sales and marketing effort that has been put into this book is, as far as I can gauge, exactly the same as any other book with my name on it would have received' (McDermid 2010).

This new visibility of lesbian writing and writers is reflective of a general shift towards greater LGBT+ inclusion, and in the past decade Virago has played its part in furthering this, publishing a good number of lesbian writers and/or novels containing lesbian themes – for example, contemporary work by authors such as Sarah Waters, Stella Duffy and Emma Donoghue, as well as reprinted novels by Jane Rule, Carol Anshaw and Patricia Highsmith. Virago has continued, then, to fulfil its role of providing literature that conveys messages about equality and diversity, arguably helping mainstream what once would have been considered 'alternative' identities. The role of the publisher remains vital, especially if, as Kaitlynn Mendes notes, feminism is once again being promulgated through literary rather than academic texts (as was the case during the third wave, when much feminist discussion was situated in the academy): 'feminist discourses are no longer the reserve of academia and have permeated popular culture' (Mendes 2011, 136). Virago's dissemination of feminist messages in the 'everyday' language of (especially) fiction writing avoids the exclusionary nature of academic texts. Goodings is not unaware of this and explains how Virago attempts to convey its feminist politics through its fiction: 'I've always said the message is in the book.'[8]

The fourth wave has seen a renewal of popular engagement with feminist politics. As feminist scholars moved into the academy in the 1970s and 1980s, and university courses on gender and feminism were instituted, feminism's increasingly sophisticated intellectual agenda became more entrenched in the academy. This was a positive result of women's incursion into the intellectual field, but an unfortunate effect was to alienate rather than engage women: 'academic feminism has developed a language that makes sense only to a closed circle of initiates. Too many women feel shut out, alienated' (Walters 2005, 140). Gloria Steinem makes the following point: 'the causes of feminism are not always best served by its professors and theorists. "I always wanted to put a sign up on the road to Yale saying, 'Beware: Deconstruction Ahead'. Academics are forced to write in a language no one can understand so that they get tenure. They have to say 'discourse', not 'talk'. Knowledge that is not accessible is not helpful"' (Denes 2005).

There has certainly been a shift in Virago's fourth decade towards a less 'academic' feminism, rooted in online engagement, direct action and, still, books. In the past decade, then, Virago has continued its project of publishing books intended to address feminism's multiple and sometimes contradictory positions. We can see evidence of this by looking at both the content and the form of its lists over the past ten years. For example, as UK feminism has increasingly come to engage with global perspectives of women's lives, Virago has outputted a growing number of texts by and/or about BME women and women in non-Western cultures. Virago writer Natasha Walter explains on the press' website that 'some of the most pressing problems faced by women in the world today are in non-Western societies . . . I'm certainly very aware of the international context to women's struggles for human rights and what I see of women's experiences in other countries makes me absolutely certain that feminism is internationally relevant'.[9]

As postcolonial feminism has become a key aspect of feminist academic writing and research, it has been reflected in the engagement of both popular and literary culture with global feminist issues: 'it has brought about a "worlding" of mainstream feminist theory; feminist theory has moved from a rather parochial concern with white, middle-class English-speaking women, to a focus on women in different national and cultural contexts' (Mills in Mills and Jones 1998, 98). Virago has reflected this shift, doubling the number of texts it published by BME women or women from non-Western cultures compared to the previous ten years.

The increasingly joined-up nature of communications thanks to the proliferation of online communities means that contemporary UK feminism is now more engaged than ever with global issues such as poverty, religion, ecology, the environment and technology. The seismic effect of the 'Arab Spring' demonstrations and protests of 2010–12, first in Tunisia, then Egypt, Libya and many other countries of the Arab League, initially inspired hope among Western feminists that women's rights in these countries might at last be put on the agenda. But it was to be a short-lived optimism: 'a revolution has come and gone, but done little for Arab women. There are only eight women in Egypt's new 500-seat parliament – and not one female presidential candidate. Domestic violence, forced marriage and female genital mutilation are still part of the status quo across a region covering more than 20 countries and 350 million people' (Chulov and Hussein 2012). Consequently, there has been a renewal of engagement by UK feminists with non-Western women's rights and a more global configuring of the battles that twenty-first-century feminism must fight. Use of online social networks underpins the new global protest movement that has emerged this millennium. Feminism in this country is now looking outward, adding the issues facing women in different countries and cultures to its agenda for change. Virago evidences this global outlook in the almost 6 per cent of its published output that presents global perspectives of women's lives.

Virago has also continued its project of using memoir writing, as well as biography, to convey feminist ideas and messages (see Chapter 4). The proportion of autobiographical and biographical writing published by Virago has risen steadily during the past two decades – from around 13 per cent of its total lists in its third decade to almost 19 per cent in the past ten years. This is up from around 9 per cent in its first two decades, showing that Virago understands the cultural and literary shift in the United Kingdom towards individuation rather than collectivism; the way to disseminate a message in this context is to exemplify it through the story of an individual. Goodings concurs that the shift is deliberate: 'subversion is the way forward. I don't think you can change people by banging them over the head. That's why I think the memoirs are really working now, actually'.[10]

Virago seeks to communicate its feminism through publication of real people's stories, and it is this that continues to render it both relevant and necessary: relevant because even in our internet age, books are still a way for people to connect with each other, and to share ideas and experiences; and necessary because the fight for gender equality has not yet been won. Goodings puts the case for Virago's continued vitality: 'I believe in the sheer inventiveness of our industry . . . and in the endless genius and imagination of writers. I have faith in authors and I have faith in readers. I have seen too much evidence that shows us that books continue to matter, that good writing will move and nourish us. That essential fact is not going to change' (Tonkin 2011). As Virago hits middle age with the passing of its fortieth birthday milestone, there are plenty of challenges ahead for both the imprint and for feminism in the United Kingdom and across the world.

Notes

1. Interview with Lennie Goodings, 8 November 2004.
2. Established in March 2015, the Women's Equality Party was cofounded by Catherine Mayer and Sandi Toksvig, and is led by Sophie Walker. It has seven core objectives: equal pay, parenting, education, health, representation in politics and business, equality in the media and an end to violence against women.
3. Interview with Lennie Goodings, 8 November 2004.
4. Ibid.
5. Interview with Ursula Owen, 5 February 2009.
6. Retrieved 26 September 2017 from http://www.fawcettsociety.org.uk/our-work/campaigns/gender-pay-gap.

7. Interview with Sarah Waters, 12 July 2004.
8. Interview with Lennie Goodings, 8 November 2004.
9. Retrieved 3 July 2012 from http://www.viragobooks.net/sexism-stereotypes-and-slutwalks-natasha-walter-talks-to-virago-book-club-members.
10. Interview with Lennie Goodings, 8 May 2008.

Conclusion

Virago's establishment in 1973 marked the beginning of the UK's second-wave feminist publishing phenomenon. Carmen Callil and cofounder Marsha Rowe both recalled, in my interviews with them, the sense of condescension, ridicule or occasional downright hostility that greeted their venture, evidencing the sexist culture into which they were launching themselves as publishers. The reasons for their venture were clearly stated from the outset: 'Virago was founded to publish books which, focusing on the lives, history and literature of women, would provide some balance to dominant views of human experience' (Callil 1980, 1001). Callil's desire to establish a publisher devoted to women's writing, and run by women, was generated in and by a culture that positioned women as unequal to men. She sought to redress this imbalance through the provision of literature that questioned the patriarchal hegemony of contemporary 1970s culture and the fact that women had been similarly limited throughout history – as well as through publication of women's literary attempts to defy these limitations. Virago thus sought to highlight the ways in which women were disadvantaged because of their gender as readers, as writers, as publishers and, indeed, as people.

The goals of second-wave feminism – parity of pay, equal sharing of domestic and parental responsibilities, freedom from sexual exploitation and the right to an empowered sexuality – were all addressed in the range of material published by Virago in its early years and continue to be themes in the books that it now publishes. This reflects the fact that although contemporary UK culture is greatly changed from that of the early 1970s, the original goals of second-wave feminism have not been attained. Callil's original desire to change the publishing industry, the feminist movement and culture itself in order to benefit women continues to have resonance, as Goodings says: 'things haven't changed enough. A lot of things have changed: there's a lot more women studied in universities and schools, those kinds of things, they're shifts. And there are astonishing shifts too, from ten years ago, fifteen, thirty years ago. A lot of things have changed hugely. It's the more subtle things that one still hasn't got across, got through yet'.[1]

Changing the Literary Landscape

Virago has certainly effected some lasting changes. First, its engagement with the project of unearthing and reprinting lost and forgotten historical women's writing has without doubt shifted forever the false assertion that women in the past had not written, or not written well. The canon, and literary study itself, has been irrevocably reshaped by Virago's Modern Classics, part of the project of excavating excellent women's writing from the past: 'people are apt to forget, now, how much Virago shifted the landscape not only of publishing, but of academia, too. In 2008, publishers ignore women readers and writers at their peril, while schools and universities have been forced, after decades of neglect, to include women writers in syllabuses (Cooke 2008). The Modern Classics are still a major component of Virago's publishing schedule, comprising over a third of its output during the last decade – evidence of the continued demand for women's writing from the past, as well as Virago's canny ability to provide this material, packaged in such a way to make it appealing to contemporary audiences.

Virago author Sarah Waters argues that the Modern Classics series is still really exciting: 'partly because it's just keeping books in print – for me, regardless or not of whether they're by women. I think it's exciting that there are all these wonderful books by women, and it's really important to keep them alive and there aren't really any other publishers doing that'.[2] The Modern Classics have broadened the parameters of literary judgement, expanding the historically constructed boundaries of fiction writing to include women's contribution. They have also enlightened understanding of women's lived experiences in the past, and Goodings is adamant that the list should continue to be developed by the addition of new titles, but also that the back catalogue of Modern Classics must be kept in circulation so that it can engage new readers and thus teach the same lessons anew:

> There are different kinds of work to be done now – it's keeping that list alive. It's a challenge. It's a challenge because it's been out there for a long time, it's a challenge because the way bookshops go now they don't stock back titles, which they used to do. So you have to keep thinking of new ways.[3]

Virago continues to innovate in order to maintain the Modern Classics' vitality, building on Callil's example of utilizing marketing and production techniques in order to get the press' books out to as wide an audience as possible. For Goodings, as for Callil, the Modern Classics continue to play a vital part in Virago's remit: 'we made a big fuss getting them back in print! So it's good we haven't let them go'.[4] It has also added authors like Angela Carter, Daphne du Maurier and Patricia Highsmith to the list, a further attempt to broaden the boundaries of the canon to incorporate more contemporary female writers – and a successful one, as these writers are indeed now taught on many university courses. Spicer is right, then, to argue that the Modern Classics series 'is a contributor to the very substantial shift in women's writing, appreciation of, and the value of just looking at it in and of itself'.[5]

In addition, Virago continues to jockey for a fair share of the review press' coverage, challenging the historical bias of a literary culture that has long served to edge out women's contributions. Having established its reputation as a 'quality' imprint and now being the publisher of contemporary big-hitting authors such as Margaret Atwood, Sarah Waters, Ali Smith and Shirley Hazzard, Virago demands attention for its books and its writers in a marketplace that continues to sideline women's efforts. Recent analysis shows a review press still dominated by men, with Vida's 2013 research pointing out that 'not one of the literary publications it analysed reviewed more books by female authors than male authors' (Cochrane 2013). This is down to the prevailing cultural bias that allocates greater authority to men's work – although the boundaries of the canon have shifted, there is further to go before literary and wider culture can shake off men's historical dominance of the intellectual world. So if it remains true that 'women are interested in literary fiction by men and women, and men only in literary fiction by men, then perhaps it's not surprising that more male authors might be reviewed and published' (Cochrane 2013).

Virago's purpose remains, then, to challenge the notion that women's writing is somehow limited to a female audience. 'Even now people say to me that it's niche publishing and I say it's not actually, it really isn't', says Goodings. 'It gives priority and it highlights women but that's not niche publishing. Niche publishing is cookery writing or something, or gardening, something particular. And what we're publishing is the world through women's eyes.'[6] Virago's continuing relevance thus lies in its provision of diverse, empowered and empowering female role models, conveying important messages because, as Callil always maintained, fiction teaches us things. Virago writers such as Angela Carter, Margaret Atwood, Michéle Roberts and Maya Angelou have done much to change perceptions of the notion of 'appropriate' female behaviour through their writing. In publishing their work, Virago has therefore played a part in changing culture itself. With contemporary writers such as Sarah Waters, Stella Duffy and Gillian Slovo the press similarly provides a platform for women seeking to examine cultural constructions of sex and gender, and to challenge the status quo. In publishing so many award-winning authors whose work refuses the usual categories into which women's writing – and identity – has so often been shoehorned, Virago's books continue to challenge the historical pejoration of female fiction.

The difference of a woman-only publishing house still counts, as author Kamila Shamsie described in setting out her call for a 'Year of Publishing Women' in 2018 – her solution to the continuing discrepancy in the proportion of men's to women's writing submitted to book prize panels. Mainstream publishers still submit a ratio of 6:4 male to female writing for consideration in these prizes, and Shamsie is clear that the existing publishing process will not suffice in getting that figure to 50:50. She says: 'ask what actually helped to change literary culture in the UK? Two things come to mind: the literary presses of the 70s, of which Virago is the most notable; and the Women's Prize for Fiction. In part, what both the presses and the prize did was to create a space for women in a male-dominated world, giving voice and space to those who wouldn't find them elsewhere' (Shamsie 2015). Virago continues to play this important role, putting forward only women's literary efforts in its annual engagement with the literary prize industry.

The fact that many of Virago's writers are award-winning is also significant. Book prizes lists make a huge difference to sales, so being featured on the long- and short-lists of the Women's Prize for Fiction as well as the Man Booker and Costa Book Awards means Virago's books take their challenge to as wide an audience as possible. Atwood, Waters, Smith and Hazzard, for example, have broken into the mainstream through their attainment of these literary prizes, which hold great sway. One of Virago's achievements, then, and one of the reasons it retains its vitality, is in its success in putting forward its writers for these awards. 'Our role is still to inspire, actually', says Goodings, 'and to put out financially viable, stylish work that inspires men and women and looks at the world through women's eyes.'[7]

The Virago project, and the combined influence of all the feminist publishing houses that were instituted during the second wave, also succeeded in effecting one further change to the literary landscape. Their legacy includes the addition of a range of new genres of writing to the category 'women's writing', with feminist sci-fi, feminist crime and feminist romance fiction all having been enabled by the existence of publishing houses willing to output their stories. These genres helped broaden the remit of 'female' writing styles, and their influence can be seen in the work of contemporary authors such as Karen Russell, Gillian Flynn and Tana French, and even Stephanie Meyers and J.K. Rowling. Having helped enable the emergence of such writing, particularly by instituting dedicated crime and sci-fi series, Virago has had a lasting impact on the kinds of writing now considered publishable and popular.

Publishing Feminist Writing

As well as changing the literary landscape, Virago has played a significant role in changing the feminist landscape, publishing a range of key texts over the course of its nearly fifty years of business. In its early years, thanks in large part to its Advisory Group of historians, writers, teachers and researchers, Virago was at the vanguard of feminist politicking and published a broad range of nonfiction that examined the problems of sexist culture, as well as proposals for change. Second-wave feminism's problematization of the gendered stereotypes of mother, housewife and sex object were key themes in the critical writing Virago published in the 1970s and 1980s, as well as many of its fiction titles (for example, the works of Carter and Atwood). Its status as a publisher of feminist theory/polemic became more complex as the second wave gave way to the third, and feminist theory became more entrenched in the academy even while feminism itself came to be contested in popular culture. The separation of academic rhetoric from more mainstream critical writing was a positive outcome, allowing female scholars to take their place in the academy and feminist theory to become embedded as an intellectual discipline. But for Virago, which is not an academic publisher, it meant a lessening of its ability to act as a conduit for theoretical feminist writing.

However, as Goodings has always asserted, Virago's intent remained distinctly feminist. Through third-wave formulations of feminism, and the simultaneous disavowal of the f-word in mainstream popular culture, it steered a course that allowed engagement with some of the theory being played out in the academy, while also publishing literary fiction that explored new formulations of feminist positions through storytelling. For example, as queerer ideas of identity took hold while a new commodity culture increasingly drew focus to the 'power' of the individual, Virago published Sarah Waters' lesbian cross-dressing narratives alongside Natasha Walter's critical exploration of the selling of sex-as-empowerment. Virago continued to use its position to publish books that added to the multiple directions of third-wave feminist discourse(s).

More recently, Virago has published some fourth-wave writing, including its recent compendium by new as well as more established writers, *Fifty Shades of Feminism* (Appignanesi et al. 2013). In addition, it has continued to place an emphasis on publishing what Callil describes as 'politics through memoirs, politics through stories of . . . life stories. Which is very much actually the way people today absorb things'.[8] An examination of Virago's nonfiction lists reveals that its output of autobiographical and biographical writing has more than doubled in its third and fourth decades: such texts made up 10 per cent of its lists in the years up to the mid 1990s, but now comprise almost a fifth of its total published output. Virago is engaging with contemporary culture's reification of the individual and the subsequent literary shift towards expression of politics through individual's stories. Goodings concurs that the shift is deliberate: 'subversion is the way forward. I don't think you can change people by banging them over the head. That's why I think the memoirs are really working now, actually'.[9]

Feminism remains at the heart of Virago's lists and so, while literary and mainstream culture persists in excluding, devaluing and suppressing women's contributions, it continues to have a role. In contemporary culture there is plenty of evidence of the need for a sustained feminist challenge, with the three stereotypes of wife, mother and sex object continuing to limit women in the United Kingdom at work, at home and in public spaces. Virago's founders are right that the press still has work to do, as Rowe explains: 'this is still going on – these complex questions about men and women and life and power. I think it is in places like women-only publishing houses that you can be alert to these things'.[10] Rowe correctly identifies publishing houses as a vital conduit in the transmission of ideas that challenge the prevailing cultural order. While women continue to be devalued in literary and public life, Virago continues to have a useful role.

Setting an Example in Female Enterprise and Industry

Finally, Virago's significance lies in the example it set as a female-run business, launching itself into sexist literary and financial domains, and succeeding in spite of the disadvantages its founders' gender posed within both sets of parameters. The Virago team has always innovated in order to succeed, introducing new formats such as the Midway paperbacks and new ideas such as the Modern Classics series. More recently, Goodings has overseen the introduction of web-based initiatives, including print-on-demand and online book clubs, continuing the Virago tradition of engaging as wide a readership as possible through inventive and original ways of doing business.

Spicer is emphatic that Virago's example remains vital: 'it's a valuable publishing resource. I'm absolutely one hundred per cent behind it continuing, and it is something entirely different'.[11] Virago sets an example through its female workforce enacting their own – very successful – methods of doing business: feminism as praxis. Callil always emphasized that succeeding in business terms was as vital a part of Virago's remit as its publication of women's literature. Today, Goodings similarly argues that the example Virago sets in terms of being a female-run business venture remains relevant and, indeed, vital: 'people want meaning, people want inspiration . . . Individually, I think the books obviously have their own route but together, I think that's the job actually, to still be visible. That's it, you know'.[12]

Virago's example helped shift the constitution of the publishing industry itself. It is one of the few areas of business in which women make up a significant proportion of senior leaders (see Chapter 7), and although men currently lead three of the four major publishing groups in the United Kingdom, over the span of Virago's more-than-forty years of operations, women have taken the helm at most of the major UK publishing companies as well as the new conglomerates that have recently incorporated many of these corporations enterprises within them. Women like Liz Calder, Gail Rebuck, Victoria Barnsley and Virago's own Alexandra Pringle – as well as, of course, Lennie Goodings – have shown that women can lead publishing houses to spectacular success, in spite of the limitations of, for example, parental leave provision and the structural expectation that childrearing is incompatible with women's careers (but not men's). These women have inspired others to follow in their footsteps, changing the publishing industry so that it is no longer dominated by 'gentlemen in trousers' – a fact made even more important because of women's continuing lack of representation in senior positions in other industries.

Virago today is something entirely different from the Virago of 1973. This is both a positive indication of the extent to which women have come over the past forty-five years – as readers, as writers, as publishers, as feminists – as well as a sign of the new battles that women face in a greatly changed cultural and literary setting. In the act of publishing 'books by women, for everyone', Virago prioritizes women's writing in order to elide the differences between the sexes and to change cultural formations of gender. It is, as Harriet Spicer says, 'a brand that can be used as a shorthand to represent women's literary achievement, women's business achievement, women's abilities'.[13] It has a rich and important legacy, but, perhaps more critically, it continues to look to the future, recognizing that there is still work to do. We need Virago because it continues to engage in the battle for equality in literature and culture, and to mark out the difference of a female perspective on the world, and to insist that this perspective is important. That is the point and purpose of Virago's publishing agenda, and it is one that will still count until gender itself no longer determines how we read, write and publish great literature.

Notes

1. Interview with Lennie Goodings, 8 November 2004.
2. Interview with Sarah Waters, 12 July 2004.
3. Interview with Lennie Goodings, 8 November 2004.
4. Ibid.
5. Interview with Harriet Spicer, 20 October 2004.
6. Interview with Lennie Goodings, 8 November 2004.
7. Ibid.
8. Interview with Carmen Callil, 10 November 2004.
9. Interview with Lennie Goodings, 8 May 2008.
10. Interview with Marsha Rowe, 15 July 2004.
11. Interview with Harriet Spicer, 20 October 2004.
12. Interview with Lennie Goodings, 8 November 2004.
13. Interview with Harriet Spicer, 20 October 2004.

Bibliography

Adams, Andrea, with Neil Crawford. 2014. *Bullying at Work: How to Confront and Overcome it.* London: Virago.

Adams, Carol, and Rae Laurikietis. 1976. *The Gender Trap: A Closer Look at Sex Roles.* London: Virago, 1976.

Adams, Tim. 2005. 'New Kid on the Newsstand', *The Observer,* 23 January.

Ahmad, Rukhsana. 1991. 'What's Happening to the Women's Presses?', *Spare Rib* 223: May.

Aitchison, Cathy. 1995. 'She's Not One of the Boys', *The Independent,* 16 February.

Alexander, Sally. 1984. *Studies in the History of Feminism 1850s–1930s.* London: University of London.

Allen, Katie. 2010. 'Indie Literary Sites Start Coming of Age', *The Bookseller,* 8 October.

Altbach, Philip G., and Edith S. Hoskins (eds). 1995. *International Book Publishing: An Encyclopaedia.* London: Fitzroy Dearborn Publishers.

Anderson, Kristin J. 2015. *Modern Misogyny: Anti-feminism in a Post-feminist Era.* Oxford: Oxford University Press.

Angelou, Maya. 1984. *I Know Why the Caged Bird Sings.* London: Virago.

Angier, Natalie. 1999. *Woman: An Intimate Geography.* London: Virago.

Anon. 1984. 'Books and Book Women', *Sunday Times,* 25 November 1984.

———. 1991. 'The Dearth Moves for Attallah the Fun', *Sunday Times,* 7 April.

———. 1993. 'Feminist Publishing', *The Economist.* 12 June.

———. 1975. 'Lookout! Column', *Sunday Times.* 7 September.

———. 1981. *Love Your Enemy? The Debate between Heterosexual Feminism and Political Lesbianism.* London: Onlywomen.

Appignanesi, Lisa, Rachel Holmes and Susie Orbach (eds). 2013. *Fifty Shades of Feminism.* London: Virago.

Arcana, Judith. 1983. *Every Mother's Son: The Role of Mothers and the Making of Men.* London: The Women's Press.

———. 1981. *Our Mothers' Daughters.* London: The Women's Press.

Ardill, Susan, and Sue O'Sullivan. 1985. 'Dizzy Pace in Women's Publishing', *New Statesman.* 25 October.

Armitt, Lucie (ed.). 1991. *Where No Man Has Gone Before: Women and Science Fiction.* London: Routledge.

Assiter, Alison, and Carol Avedon (eds). 1993. *Bad Girls and Dirty Pictures: The Challenge to Reclaim Feminism.* London: Pluto Press.

Athill, Diana. 2000. *Stet.* London: Granta.

Attallah, Naim. 2007. *Fulfilment and Betrayal: 1975–1995.* London: Quartet Books.

Atwood, Margaret. 1997. *Alias Grace.* London: Virago.

——— (ed.). 1987. *The Canlit Foodbook: From Pen to Palate. A Collection of Tasty Literary Fare.* Toronto: Totem Books.

————. 2005. *Curious Pursuits: Occasional Writing 1970–2005*. London: Virago.

————. 1980. *The Edible Woman*. London: Virago.

————. 1987. *The Handmaid's Tale*. London: Virago.

————. 1982a. *Lady Oracle*. London: Virago.

————. 1982c. *Life Before Man*. London: Virago.

————. 2013. *Maddaddam*. London: Virago.

————. 2004. *Oryx and Crake*. London: Virago.

————. 1994. *The Robber Bride*. London: Virago.

———— (ed.). 1982b. *Second Words: Selected Critical Prose*. Toronto: Anansi.

Baehr, Helen, and Gillian Dyer (eds). 1987. *Boxed in: Women and Television*. London: Pandora.

Baines, Elizabeth. 1983. *The Birth Machine*. London: The Women's Press.

Banyard, Kat. 2010. *The Equality Illusion: The Truth about Men and Women Today*. London: Faber & Faber.

Barker, Paul. 1995. 'The Return of the Magic Storyteller', *The Independent on Sunday*, 8 January.

Barr, Marleen S. 1992. *Feminist Fabulation: Space/Postmodern Fiction*. Iowa City: University of Iowa Press.

Bartlett, Jane. 1994. *Will You Be Mother?: Women Who Choose to Say No*. London: Virago.

Bates, Laura. 2014. *Everyday Sexism: The Project that Inspired a Worldwide Movement*. London: Simon & Schuster.

Battersby, Matilda. 2015. 'Baileys Prize 2015: Why We Sadly Still Need Women-Only Book Prizes', *The Independent*. 4 June.

Baumgardner, Jennifer, and Amy Richards. 2000. *ManifestA: Young Women, Feminism and the Future*. New York: Farrar, Straus & Giroux.

Baxter, Sarah. 1995. 'Why Did the Apple Crumble?', *The Observer*. 29 October.

————. 2004. 'Women, the True Winners at Work', *Sunday Times*, 11 January.

Beauman, Nicola. 1993. *A Very Great Profession: The Woman's Novel 1914–1939*. London: Virago.

Beckett, Andy. 2006. 'The Man Who Rocks the Cradle', *The Guardian*, 9 June.

Bedell, Geraldine. 2005. 'Textual Politics', *The Guardian*, 6 March.

Bell, Rachel. 2007. 'University Challenge', *The Guardian*, 9 February.

Bennett, Catherine. 1993. 'The House that Carmen Built', *The Guardian*, 14 June.

————. 1988. 'Women's Side of the Story . . . But Not the Boys: Who is Looking to Feminist Book Fortnight?', *The Times*, 25 March.

Benson, Mary, and McDermid, Anne. 1993. 'A Kind of Innocence: Obituary of Ros de Lanerolle', *The Guardian*, 25 September.

Benstock, Shari (ed.). 1988. *The Private Self: Theory and Practice of Women's Autobiographical Writings*. London: Routledge.

Berger, Melody (ed.). 2006. *We Don't Need Another Wave: Dispatches from the Next Generation of Feminists*. Emeryville: Seal Press.

Berman, Jennifer. 2001. *For Women Only: A Revolutionary Guide to Reclaiming Your Sex Life*. London: Virago.

Berrington, Lucy. 1992. 'Well Versed', *The Guardian*, 16 April.

Betterton, Rosemary. 1987. *Looking on: Images of Femininity in the Visual Arts and Media*. London: Pandora.

Betz, Phyllis M. 2006. *Lesbian Detective Fiction: Woman as Author, Subject and Reader.* Jefferson, NC: MacFarland & Company.

Black, Clementina (ed.). 1983. *Married Women's Work: Being the Report of an Enquiry Undertaken by the Women's Industrial Council.* London: Virago.

Bland, Lucy and Laura Doan. 1998. *Sexology Uncensored: The Documents of Sexual Science.* Cambridge: Polity Press.

Bloom, Harold (ed.). 2000. *Modern Critical Views: Margaret Atwood.* Philadelphia: Chelsea House Publishers.

Blum, Linda, and Vicki Smith. 1988. 'Women's Mobility in the Corporation: A Critique of the Politics of Optimism', *Signs* 13(3) (Spring).

Bostridge, Mark. 2003. 'The Apple Bites Back', *The Independent,* 18 May.

Bourke, Joanna. 2009. 'Women Beware Women', *The Guardian,* 30 May.

Bovey, Shelley. 1989. *Being Fat is Not a Sin.* London: Pandora.

———. 1995. *The Empty Nest: When Children Leave Home.* London: Pandora.

———. 2000. *Sizeable Reflections.* London: The Women's Press.

———. 2002. *What Have You Got to Lose? The Great Weight Debate and How to Diet Successfully.* London: The Women's Press.

Bown, Jane. 1999. 'National Portraits', *The Guardian,* 17 October.

Braid, Helen (ed.). 1997. *A Stranger at My Table: Women Write about Mothering Adolescents.* London: The Women's Press.

Briscoe, Joanna. 1990a. 'Feminist Fatales', *The Guardian,* 1 February.

———. 1990b. 'Feminist Presses: Who Needs Them?', *The Guardian,* 6 June.

———. 1989. 'Femme Fatalities', *The Guardian,* 26 April.

Bristow, Joseph, and Trev Lynn Broughton (eds). 1997. *The Infernal Desires of Angela Carter: Fiction, Femininity, Feminism.* London: Longman.

Broughton, Ellie. 2010. 'The Bookseller Industry Awards 2010', *The Bookseller,* 7 May.

Brown, Helen. 2006. 'The Other One', *Daily Telegraph,* 11 March.

Brown, Louise. 2000. *Sex Slaves: The Trafficking of Women in Asia.* London: Virago.

Brownmiller, Susan. 1975. *Against Our Will: Men, Women and Rape.* New York: Ballantine Books.

Bunch, Charlotte. 1982. 'Feminist Journals: Writing for a Feminist Future', in J. Hartman and E. Messer-Davidow (eds), *Women in Print II: Opportunities for Women's Studies Publication in Language and Literature.* New York: Modern Language Association of America.

Bunting, Madeleine. 2007. 'Baby, This Just isn't Working for Me', *The Guardian,* 1 March.

Burchill, Julie. 2000. 'Nagging Doubts', *The Guardian,* 8 July.

Butler, Judith. 1990. *Gender Trouble: Feminism and the Subversion of Identity.* New York: Routledge.

Byrnes, Sholto. 2003. 'Feminist Institution Needs to Pile on the Pounds', *The Independent,* 9 July.

Cadman, Eileen, Gail Chester and Agnes Pivot (eds). 1981. *Rolling Our Own: Women as Printers, Publishers and Distributors.* London: Minority Press Group.

Callil, Carmen. 1992. 'Flying Jewellery', *Sunday Times,* 23 February.

———. 2008. 'The Stories of Our Lives', *The Guardian,* 26 April.

———. 1973. 'Untitled', publicity pamphlet.

————. 1980. 'Virago Reprints: Redressing the Balance', *The Times Literary Supplement*, 12 September.

Caro, Jane and Catherine Fox. 2008. *The F Word: How We Learned to Swear by Feminism*. Sydney: University of New South Wales Press.

Carter, Angela. 1984. *Nights at the Circus*. London: Virago.

————. 1982. *The Passion of New Eve*. London: Virago.

————. 1979. *The Sadeian Woman*. London: Virago.

———— (ed.). 1990. *The Virago Book of Fairy Tales*. London: Virago.

————. 1992. *Wise Children*. London: Virago.

Ceulemans, Mieke, and Fauconnier, Guido. 1979. *Mass Media: The Image, Role, and Social Conditions of Women. A Collection and Analysis of Research Materials*. Paris: Unesco.

Chamberlain, Mary. 1975. *Fenwomen*. London: Virago.

———— (ed.). 1988. *Writing Lives: Conversations between Women Writers*. London: Virago.

Chasseguet-Smirgel, Janine. 1981. *Female Sexuality*. London: Virago.

Chernin, Kim. 1986. *The Hungry Self: Women, Eating and Identity*. London: Virago.

————. 1983. *Womansize: The Tyranny of Slenderness*. London: The Women's Press.

Chester, Gail, and Julienne Dickey (eds). 1988. *Feminism and Censorship: The Current Debate*. Dorset: Prism Press.

Chester, Gail, and Sigrid Neilsen (eds). 1987. *In Other Words: Writing as a Feminist*. London: Hutchinson.

Chodorow, Nancy. 1978. *The Reproduction of Mothering: Psychoanalysis and the Sociology of Gender*. Berkeley: University of California Press.

Christian, Barbara. 1980. *Black Women Novelists: The Development of a Tradition 1892–1976*. Westport, CT: Greenwood Press.

Chulov, Martin, and Rahman Hussein. 2012. 'After the Arab Spring, the Sexual Revolution?', *The Guardian*, 27 April.

Clapp, Susannah. 1991. 'On Madness, Men and Fairy-Tales', *The Independent on Sunday*, 9 June.

Clark, Giles. 2001. *Inside Book Publishing*. London: Routledge.

Clay, Rosamund. 1990. *Only Angels Forget*. London: Virago.

Cochrane, Kira. 2007. 'Got it, Bought the T-shirt', *The Guardian*, 9 March.

————. 2013. 'Has Virago Changed the Publishing World's Attitudes towards Women?', *The Guardian*, 14 March.

————. 2010. *Women of the Revolution: Forty Years of Feminism*. London: Guardian Books.

Coe, Jonathan. 2007. 'My Literary Love Affair', *The Guardian*, 6 October.

Colgan, Jenny. 2001. 'We Know the Difference between *Foie Gras* and Hula Hoops, Beryl, But Sometimes We Just Want Hula Hoops', *The Guardian*, 24 August.

Collins, Patricia Hill. 2000. *Black Feminist Thought: Knowledge, Consciousness and the Politics of Empowerment*. New York: Routledge.

Connell, R.W. 2002. *Gender*. Cambridge: Polity Press.

Cooke, Rachel. 2008. 'Taking Women off the Shelf', *The Observer*, 6 April.

————. 2006. 'Warning! These Pretty Packages May Contain a Lot of Long Words', *The Guardian*, 23 July.

Cooper, Charlotte. 1998. *Fat and Proud: The Politics of Size*. London: The Women's Press.

Cooper, Leonie. 2008. 'Books Lost and Found', *The Guardian,* 8 February.

Cooper-Clark, Diana. 1983. *Designs of Darkness: Interviews with Detective Novelists.* Bowling Green, OH: Bowling Green State University Popular Press.

Coote, Anna, and Tess Gill. 1974. *Women's Rights: A Practical Guide.* Harmondsworth: Penguin.

Cornillon, Susan Koppelman (ed.). 1972. *Images of Women in Fiction: Feminist Perspectives.* Bowling Green, OH: Bowling Green University Press.

Corp, Anna. 1997. 'A Life Less Ordinary? Well, Excuse Us for Fantasising. . .', *The Independent,* 1 December.

Coser, Lewis A., Charles Kadushin and Walter W. Powell. 1982. *Books: The Culture and Commerce of Publishing.* New York: Basic Books Inc.

Cosslett, Tess, Alison Easton and Penny Summerfield (eds). 1996. *Resistance: An Introduction to Women's Studies.* Buckingham: Open University Press.

Cranny-Francis, Ann. 1990. *Feminist Fiction: Feminist Uses of Generic Fiction.* New York: St Martin's Press.

Criado-Perez, Caroline. 2015. *Do it Like a Woman . . . and Change the World.* London: Portobello.

Crown, Sarah. 2012. 'The Future isn't Orange: Literary Prize Sponsor Pulls out', *The Guardian,* 22 May.

———. 2011. 'Judging Books' Covers: The New Virago Modern Classics Series', *The Guardian,* 2 August.

Curtis, Polly. 2006. 'One in Five Firms Break Law over Women's Pay', *The Guardian,* 27 January.

Curtis, Richard. 1998. *This Business of Publishing: An Insider's View of Current Trends and Tactics.* New York: Allworth Press.

Dalley, Janet. 1995. 'Was Virago Too Successful? On the Sale of a Feminist Icon which Failed to Reinvent Itself', *The Independent on Sunday,* 20 October.

Davidson, Marilyn. 1985. *Reach for the Top: A Woman's Guide to Success in Business and Management.* London: Piatkus Press.

Davies, Kath, Julienne Dickey and Teresa Stratford (eds). 1987. *Out of Focus: Writings on Women and the Media.* London: The Women's Press.

De Beauvoir, Simone. 1997. *The Second Sex.* London: Vintage.

de Bellaigue, Eric. 2004. *British Book Publishing as a Business since the 1960s: Selected Essays.* London: British Library.

———. 1984. *The Business of Books: The de Bellaigue Report.* London: Hutchinson.

———. 1998. 'Wooing and Winning Virago', *The Bookseller,* 15 May.

De Grazia, Victoria, with Ellen Furlough (eds). 1996. *The Sex of Things: Gender and Consumption in Historical Perspective.* Berkeley: University of California Press.

De Marneffe, Daphne. 2006. *Maternal Desire: On Children, Love and the Inner Life.* London: Virago.

Dean, Jonathan. 2010. *Rethinking Contemporary Feminist Politics.* Basingstoke: Palgrave Macmillan.

Delacoste, Frédérique and Priscilla Alexander (eds). 1988. *Sex Work: Writings by Women in the Sex Industry.* London: Virago.

Denes, Melissa. 2005. '"Feminism? It's Hardly Begun". Interview with Gloria Steinem', *The Guardian,* 17 January.

Dinesen, Betzy (ed.). 1981. *Rediscovery: 300 Years of Stories by and about Women.* London: The Women's Press.

Diski, Jenny. 2003. *View from the Bed and Other Observations.* London: Virago.

Dix, Carol. 1988. 'The Rights Stuff', *The Guardian,* 26 January.

Dougary, Ginny. 1994. *The Executive Tart and Other Myths: Media Women Talk Back.* London: Virago.

Douglas, Susan J. 2010. *Enlightened Sexism: The Seductive Message that Feminism's Work is Done.* New York: Times Books.

Dowrick, Stephanie, and Sibyl Grundberg. 1980. *Why Children?* London: The Women's Press.

Duffy, Maureen. 1983. *That's How it was.* London: Virago.

Duncker, Patricia. 1992. *Sisters and Strangers: An Introduction to Contemporary Feminist Fiction.* Oxford: Blackwell.

———. 2002. *Writing on the Wall: Selected Essays.* London: Pandora.

Dunn, Jane. 1998. *Antonia White: A Life.* London: Jonathan Cape.

Durrant, Sabine. 1993. 'How We Met: Carmen Callil and Harriet Spicer', *The Independent on Sunday,* 23 May.

Dworkin, Andrea. 1981. *Pornography: Men Possessing Women.* London: The Women's Press.

Dybikowski, Ann, Victoria Freeman, Daphne Marlatt, Barbara Pulling and Betsy Warland (eds). 1985. *In the Feminine: Women and Words/Les Femmes et les Mots (Conference Proceedings 1983).* Edmonton: Longspoon Press.

Easton, Alison (ed.). 2000. *Angela Carter.* Basingstoke: Macmillan.

Editorial. 1988. 'Bestsellers', *The Guardian,* 15 July.

———. 1984. 'Books and Book Women', *Sunday Times,* 25 November.

———. 1989. 'Women in the 1980s: What Happened?', *The Guardian,* 28 December.

Eisenbach, Helen. 1997. *Lesbianism Made Easy.* London: Virago.

English, James F. (ed.). 2006. *A Concise Companion to Contemporary British Fiction.* Oxford: Blackwell.

Evans, Adrienne, and Sarah Riley. 2015. *Technologies of Sexiness: Sex, Identity and Consumer Culture.* Oxford: Oxford University Press.

Evans, Mari (ed.). 1985. *Black Women Writers: Arguments and Interviews.* London: Pluto Press.

Evans, Sarah Jane. 1986. 'Open Space: Shades of the Colour Purple', *The Guardian,* 8 July.

Ezard, John. 2005. '*Small Island* Novel Wins Biggest Orange Prize', *The Guardian,* 4 October.

Fairbairns, Zoe 1979. *Benefits.* London: Virago.

Faludi, Susan. 1992. *Backlash: The Undeclared War against Women.* London: Chatto & Windus.

Farrell, Amy Erdman. 1995. 'Feminism and the Media: Introduction', *Signs* 20(3) (Spring).

———. 1998. *Yours in Sisterhood: 'Ms' Magazine and the Promise of Popular Feminism.* Chapel Hill: University of North Carolina Press.

Felman, Shoshana. 1993. *What Does a Woman Want? Reading and Sexual Difference.* Baltimore: Johns Hopkins University Press.

Ferguson, Marjorie. 1990. 'Images of Power and the Feminist Fallacy', *Critical Studies in Mass Communication* 7(3) (September).

Figes, Eva. 1978. *Patriarchal Attitudes: Women in Society.* London: Virago.

Figes, Kate. 2007. *The Big Fat Bitch Book.* London: Virago.

Fine, Cordelia. 2010. *Delusions of Gender: The Real Science behind Sex Differences.* London: Icon Books.

Firestone, Shulamith. 1970. *The Dialectic of Sex: The Case for Feminist Revolution.* London: Jonathan Cape.

Flanagan, Caitlin. 2006. *To Hell with All That: Loving and Loathing Our Inner Housewife.* London: Virago.

Fleisher, Julian. 1997. *The Drag Queens of New York: An Illustrated Field Guide.* London: Pandora.

Flood, Alison. 2011. 'Australian "Orange Prize" to Promote Women Writers' Status', *The Guardian,* 4 May.

Fowler, Rebecca, and Lesley Thomas. 1995. 'Taking on the Men', *Sunday Times,* 19 February.

Frame, Janet. 1984. *An Angel at My Table.* London: The Women's Press.

———. 1985. *The Envoy from Mirror City.* London: The Women's Press.

———. 1983. *To the Island.* London: The Women's Press.

France, Louis, and Eva Wiseman. 2007. 'The New Feminists', *The Guardian,* 9 September.

Franks, Suzanne. 2000. *Having None of it: Women, Men and the Future of Work.* London: Granta.

Freely, Maureen. 2000. *The Parent Trap: Children, Families and the New Morality.* London: Virago.

———. 1998. 'Sugar and Spite. Virago: Her Story', *The Observer,* 18 January.

Friday, Nancy. 1975. *My Secret Garden: Women's Sexual Fantasies.* London: Virago.

Friedan, Betty. 1963. *The Feminine Mystique.* London: Victor Gollancz.

———. 1982. *The Feminine Mystique.* London: Penguin.

Friedman, Leslie J. 1977. *Sex Role Stereotyping in the Mass Media: An Annotated Bibliography.* New York: Garland Publishing.

Furman, Laura. 1970. '"A House Is Not a Home": Women in Publishing' in *Sisterhood Is Powerful: An Anthology of Writings from the Women's Liberation Movement.* Morgan, Robin (ed.). New York: Random House.

Gamman, Lorraine, and Margaret Marshment (eds). 1988. *The Female Gaze: Women as Viewers of Popular Culture.* London: The Women's Press.

Garden, Nancy. 1988. *Annie on My Mind.* London: Virago.

Garrett, Laurie. 1995. *The Coming Plague: Newly Emerging Diseases in a World out of Balance.* London: Virago.

Gavron, Hannah. 1968. *The Captive Wife: Conflicts of Housebound Mothers.* Harmondsworth: Penguin.

Gerard, Jasper. 2000. 'The First Lady of Letters is Smiling at Last', *Sunday Times,* 12 November.

Gerrard, Nicci. 1989. *Into the Mainstream: How Feminism Has Changed Women's Writing.* London: Pandora.

Ghazi, Polly. 2003. *The 24-Hour Family: A Parent's Guide to the Work-Life Balance.* London: The Women's Press.

Gibbons, Fiachra. 2001a. 'The Route to Literary Success: Be Young, Gifted But Most of All Gorgeous', *The Guardian,* 28 March.

————. 2001b. 'Women Lead the Way in "Hottest" Books List', *The Guardian*, 29 December.

Gibbs, Liz (ed.). 1994. *Daring to Dissent: Lesbian Culture from Margin to Mainstream.* London: Cassell.

Gilbert, Harriett. 1987. *A Women's History of Sex.* London: Pandora.

Gilbert, Sandra M., and Susan Gubar (eds). 1985. *The Norton Anthology of Literature by Women: The Tradition in English.* New York: Norton.

Gillis, Stacey, Gillian Howe and Rebecca Munford (eds). 2004. *Third Wave Feminism: A Critical Exploration.* Basingstoke: Palgrave Macmillan.

Gilman, Charlotte Perkins. 1981. *The Yellow Wallpaper.* London: Virago.

Glendinning, Victoria, and Matthew Glendinning. 1996. *Sons and Mothers.* London: Virago.

Gold, Tanya. 2012. 'For Women in Work This is a Perfect Storm of Inequality', *The Guardian*, 2 April.

Goldsworthy, Joanna (ed.). 1993. *A Certain Age: Reflecting on the Menopause.* London: Virago.

————. 1995. *Mothers: By Daughters.* London: Virago.

Goodings, Lennie. 1993a. 'Call Me Old-Fashioned, But that Advertisement's Sexist', *The Independent on Sunday*, 20 June.

————. 1993b. 'Cleaning the Office, Changing the World', *The Bookseller*, 4 June.

Goodison, Lucy. 1990. *Moving Heaven and Earth: Sexuality, Spirituality and Social Change.* London: The Women's Press.

Görtschacher, Wolfgang, and Holger Klein, in association with Claire Squires. 2006. *Fiction and Literary Prizes in Great Britain.* Vienna: Praesens Verlag.

Grant, Linda. 2012. 'Orange is Not the Only Fruit: Why Book Prizes, Not Sponsors, Matter to Writers', *The Guardian*, 22 May.

Greer, Germaine. 1970. *The Female Eunuch.* London: MacGibbon & Kee.

————. 1974. 'Flying Pigs and Double Standards', *The Times Literary Supplement*, 26 July.

————. 1999. *The Whole Woman.* London: Transworld.

Griffey, Harriet. 1998. 'The Women's Boom', *The Guardian*, 17 February.

Griffin, Susan. 1981. *Pornography and Silence: Culture's Revenge against Nature.* London: The Women's Press.

Groskop, Viv. 2011. 'There's Nothing Wrong with Judging a Book by its Cover', *The Guardian*, 4 September.

————. 2010. 'What Happened Next? Feminism', *The Guardian*, 27 December.

Gunkel, Henriett, Chrysanthi Nigianni and Fanny Soderback (eds). 2012. *Undutiful Daughters: New Directions in Feminist Thought and Practice.* New York: Palgrave Macmillan.

Hadjifotiou, Nathalie. 1983. *Women and Harassment at Work.* London: Pluto Press.

Hadley, Janet. 1996. *Abortion: Between Freedom and Necessity.* London: Virago.

Halberstam, Judith. 2005. *In a Queer Time and Place: Transgender Bodies, Subcultural Lives.* New York: New York University Press.

Hales, Dianne R. 1999. *Just Like a Woman: How Gender Science is Redefining What Makes Us Female.* London: Virago.

Hall, Radclyffe. 1981. *The Unlit Lamp.* London: Virago.

————. 1982. *The Well of Loneliness.* London: Virago.

Hamilton, Marybeth. 1996. *The Queen of Camp.* London: Pandora.

Hanscombe, Gillian E. 1982. *The Art of Life: Dorothy Richardson and the Development of Feminist Consciousness.* London: Owen.

Hanscombe, Gillian E., and Jackie Forster. 1982. *Rocking the Cradle. Lesbian Mothers: A Challenge in Family Living.* London: Sheba.

Harpwood, Diane. 1981. *Tea and Tranquillisers: The Diary of a Happy Housewife.* London: Virago.

Harron, Mary. 1984. "'I'm a Socialist, Damn it. How Can You Expect Me to Be Interested in Fairies?'", *The Guardian,* 25 September.

Hartley, Jenny. 2003. *The Reading Groups Book.* Oxford: Oxford University Press.

Hartman, Joan E. 1972. 'Part II: Editing and Publishing Freshman Textbooks', *College English* 34(1) (October).

Hartman, Joan E., and Ellen Messer-Davidow (eds). 1982. *Women in Print II: Opportunities for Women's Studies Publication in Language and Literature.* New York: Modern Language Association of America.

Hattenstone, Simon. 2001. 'Voices from the Margins', *The Guardian,* 21 July.

Healey, Emma. 1996. *Lesbian Sex Wars.* London: Virago.

Healey, Emma, and Angela Mason (eds). 1994. *Stonewall 25: The Making of the Lesbian and Gay Community in Britain.* London: Virago.

Hearn, Jeff. 1998. 'It's Goodbye He-Man, Hello She-Man', *The Times Higher Education Supplement,* 13 February.

Heilbrun, Carolyn G. 1979. *Reinventing Womanhood.* London: Victor Gollancz.

Hemmings, Clare. 2011. *Why Stories Matter: The Political Grammar of Feminist Theory.* Durham, NC: Duke University Press.

Heywood, Leslie, and Jennifer Drake (eds). 1997. *Third Wave Agenda: Being Feminist, Doing Feminism.* Minneapolis: University of Minnesota Press.

Hines, Helen (ed.). 2002. *Perfect: Young Women Talk about Body Image.* London: The Women's Press.

Hite, Shere. 1976. *The Hite Report: A Nationwide Study on Female Sexuality.* New York: Macmillan.

————. 1987, *The Hite Report: On Female Sexuality.* London: Pandora.

Hoagland, Sarah Lucia, and Julia Penelope (eds). 1988. *For Lesbians Only: A Separatist Anthology.* London: Onlywomen.

Hoff Sommers, Christina. 1994. *Who Stole Feminism? How Women Have Betrayed Women.* New York: Simon & Schuster.

Hole, Judith, and Ellen Levine. 1971. *Rebirth of Feminism.* New York: Quadrangle Books.

Hollows, Joanne, and Rachel Moseley (eds). 2006. *Feminism in Popular Culture.* Oxford: Berg.

Homes, A.M. 1994. *In a Country of Mothers.* London: Virago.

hooks, bell. 1982. *Ain't I a Woman? Black Women and Feminism.* London: Pluto Press.

————. 1989. *Talking Back: Thinking Feminist – Thinking Black.* Boston: Sheba.

Hooper, Anne. 1980. *The Body Electric.* London: Virago.

————. 1987. *The Body Electric.* London: Pandora.

Howells, Coral Ann. 2005. *Margaret Atwood.* Basingstoke: Palgrave MacMillan.

Humm, Maggie. 1991. *Border Traffic: Strategies of Contemporary Women Writers.* Manchester: Manchester University Press.

———. 1986. *Feminist Criticism: Women as Contemporary Critics.* Brighton: Harvester.

Ingersoll, Earl (ed.). 1990. *Margaret Atwood: Conversations.* Ontario: Ontario Review Press.

Itzin, Catherine (ed.). 1980. *Splitting up: Single Parent Liberation.* London: Virago.

Jackson, Christine. 1989. *Arts and Equality.* Darlington: Arts Development Association.

Jackson, Rosie. 1994. *Mothers Who Leave: Behind the Myth of Women without Their Children.* London: Pandora.

Jaggi, Maya. 2005. 'Wizard Talent', *The Observer,* 2 July 2005.

Jardine, Cassandra. 2000. 'Reading the Booker Winner, Then? Margaret Atwood's Victory Met a Mixed Response', *The Daily Telegraph,* 9 November.

Jarrett, Lucinda. 1997. *Stripping in Time: A History of Erotic Dancing.* London: Pandora.

Jay, Karla (ed.). 1996. *Dyke Life: From Growing Up to Growing Old – A Celebration of the Lesbian Experience.* London: Pandora.

Jeffreys, Sheila. 1990. *Anticlimax: A Feminist Perspective on the Sexual Revolution.* London: The Women's Press.

Jeffreys, Susan. 1996. 'Women Caught in a War of Words', *Sunday Times,* 21 April.

Jelinek, Estelle C. 1986. *The Tradition of Women's Autobiography: From Antiquity to the Present.* Boston: Twayne Publishers.

Jenkins, Emily. 1999. *Tongue First: Adventures in Physical Culture.* London: Virago.

Johnston, Sue. 1989. *Hold on to the Messy Times.* London: Pandora.

Jones, Nicolette. 1991a. 'A Way with Words', *The Guardian,* 30 May.

———. 1991b. 'The Need to Publish and Be Feminist: Takeovers and Recession Have Brought Crises to Several Women's Presses', *The Independent,* 11 September.

Jones, Philip. 2009. 'Virago Aims to Push New Waters', *The Bookseller,* 6 February.

Kahn, Paula. 1995. 'Still Grey Suits at the Top', *The Bookseller,* 17 February.

Kean, Danuta. 1999. 'A Suitable Place for a Woman', *The Bookseller,* 17 December.

Kemp, Philip. 2006. 'Filthy Rich and Female', *BBC News,* 26 January. Retrieved 27 September 2017 from http://news.bbc.co.uk/1/hi/business/4648282.stm.

Kinney, M.M. 1982. 'Boards and Paper: Feminist Writing and Trade Publishing' in *Women in Print II: Opportunities for Women's Studies Publication in Language and Literature.* J Hartman and E Messer-Davidow (eds). New York: Modern Language Association of America.

Kinnock, Glenys, and Fiona Millar (eds). 1993. *By Faith and Daring: Interviews with Remarkable Women.* London: Virago.

Klein, Naomi. 2000. *No Logo.* London: Flamingo.

Kolodny, Annette. 1975. 'Some Notes on Defining a "Feminist Literary Criticism"', *Critical Inquiry* 2 (Autumn).

Lakoff, Robin. 1975. *Language and Woman's Place.* New York: Harper Colophon Books.

Lambert, Angela. 1990. 'Should Feminists Use a Maiden So?', *The Independent,* 26 September.

Latifa. 2002. *My Forbidden Face: Growing up under the Taliban: A Young Woman's Story.* London: Virago.

Laughlin, Kathleen A., and Jacqueline L. Castledine (eds). 2011. *Breaking the Wave: Women, Their Organisations, and Feminism, 1945–1985.* New York: Routledge.

Lawrence, Marilyn. 1984. *The Anorexic Experience*. London: The Women's Press.

———— (ed.). 1987. *Fed Up and Hungry: Women, Oppression and Food*. London: The Women's Press.

Laws, Sophie. 1981. *Down There: An Illustrated Guide to Self-Examination*. London: Onlywomen.

Lazarre, Jane. 1981. *On Loving Men*. London: Virago.

Le Guin, Ursula K. 1989. *The Language of the Night: Essays on Fantasy and Science Fiction*. London: The Women's Press.

Lee, Hermione (ed.). 1984. Virginia Woolf's '*A Room of One's Own*' and '*Three Guineas*'. London: The Hogarth Press.

Lefanu, Sarah. 1985. *Despatches from the Frontiers of the Female Mind: An Anthology of Original Stories*. London: The Women's Press.

————. 1988. *In the Chinks of the World Machine: Feminism and Science Fiction*. London: The Women's Press.

Lerner, Betsy. 2003. *Food and Loathing*. London: Virago.

Lessing, Doris. 1983. *The Diaries of Jane Somers*. London: Michael Joseph.

Levy, Ariel. 2006. *Female Chauvinist Pigs: Women and the Rise of Raunch Culture*. London: Pocket Books.

Lewis, Jeremy. 1996. *Kindred Spirits: Adrift in Literary London*. London: HarperCollins.

Llewelyn Davies, Margaret (ed.). 1978. *Maternity: Letters from Working-Women Collected by the Women's Co-operative Guild*. London: Virago.

Lont, Cynthia (ed.). 1995. *Women and Media: Content/Careers/Criticism*. California: Wadsworth.

Lorde, Audre. 1984. *Zami: A New Spelling of My Name*. London: Sheba.

Lovenduski, Joni, and Vicky Randall. 1993. *Contemporary Feminist Politics: Women and Power in Britain*. Oxford: Oxford University Press.

Lowry, Suzanne. 1983. 'Cover Stories', *The Sunday Times*, 6 February.

————. 1980. *The Guilt Cage: Housewives and a Decade of Liberation*. London: Elm Tree Books.

————. 1977. 'Three's Company', *The Guardian*, 19 August.

Lury, Celia. 1996. *Consumer Culture*. Cambridge: Polity Press.

Lyndon, Neil. 1984. 'Carmen Callil on Her Own Terms', *Sunday Times*, 29 January.

MacAlister, Terry. 2007. 'Women Bosses Left Behind by Men's Pay', *The Guardian, 29* August.

Macaskill, Hilary. 1989. 'Publishing: A Woman's Place?', *British Book News*, April.

MacLeod, Sheila. 1981. *The Art of Starvation*. London: Virago.

Maddock, Su. 1999. *Challenging Women: Gender, Culture and Organisation*. London: Sage.

Mahony, Pat, and Carol Jones (eds). 1989. *Learning Our Lines: Sexuality and Social Control in Education*. London: The Women's Press.

Mansfield, Paul. 1990. 'Tell-Tale Sisters', *The Guardian, 25* October.

Marks, Elaine, and Isabelle de Courtivron (eds). 1980. *New French Feminisms: An Anthology*. Amherst: University of Massachusetts Press.

Marshall, Judi. 1984. *Women Managers: Travellers in a Male World*. Chichester: John Wiley & Sons.

Martinson, Jane. 2005. 'The Narnia Publisher Who Has Worked Her Own Magic with the Balance Sheet', *The Guardian, 7* December.

Maushart, Susan. 1999. *The Mask of Motherhood: How Becoming a Mother Changes Everything and Why We Pretend It Doesn't.* London: Pandora.

McBean, Samantha. 2016. *Feminism's Queer Temporalities.* London: Routledge.

McCabe, Jess. 2007. 'Leading from the Front Page', *The Guardian,* 13 July.

McCrum, Robert. 2006. 'Our Top 50 Players in the World of Books', *The Guardian,* 5 March.

McDermid, Val. 2010. 'Niche off the Leash: Val McDermid on Progress in Lesbian Fiction', *The Independent on Sunday,* 12 September.

McEwen, Christine (ed.). 1988. *Naming the Waves: Contemporary Lesbian Poetry.* London: Virago.

McEwen, Christine, and Sue O'Sullivan (eds). 1988. *Out the Other Side: Contemporary Lesbian Writing.* London: Virago.

McFerran, Ann. 1998. *Motherland: Interviews with Mothers and Daughters.* London: Virago.

McGlone, Jackie. 2003. 'Hand-Made Tales from a Gene Genie', *Scotland on Sunday,* 27 April.

McLoughlin, Jane. 1992. *Up and Running: Women in Business.* London: Virago.

McNair, Brian. 2002. *Striptease Culture: Sex, Media and the Democratisation of Desire.* London: Routledge.

McNeil, Gil (ed.). 1994. *Soul Providers: Writings by Single Parents.* London: Virago.

McRobbie, Angela. 2009. *The Aftermath of Feminism: Gender, Culture and Social Change.* London: Sage.

———. 2006. 'Female Celebrities Must Work Just as Hard Off-Stage', *The Guardian,* 8 June.

McVeigh, Tracy. 2012. 'Why Stay-at-Home Dads are Still the Invisible Men of the House', *The Observer,* 29 January.

Mellor, Mary. 1997. *Feminism and Ecology.* Cambridge: Polity Press.

Mendes, Kaitlynn. 2011. *Feminism in the News: Representations of the Women's Movement since the 1960s.* Basingstoke: Palgrave Macmillan.

Merchant, Carolyn. 1992. *Radical Ecology: The Search for a Liveable World.* New York: Routledge.

Messent, Peter (ed.). 1997. *Criminal Proceedings: The Contemporary American Crime Novel.* London: Pluto Press.

Meulenbelt, Anja. 1981. *For Ourselves: From Women's Point of View – Our Bodies and Sexuality.* London: Sheba.

Michael, Magali Cornier. 1994. 'Angela Carter's *Nights at the Circus*: An Engaged Feminism via Subversive Postmodern Strategies', *Contemporary Literature* 35(3) (Autumn).

Middlebrook, Diane Wood. 1998. *Suits Me: The Double Life of Billy Tipton.* London: Virago.

Millar, Eloise. 2007. 'A Classic Example for Other Publishers', *The Guardian,* 26 November.

Miller, Casey, and Kate Swift. 1980. *The Handbook of Non-sexist Writing for Writers, Editors and Speakers.* London: The Women's Press.

Miller, Casey, and Kate Swift. 1977. *Words and Women.* London: Victor Gollancz.

Miller, Jacques-Alain (ed.). 1992. *The Ethics of Psychoanalysis 1959–1960: The Seminar of Jacques Lacan.* London: Tavistock/Routledge.

Miller, Jane Eldridge. 1994. *Rebel Women: Feminism, Modernism and the Edwardian Novel.* London: Virago.

Millett, Kate. 1970. *Sexual Politics.* London: Granada.

———. 1977. *Sexual Politics.* London: Virago.

———. 1977. *Sita.* London: Virago.

Mills, Eleanor with Kira Cochrane (eds). 2005. *Cupcakes and Kalashnikovs: 100 Years of the Best Journalism by Women.* London: Constable.

Mills, Jane. 1978. *Make it Happy: What Sex is All About.* London: Virago.

Mills, Sara, and Jackie Jones (eds). 1998. *Contemporary Feminist Theories.* Edinburgh: Edinburgh University Press.

Mirza, Heidi Safia (ed.). 1997. *Black British Feminism: A Reader.* London: Routledge.

Mitchell, Juliet. 1971. *Woman's Estate.* Harmondsworth: Penguin.

———. 1984. *Women: The Longest Revolution: Essays on Feminism, Literature and Psycho- analysis.* London: Virago.

Modleski, Tania. 1991. *Feminism without Women: Culture and Criticism in a 'Postfeminist' Age.* London: Routledge.

———. 1988. *Loving with a Vengeance: Mass-Produced Fantasies for Women.* New York: Routledge.

Moers, Ellen. 1976. *Literary Women.* New York: Doubleday & Co.

Moi, Toril, and Janice Radway (eds). 1994. *Materialist Feminism.* Durham, NC: Duke University Press.

Moore, Suzanne. 2012. 'Naomi Wolf's Book *Vagina*: Self-Help Marketed as Feminism', *The Guardian,* 5 September.

Moorhead, Caroline. 1978. 'Paper Tigresses', *The Times,* 11 February.

Moorhead, Joanna. 2007. 'Girl Power Comes of Age', *The Guardian,* 24 October.

Moran, Joe. 2000. *Star Authors: Literary Celebrity in America.* London: Pluto Press.

Morgan, Elaine. 2007. 'Were Those the Days, My Friends?', *The Guardian,* 12 January.

Morgan, Robin (ed.). 1970. *Sisterhood is Powerful: An Anthology of Writings from the Women's Liberation Movement.* New York: Random House.

Morland, Iain, and Annabelle Wilcox (eds). 2005. *Queer Theory.* Basingstoke: Palgrave Macmillan.

Morris, Pam. 1993. *Literature and Feminism: An Introduction.* Oxford: Blackwell.

Mort, Frank. 1996. *Cultures of Consumption: Masculinities and Social Space in Late Twentieth-Century Britain.* London: Routledge.

Mosse, Kate. 1993. *Becoming a Mother.* London: Virago.

Muir, Anne Ross. 1987. *A Woman's Guide to Jobs in Film and Television.* London: Pandora.

Mullen, Jean S. 1972. 'Women Writers in Freshman Textbooks', *College English* 34(1) (October).

Munt, Sally R. 1994. *Murder by the Book? Feminism and the Crime Novel.* London: Routledge.

Murphy, Nicola. 1990. 'Disquiet on the Home Front', *The Times,* 14 December.

Murray, Simone. 1998. '"Books of Integrity": The Women's Press, Kitchen Table Press and Dilemmas of Feminist Publishing', *European Journal of Women's Studies* 5(2) (May).

———. 2004. *Mixed Media: Feminist Presses and Publishing Politics.* London: Pluto Press.

Negra, Dian. 2009. *What a Girl Wants? Fantasising the Reclamation of Self in Postfeminism.* London: Routledge & Kegan Paul.

Neustatter, Angela. 1988. 'A Cause for Celebration', *The Guardian,* 13 April.

Nicholson, Joyce. 1977. *What Society Does to Girls.* London: Virago.

NUJ Equality Working Party. 1997. *Images of Women: Guidelines for Promoting Equality through Journalism.* London: NUJ.

Nye, Robert. 1984. 'Daring Young Woman', *The Guardian,* 27 September.

Oakes, Philip. 1974. 'Coming on Column', *Sunday Times,* 12 May.

Oakley, Ann. 1990. *Matilda's Mistake.* London: Virago.

———. 1988. *The Men's Room.* London: Virago.

———. 1972. *Sex, Gender and Society.* London: Temple Smith.

Oakley, Ann, and Juliet Mitchell (eds). 1997. *Who's Afraid of Feminism? Seeing through the Backlash.* London: Hamish Hamilton.

O'Connor, Noreen, and Joanna Ryan (eds). 1993. *Wild Desires and Mistaken Identities: Lesbianism and Psychoanalysis.* London: Virago.

O'Toole, Emer. 2015. *Girls Will Be Girls: Dressing up, Playing Parts and Daring to Act Differently.* London: Orion.

Olsen, Tillie. 1980. *Silences.* London: Virago.

Orbach, Susie. 1979. *Fat is a Feminist Issue: How to Lose Weight Permanently . . . without Dieting.* London: Hamlyn.

Owen Peter (ed.). 1988. *Publishing – the Future.* London: Peter Owen Publishers.

Owen, Ursula (ed.). 1983. *Fathers: Reflections by Daughters.* London: Virago.

———. 'True Tales from a Revolution: The Non-Fiction Classics Now Hidden from Feminist History', *The Independent,* 7 May.

Page, Benedicte. 2010. 'Climate Worsens for Literary Debuts', *The Bookseller,* 27 June.

Paglia, Camille. 1990. *Sexual Personae: Art and Decadence from Nefertiti to Emily Dickinson.* New Haven: Yale University Press.

Pallister, David. 1991. 'Under Pressure', *The Guardian,* 27 March.

Parker, Roszkia. 1995. *Torn in Two: The Experience of Maternal Ambivalence.* London: Virago.

Payne, Karen (ed.). 1994. *Between Ourselves: Letters between Mothers and Daughters 1750–1982.* London: Virago.

Pepinster, Catherine. 2003. 'When Pigoons Attack, Readers Run for Cover', *The Independent on* Sunday, 1 June.

Phillips, Anne. 1987. *Divided Loyalties: Dilemmas of Sex and Class.* London: Virago.

Piercy, Marge. 1979. *Woman on the Edge of Time.* London: The Women's Press.

Pitman, Joanna. 1995. 'The Mother of All Rows', *The Times,* 18 November.

Plain, Gill. 2001. *Twentieth-Century Crime Fiction: Gender, Sexuality and the Body.* Edinburgh: Edinburgh University Press.

Radway, Janice A. 1994. *Reading the Romance: Women, Patriarchy, and Popular Literature.* London: Verso.

Rake, Katherine. 2006a. Let's Reclaim the F-word', *The Guardian,* 8 August.

———. 2006b. 'The New Mass Women's Lobby Must Include Men', *The Guardian,* 2 February.

Reach, Kirsten. 2013. 'Are There Any Female CEOs Left in the Big Five?', 3 July. Retrieved 27 September 2017 from https://www.mhpbooks.com/are-there-any-female-ceos-left-in-the-big-five.

Redclift, Nanneke, and Thea M. Sinclair (eds). 1991. *Working Women: International Perspectives on Labour and Gender Ideology.* London: Routledge.

Reddy, Maureen T. 1988. *Sisters in Crime: Feminism and the Crime Novel*. New York: Continuum.

Redfern, Catherine and Kristin Aune. 2010. *Reclaiming the F Word: The New Feminist Movement*. London and New York: Zed Books.

Reeves, Richard. 2004. 'Men Remain Stuck in Cages of Their Own Creation', *New Statesman*, 16 August.

Reiter, Rayna R. (ed.). 1975. *Toward an Anthropology of Women*. New York: Monthly Review Press.

Reynolds, Margaret (ed.). 1990. *Erotica: An Anthology of Women's Writing*. London: Pandora.

Rich, Adrienne. 1981. *Compulsory Heterosexuality and Lesbian Existence*. London: Onlywomen.

———. 1977. *Of Woman Born: Motherhood as Experience and Institution*. London: Virago.

———. 1980. *On Lies, Secrets and Silence. Selected Prose 1966–1978*. London: Virago.

Richardson, Sarah (ed.). 1996. *Writing on the Line: Twentieth Century Working-Class Women Writers*. London: Working Press.

Riley, Denise. 1983. *War in the Nursery: Theories of the Child and Mother*. London: Virago.

Ritchie, Harry. 1993. 'Come into the Garden', *Sunday Times*, 10 October.

Roberts, Helen (ed.). 1981. *Doing Feminist Research*. London: Routledge & Kegan Paul.

Roberts, Michéle. 1994. *During Mother's Absence*. London: Virago.

———. 1983. *The Visitation*. London: The Women's Press.

Roberts, Yvonne. 1992. *Mad about Women: Can There Ever Be Fair Play between the Sexes?* London: Virago.

Roe, Sue (ed.). 1987. *Women Reading Women's Writing*. Brighton: The Harvester Press.

Roiphe, Anna. 1997. *A Mother's Eye: Motherhood and Feminism*. London: Virago.

Roiphe, Katie. 1993. *The Morning After: Sex, Fear and Feminism on Campus*. Boston: Little, Brown.

Romaine, Suzanne. 1999. *Communicating Gender*. Mahwah, NJ: Lawrence Erlbaum Associates.

Root, Jane. 1984. *Pictures of Women: Sexuality*. London: Pandora Press.

Rosenberg, Betty. 1982. *Genreflecting: A Guide to Reading Interest in Genre Fiction*. Littleton, CO: Libraries Unlimited Inc.

Rothblatt, Martine. 1995. *The Apartheid of Sex: A Manifesto on the Freedom of Gender*. London: Pandora.

Rowbotham, Sheila. 1983. *Dreams and Dilemmas: Collected Writings*. London: Virago.

———. 1974. *Hidden from History*. London: Pluto.

———. 1989. *The Past is before Us: Feminism in Action since the 1960s*. London: Pandora Press.

———. 1973. *Woman's Consciousness, Man's World*. Harmondsworth: Penguin.

———. 1972. *Women, Resistance and Revolution*. London: Allen Lane.

Rubin, Bernard (ed.). 1980. *Small Voices and Great Trumpets: Minorities and the Media*. New York: Praegar.

Rubin, Gayle. 1975. 'The Traffic in Women: Notes on the "Political Economy" of Sex' in *Toward an Anthropology of Women*. Reiter, Rayna R. (ed.). New York: Monthly Review Press.

Rush, Ramona, and Donna Allen (eds). 1989. *Communications at the Crossroads: The Gender Gap Connection.* Norwood, NJ: Ablex Publishing.

Rustin, Susanna. 2013. 'Lennie Goodings: "Virago survived because it's a brand with a philosophy"', *The Guardian,* 20 July.

Sage, Lorna. 1994. *Angela Carter.* Plymouth: Northcote House Publishers.

———. 1987. 'Behind the Lines', *The Times Literary Supplement,* 10 July.

Said, Edward. 1993. *Culture and Imperialism.* London: Vintage.

———. 1973. *Orientalism.* London: Penguin.

Sarton, May. 1985. *Journal of a Solitude.* London: The Women's Press.

Scanlon, Jean, and Julia Swindells. 1994. 'Bad Apple', *Trouble and Strife* 28 (Spring).

Scanlon, Jennifer (ed.). 2000. *The Gender and Consumer Culture Reader.* New York: New York University Press.

Scanlon, Joan (ed.). 1990. *Surviving the Blues: Growing up in the Thatcher Decade.* London: Virago.

Scharff, Christina. 2012. *Repudiating Feminism: Young Women in a Neoliberal World.* Farnham: Ashgate.

Segal, Lynne (ed.). 1997. *New Sexual Agendas.* Basingstoke: Macmillan.

———. 1990. *Slow Motion: Changing Masculinities, Changing Men.* London: Virago.

———. 1997. *Slow Motion: Changing Masculinities, Changing Men.* London: Virago.

———. 1994. *Straight Sex: The Politics of Pleasure.* London: Virago.

———. 1999. *Why Feminism? Gender, Psychology and Politics.* London: Polity Press.

Segal, Lynne, and Mary McIntosh (eds). 1992. *Sex Exposed: Sexuality and the Pornography Debate.* London: Virago.

Senior, Jennifer. 2015. *All Joy and No Fun: The Paradox of Modern Parenthood.* London: Virago.

Shahrukh, Husain. 1995. *Women Who Wear the Breeches: Delicious and Dangerous Tales.* London: Virago.

Shamsie, Kamila. 2015. 'Let's Have a Year of Publishing Only Women: A Provocation', *The Guardian,* 5 June.

Shaw, Fiona. 2001. *Out of Me: The Story of a Postnatal Breakdown.* London: Virago.

Showalter, Elaine. 1982. *A Literature of Their Own: British Women Novelists from Brontë to Lessing.* London: Virago.

——— (ed.). 1986. *The New Feminist Criticism: Essays on Women, Literature and Theory.* London: Virago.

———. 1971. 'Women and the Literary Curriculum', *College English* 32(8) (May).

Shriver, Lionel. 2006. '"It Pains Me that I Can No Longer Feel Sorry for Myself"', *The Guardian,* 13 March.

Siegel, Deborah. 2007. 'What Next for the Sexual Revolution?', *The Guardian,* 31 August.

Simons, Judy, and Kate Fullbrook (eds). 1998. *Writing: A Women's Business – Women, Writing and the Marketplace.* Manchester: Manchester University Press.

Smedley, Agnes. 1984. *China Correspondent.* London: Pandora.

Smith, David. 2004. 'Girls Will Be Girls and Boys Will Be Boss (Now There's a Surprise)', *The Guardian,* 28 November.

———. 2003. 'Women Celebrate a Turn-Up for the Books', *The Observer,* 21 September.

Smith, Joan. 2007. 'Women Need Their Own Voice on Equality', *The Guardian,* 25 July.

Smith, Sidonie. 1987. *A Poetics of Women's Autobiography: Marginality and the Fictions of Self-Representation.* Bloomington: Indiana University Press.

Snitow, Ann, Christine Stansell and Sharon Thompson (eds). 1984. *Desire: The Politics of Sexuality.* London: Virago.

Spacks, Patricia Meyer. 1976. *The Female Imagination: A Literary and Psychological Investigation of Women's Writing.* London: George Allen & Unwin.

Spender, Dale. 1985. 'Inner Thoughts from Outer Space', *The Guardian,* 10 January.

———. 1980. *Man Made Language.* London: Pandora.

———. 1986. *Mothers of the Novel: 100 Good Women Writers before Jane Austen.* London: The Women's Press.

———. 1982. *Women of Ideas and What Men Have Done to Them: From Aphra Behn to Adrienne Rich.* London: Routledge & Kegan Paul.

———. 1989. *The Writing or the Sex? Or Why You Don't Have to Read Women's Writing to Know it's No Good.* New York: Teacher's College Press.

Spender, Lynne. 1983. *Intruders on the Rights of Men: Women's Unpublished Heritage.* London: Pandora.

Spring Rice, Margery 1981. *Working-Class Wives: Their Health and Conditions.* London: Virago.

Squires, Claire. 2007. *Marketing Literature: The Making of Contemporary Writing in Britain.* Hampshire: Palgrave MacMillan.

Steedman, Carolyn. 1986. *Landscape for a Good Woman: A Story of Two Lives.* London: Virago.

Steel, Mel. 1998. 'Left on the Shelf', *The Independent on Sunday,* 19 April.

Steinburg, Janet (ed.). 1992. *The Writer on Her Work.* London: Virago.

Stoller, Robert. 1968. *Sex and Gender: On the Development of Masculinity and Femininity.* London: The Hogarth Press.

Stone, Philip, and Katie Allen. 2009. 'Booker Bounces Longlist Sales', *The Bookseller,* 5 August.

Stott, Mary. 1973. *Forgetting's No Excuse.* London: Faber.

Sumner, Penny (ed.). 2001. *The Fruits of Labour: Creativity, Self-Expression and Motherhood.* London: The Women's Press.

Sutherland, John. 1981. *Bestsellers: Popular Fiction of the 1970s.* London: Routledge & Kegan Paul.

———. 1978. *Fiction and the fiction industry.* London: Athlone Press.

———. 2000. 'Why Women Make Better Publishers', *The Guardian,* 24 July.

Suthrell, Charlotte. 2004. *Unzipping Gender: Sex, Cross-dressing and Culture.* Oxford: Berg.

Tagholm, Roger. 2015. 'Leaning in – in Publishing', *Publishing Perspectives,* 20 July.

Taylor, Debbie. 1994. *My Children, My Gold: Meetings with Women of the Fourth World.* London: Virago.

Taylor, Kate. 2005. 'Orange Appeal', *The Guardian,* 8 June.

———. 2006. 'Today's Ultimate Feminists are the Chicks in Crop Tops', *The Guardian,* 23 March.

Teather, David. 2000. 'Bloomsbury Set: Publisher Thrives on Atwood's Booker Win', *The Guardian,* 25 November.

Teeman, Tim. 2004. 'Alice Walker', *The Times,* 24 April.

Thompson, Dorothy. 1983. *Over Our Dead Bodies: Women against the Bomb*. London: Virago.

Thompson, William. 1983. *Appeal of One Half of the Human Race, Women, against the Pretensions of the Other Half, Men, to Retain Them in Political and Thence Civil and Domestic Slavery*. London: Virago.

Thorpe, Vanessa. 2004. 'Row at HarperCollins after Books Fail to Sell', *The Observer*, 17 October.

Tickle, Louise. 2006. 'No Place for a Woman', *The Guardian*, 24 June.

Todd, Richard. 1996. *Consuming Fictions: The Booker Prize and Fiction in Britain Today*. London: Bloomsbury.

———. 2006. 'Literary Fiction and the Book Trade', in James F. English (ed.), *A Concise Companion to Contemporary British Fiction*. Malden, Oxford & Carlton: Blackwell.

Tomlinson, Frances, and Fiona Colgan. 1989. *Twice as Many, Half as Powerful?: Report of a Survey into the Employment of Women in the United Kingdom Book Publishing Industry*. London: Polytechnic of North London/Women in Publishing.

Tonkin, Boyd. 2005. 'Old Myths, New Truths; Odysseus We Know – But Who was Penelope?', *The Independent*, 28 October.

———. 2011. 'Reasons to Be Cheerful: Leaders in the Business of Books Reveal What They are Optimistic about', *The Independent*, 7 January.

Turnbull, Annmarie, with Patricia de Wolfe and Anna Davin. 1980. *Women with a Past: A Brief Account of Some Aspects of Women's History in Britain in the 19th and 20th Centuries*. London: Women's Research and Resources Centre.

Valenti, Jessica. 2007. *Full Frontal Feminism: A Young Woman's Guide to Why Feminism Matters*. Berkeley: Seal Press.

Van Gelder, Lindsy, and Pamela Robin Brandt. 1992. *Are You Two – Together?: A Gay and Lesbian Travel Guide to Europe*. London: Virago.

Vance, Carole S. 1989. *Pleasure and Danger: Exploring Female Sexuality*. London: Pandora.

Vedantam, Shankar. 2007. 'The Truth about Why Women are Paid Less – Even if They Ask for More', *The Guardian*, 21 August.

Wadia-Ells, Susan (ed.). 1996. *The Adoption Reader: Birth Mothers, Adoptive Mothers and Adopted Daughters Tell Their Stories*. London: The Women's Press.

Walker, Alice. 1983. *The Color Purple*. London: The Women's Press.

Walker, Rebecca (ed.). 1995. *To Be Real: Telling the Truth and Changing the Face of Feminism*. New York: Anchor Books.

Walsh, Susan, and Catherine Cassell. 1995. *A Case of Covert Discrimination*. London: Bentinck Group's Women into Management Study.

Walter, Natasha (ed.). 1999. *On the Move: Feminism for a New Generation*. London: Virago.

———. 2006a. 'Prize Culture Lags Behind', *The Guardian*, 27 April.

———. 1993. 'Still Maligned, Still Loved, Still Needed: On the Occasion of Virago's 20th Birthday Natasha Walter Asks, What are We Celebrating?', *The Independent*, 19 June.

———. 2006b. 'Still One of the Guys', *The Guardian*, 18 February.

Walter, Natasha. 2010. *Living Dolls: The Return of Sexism*. London: Virago.

Walters, Margaret. 2005. *Feminism: A Very Short Introduction*. Oxford: Oxford University Press.

Wandor, Michelene. 1989. 'Chronicles of the Sexual Revolution', *The Sunday Times*, 4 June.
———— (ed.). 1983. *On Gender and Writing*. London: Pandora Press.
Ward, Lucy. 2005. 'Women Part-Timers Stuck in Low-Pay Jobs', *The Guardian*, 9 March.
Ward, Stephen. 1994. 'Virago's Book List is Trimmed as Sales Drop', *The Independent*, 5 June.
Warner, Marina. 1992. 'Obituary', *The Independent*, 18 February.
Warren, Karren J. (ed.). 1997. *Ecofeminism: Women, Culture, Nature*. Bloomington: Indiana University Press.
Washington, Mary Helen. 1989. *Invented Lives: Narratives of Black Women 1860–1960*. London: Virago.
Waters, Sarah. 1999. *Affinity*. London: Virago.
————. 2002. *Fingersmith*. London: Virago.
————. 2006. *The Night Watch*. London: Virago.
————. 1998. *Tipping the Velvet*. London: Virago.
Watt, Ian. 1974. *The Rise of the Novel: Studies in Defoe, Richardson and Fielding*. London: Chatto & Windus.
Watts, Carol. 1995. *Dorothy Richardson*. Plymouth, Northcote House.
Waugh, Patricia. 1989. *Feminine Fictions: Revisiting the Postmodern*. London: Routledge.
Webster, Wendy. 1990. *Not a Man to Match Her: The Marketing of a Prime Minister*. London: The Women's Press.
Weeks, Jeffrey. 1986. *Sexuality*. Chichester and London: Ellis Horwood & Tavistock Publications.
West, Celeste, and Valerie Wheat. 1978. *Booklegger's Guide To: The Passionate Perils of Publishing*. San Francisco: Booklegger Press.
Whelehan, Imelda. 2005. *The Feminist Bestseller: From 'Sex and the Single Girl' to 'Sex and the City'*. Basingstoke: Palgrave Macmillan.
Whelehan, Imelda, and Joel Gwynne (eds). 2014. *Ageing, Popular Culture and Contemporary Feminism: Harleys and Hormones*. Basingstoke: Palgrave Macmillan.
Whitbread, Helena (ed.). 1988. *I Know My Own Heart: The Diaries of Anne Lister 1791–1840*. London: Virago.
White, Antonia. 1978. *Frost in May*. London: Virago.
Wilkinson, Helen. 1994. *No Turning Back: Generations and the Genderquake*. London: Demos.
Williams, Charlotte. 2010. 'Virago Launches Online Bookclub', *The Bookseller*, 8 December.
Williams, Patricia J. 1993. *The Alchemy of Race and Rights*. London: Virago.
————. 1997. *Seeing a Colour-Blind Future: The Paradox of Race*. London: Virago.
Wilson, Elizabeth. 1980. *Only Halfway to Paradise: Women in Post-War Britain 1945–68*. London: Tavistock.
Wilson, Elizabeth, with Angela Weir. 1986. *Hidden Agendas: Theory, Politics and Experience in the Women's Movement*. London: Tavistock Publications.
Wilson, Melba. 1993. *Crossing the Boundary: Black Women Survive Incest*. London: Virago.
———— (ed.). 1994. *Healthy and Wise: The Essential Handbook for Black Women*. London: Virago.
Windrath, Helen (ed.). 1999. *A Career in Crime: Inside Information from Leading Women Writers*. London: The Women's Press.

Winship, Janice. 1987. *Inside Women's Magazines*. London: Pandora.

Wisker, Gina (ed.). 1993. *Black Women's Writing*. Basingstoke: Macmillan.

Wittig, Monique. 1992. *The Straight Mind and Other Essays*. London: Harvester Wheatsheaf.

Wittig, Monique, and Sande Zeig. 1980. *Lesbian Peoples: Materials for a Dictionary*. London: Virago.

Wolf, Naomi. 2012. *Vagina: A New Biography*. London: Virago.

Wolff, Isabel. 1994. 'Declaration of Independents', *Sunday Times,* 20 March.

Wolmark, Jenny. 1993. *Aliens and Others: Science Fiction, Feminism and Postmodernism*. New York: Harvester Wheatsheaf.

Women and Work Commission. 2007. *Towards a Fairer Future: Implementing the Women and Work Commission Recommendations*. London: Department for Communities and Local Government.

Women in Publishing. 1987. *Reviewing the Reviews: A Woman's Place on the Book Page*. London: Journeyman Press.

Woodward, Kathleen. 1983. *Jipping Street*. London: Virago.

Woodward, Kath, and Sophie Woodward. 2009. *Why Feminism Matters: Feminism Lost and Found*. Basingstoke: Palgrave Macmillan.

Woolf, Virginia. 1932. *The Common Reader Second Series*. London: Hogarth Press.

Woolfe, Sue. 1998. *Leaning towards Infinity: How My Mother's Apron Unfolds into My Life*. London: The Women's Press.

Woolsey, Marijke, and Susan King (eds). 1994. *Dear Mother . . . An Anthology of Women Writing to or about Their Mothers*. London: The Women's Press.

Worpole, Ken. 1984. *Reading by Numbers: Contemporary Publishing and Popular Fiction*. London: Comedia.

Wroe, Nicholas. 1999. 'Success is a Feminist Issue', *The Guardian,* 31 July.

Interviews

With Carmen Callil, 10 November 2004.

With Jane Chomeley, 28 September 2004.

With Lennie Goodings, 8 November 2004.

With Lennie Goodings, 8 May 2008.

With Ursula Owen, 5 February 2009.

With Marsha Rowe, 15 July 2004.

With Ali Smith, 19 July 2004.

With Harriet Spicer, 20 October 2004.

With Sarah Waters, 12 July 2004.

Index

McDermid, Anne, 25
McDermid, Val, 76, 78, 149–50
McLoughlin, Jane, 52
McRobbie, Angela, 101, 147
Mellor, Mary, 107
memoirs, 152, 158–59
men, impact of 'new' feminism on, 149
Mendes, Kaitlynn, 150
Merchant, Carolyn, 107
Meulenbelt, Anja, 39
Meyers, Stephanie, 157
Michel, Caroline, 95, 134
'Midway' concept, 19, 159
Millar, Eloise, 126
Miller, Henry, 35
Millett, Kate, 9–10, 33, 35, 140
Mills, Jane, 39
Mills, Sara, 151
Mills & Boon, 79
minority groups, feminist publishing
    for, 62
Mirza, Heidi Safia, 65
misogyny, 141
Miss America pageant, 11
Mitchell, Joni, 10
Mitchell, Juliet, 11–12
Mitchison, Naomi, 79
Mitsubishi (company), 98
'Modern Classics' series, 9, 21–22, 24,
    26, 36, 43–45, 58–59, 75, 86, 88,
    128–29, 136, 155–56, 159
Modleski, Tania, 65, 79–80
Mohin, Lillian, 92
Moore, Suzanne, 149
Moorhead, Caroline, 15
Moran, Caitlin, 141
Moran, Joe, 100
Morrison, Toni, 101
Mort, Frank, 112
Moss, Kate, 109
Mosse, Kate, 97–98, 133
motherhood, 37–38, 115, 144–46
Mslexia (magazine), 91
Mukherjee, Bharati, 69
Mullen, Jean S., 42
Murdoch, Iris, 43

Murdoch, Rupert, 61–62
Murray, Simone, 1–2, 4, 62, 87

N
National Council for Civil Liberties, 13
National Women's Liberation
    Conference, 140
Neilsen, Sigrid, 4–5, 51, 62
neoliberalism, 141–42, 147
Net Book Agreement, 90
Neustatter, Angela, 68
Neville, Richard, 16
'News and Blog' website, 129
Ngcobo, Lauretta, 70
Ngozi, Chimamanda, 108
niche publishing, 135–36, 156
Nichols, Grace, 69
Nicholson, Joyce, 10, 37
Nicholson, Katy, 57

O
Oakley, Ann, 11, 35–36
Observer, 134
Olsen, Tillie, 38, 45
Onlywomen, 5, 24, 49, 60, 62, 73, 75,
    92
Orange Prize. *See* Women's Prize for
    Fiction
Osbourne, Frances, 124
O'Sullivan, Sue, 56
O'Toole, Emer, 148
overheads, 55
Owen, Ursula, 2, 9, 17–22, 25–29,
    32–38, 44, 46, 49–50, 53–58, 65–67,
    80, 85, 140
Oz (magazine), 15–16

P
Paglia, Camille, 101, 105
Paley, Grace, 69
Pandora, 5, 25, 33, 49, 60, 73, 75, 80
'paper tigresses', 15
parenting, 37–38, 114–15, 144–46
parliament, women in, 144, 151
patriarchal culture, 13, 15, 18, 32–39,
    52, 71–72, 79, 101, 154

Penguin Books, 44, 92, 127, 134–35
Penny, Laurie, 141
Persephone (publisher), 136
Phillips, Anne, 66–67
Piatkus, Judith, 53
Piercy, Marge, 61
Pitman, Joanna, 87
Pitman, Joy, 62
Poe, Edgar Allan, 75
pole dancing, 146
'political lesbian' figure, 72–73
popular culture, 109, 111, 115–16, 147, 158
pornography, 70–73, 146
Porter, Cathy, 11
Portobello Books, 136–37
postcolonial theory, 107
post-feminism, 105, 141–2
postmodernism, 65, 111–12
power feminists, 105
power to publish, 23
praxis, publishing as, 1, 9, 27, 54, 72, 107, 131, 139, 159–60
pressure exercised by feminist publishers, 5
Pringle, Alexandra, 2, 21, 25, 29, 44–45, 49, 54–56, 77, 85, 133, 135, 160
prizes, literary, 85, 97–99, 131–33, 137, 157
publicity campaigns, 128

Q

Quartet Books, 18–20, 24, 49
queer theory and queer politics, 65–66, 74, 108–12

R

racism, 66, 69
Radical Booksellers Association, 42
radical feminism, 10, 44, 51, 70–71
Radway, Janice, 79–80
Rake, Katherine, 142, 147
Random House, 55, 61–62, 87–88, 124
Rat (magazine), 16
'raunch' culture, 146–48

Rausing, Sigrid, 136
Raw Nerve Books, 136
Read, Nikki, 136
Rebuck, Gail, 53, 87–88, 96, 135, 160
Reclaim the Night movement, 140
Reddy, Maureen T., 75, 77
Redfern, Catherine, 141
Regester, Seeley, 75
reprint series, 21–22, 44, 58. *See also* 'Modern Classics' series
review process, 39–43, 57–58, 99, 130–32, 137, 156
Rich, Adrienne, 37, 72
Richardson, Dorothy, 58
Ridout, Amanda, 95, 134
rights, women's, 14
Riley, Denise, 9, 38
Riley, Joan, 68
Riley, Sarah, 142
Rivers Oram Press, 90
Roberts, Helen, 19
Roberts, Michéle, 60–61, 80–81, 115, 156
Robinson, Marilynne, 124, 131
Roiphe, Katie, 105
role models, 13
Romaine, Suzanne, 113
romance fiction, 79–80
Root, Jane, 39, 72
Rosenberg, Betty, 76
Rothschild Ventures, 56, 86
Routledge and Kegan Paul (RKP), 19, 25, 61
Rowbotham, Sheila, 9, 11–12, 20–21, 43, 64
Rowe, Marsha, 2–3, 9–13, 16–20, 27–28, 33–34, 42, 154, 159
Rowling, J.K., 157
Rowntree Trust, 20
Rubin, Gayle, 35
Rule, Jane, 73, 150
Ruskin, John, 145
Russ, Joanna, 79
Russell, Karen, 157
Rustin, Susanna, 126–27

Virago: Advisory Group, 11–13, 21–22, 33, 37, 59, 158; choice of name, 16; closeness to its readers, 129–30; founding of, 9, 14–18, 154; location in London, 12; sale of the company, 49, 55, 85–87, 90, 92, 97, 121; titles recently published, 151–52, 159

W

Walker, Alice, 61, 68–69, 80, 91–92

Walker, Rebecca, 105

Walter, Natasha, 81, 89, 94, 97, 114, 141, 147–48, 151, 158

Walters, Margaret, 150

Wandor, Michelene, 59

Warner, Marina, 41

Warren, Karen, 107

Washington, Mary Helen, 69

Waters, Sarah, 2, 88, 100–1, 109–11, 116–17, 124, 128, 132, 136, 145, 149–50, 155–58

Waterstone's (booksellers), 90

Watt, Ian, 42

'wave' metaphor for feminism, 2, 32, 139

Weaver, Sigourney, 109

Webster, Wendy, 50

webzines, 130

Weidenfeld & Nicholson, 92

Weir, Alison, 20

Weldon, Fay, 91

West, Mae, 101

Wester, Arnold, 21

WH Smith (retailer), 57, 93

Whelehan, Imelda, 127

Whitbread Prize, 133

White, Antonia, 21, 58

White, Michael, 16

Wilde, Dolly, 101

Wildwood House (publishers), 19, 26

Wilson, Barbara, 76, 78

Wilson, Elizabeth, 11–12

Winterson, Jeanette, 60, 73, 80, 93

Wisker, Gina, 69

Wolf, Naomi, 93–94, 101, 141, 149

Wollstonecraft, Mary, 101

Wolmark, Jenny, 79

women in businesses other than publishing, 52–53, 94–95, 133, 135, 144–45, 160

Women in Media group, 16

women-only publishing, 24, 27, 34, 94, 135, 154, 157, 159

women in publishing, 3–5, 10–14, 18–23, 87, 89, 94–96, 125, 133–37, 160

Women in Publishing (WiP) group, 25, 49, 53, 57–58

women-run and women-owned companies, 1–3, 14–15, 137, 159–60

Women's Equality Party, 139

Women's Library, 91

women's movement, 9–10, 19, 23, 28, 65–67, 70, 101, 105–6, 139, 143, 146; fragmentation of, 65–66

Women's Press (publisher), The, 4–5, 18, 24–25, 28, 37–38, 44–45, 49, 52–53, 59–61, 68–80, 90–91, 110–11, 114, 149–50

Women's Prize for Fiction, 85, 97–99, 124, 132–33, 157

Women's Review (magazine), 56

women's status, 36, 95, 106, 114

women's work, 13–15, 36–37, 95–96, 114–15, 143–45

women's writing, 23, 26–30, 33, 40–45, 49, 51, 56–62, 74, 76, 80, 94, 98, 126, 130, 134–37, 140, 145, 154–57, 160; popularity of, 57; profitability of, 62

Wood, Mrs Henry, 75

Woodward, Kath and Sophie, 141, 147

Woolf, Virginia, 4, 34, 111

Worpole, Ken, 4

Writers and Readers Cooperative, 20

Writing Women (magazine), 56

Z

Zahavi, Helen, 93

Protest, Culture and Society

General editors:
Kathrin Fahlenbrach, Institute for Media and Communication, University of Hamburg
Martin Klimke, New York University Abu Dhabi
Joachim Scharloth, Technical University Dresden, Germany

Protest movements have been recognized as significant contributors to processes of political participation and transformations of culture and value systems, as well as to the development of both a national and transnational civil society. This series brings together the various innovative approaches to phenomena of social change, protest and dissent which have emerged in recent years, from an interdisciplinary perspective. It contextualizes social protest and cultures of dissent in larger political processes and socio-cultural transformations by examining the influence of historical trajectories and the response of various segments of society, political and legal institutions on a national and international level. In doing so, the series offers a more comprehensive and multi-dimensional view of historical and cultural change in the twentieth and twenty-first centuries.